This Story Is Far From Over

Bill Stacey

PRESS

Nancy,

It was nice meeting you.
Thank you for sharing your story
with us. As you read our story
I hope you'll recognize how God's
Word encouraged us during some
difficult days.

Thanks!

Bill

Philippians 4:4-7

Contents

What Others Have Said...

*I*n this heart-rending and inspiring book, Bill Stacey allows us to join him in his journey through the deep waters where we encounter our greatest trials and yet find our greatest resource in God's provision for our every need. Bill's story will bring tears, but also, the calm assurance that the Lord's grace truly is sufficient.

Dr. J. Robert White, Executive Director, Georgia Baptist Convention

As a physician who treats glioblastoma I often have to be the bearer of bad news. Occasionally, a family with extraordinary faith, dignity and graciousness will overwhelm all of the health care providers with their kindness and caring in the face of such adversity. And so it is with the family of Nancy Stacey. I commend Bill Stacey on his compilation of the Stacey family experience and his willingness to reach out to others who are dealing with the adversity of glioblastoma; faith is an incredible gift to us all.

Dr. Bryan Barnes, M.D. Georgia Neurological Surgery

I'll never forget that early summer of 2011 when my wife and I stood in the visitation line for a friend who, after a six-month battle against a brain tumor, passed away the preceding Sunday night. Because Nancy Stacey had been a physical education teacher for 30 years—not to mention being a pastor's wife for three decades as well—we felt sure that the line to pay respects to the family would be lengthy.

Sure enough, there was quite a wait to see the family—the average time was about three hours. By the time the first person in line spoke with the family and the time the last person in line offered condolences, almost 11 hours had passed.

The next day, the church was filled about an hour before services were scheduled to begin. Suffice it to say, the total number of people who attended the visitation or were in the church for the funeral is staggering.

Celebrity funerals are big affairs. The media coverage never seems to cease; and more often than not, we see photographers and TV crews jockeying for position to get the best view of a grieving family or other celebrities that might be in attendance. The funeral often quickly turns into a spectacle, with what was meant to be a time of remembrance being overshadowed by a spotlight.

There was no news crew on hand to record the events for the world at Nancy Stacey's funeral. Nor did Hollywood's "A List" turn out in black suits and sunglasses.

But what *did* happen could fill reams of paper and massive amounts of hard-drive space. Fond memories flowed like rivers; joyous recollections scaled toward the sky. I simply cannot tell you the number of times I overheard someone mentioning how Nancy encouraged someone at work ... boosted the day of someone at church ... spent a few extra moments letting someone know he or she was special. She was filled with the love of God, and she didn't mind sharing it with everyone she encountered.

A former co-worker used to refer to this type of thing as "Lifestyle Evangelism." Though he never met Nancy Stacey, I'm convinced he had her in mind when he used that phrase.

That said, it shouldn't surprise you that there is not one ounce of doubt in anyone's mind about where Nancy is spending eternity.

In a way that would please her heavenly Father, Nancy left a lasting impression on those around her. I overheard one person make the comment that watching Nancy in life was like reading the Bible—and that just goes to add credibility to the old statement that "you may be the only Bible some people read."

How will people remember *you* when, one day, they read your obituary? Will they wait in line for hours just to tell the family how much they appreciated you or to share a special story? Even more importantly, will anyone be wondering where you are spending eternity?

Follow Nancy's example. Leave a lasting impression.

In the pages that follow, you're going to learn a lot about Nancy Stacey, her life, her family, and her legacy. In fact, before you reach the end of this book, you'll consider Nancy a member of your family.

That's very fitting, as this book encompasses a broad definition of family, not just the traditional definition of a family as we know, but also how the Stacey family are part of a much bigger family— God's family. And, in a day and time when the family is under attack, what you are about to read offers in vivid detail just how important it is to be a family in God's family.

Again, I say, follow Nancy's example

Danny Jones
Editor-In-Chief
Singing News Magazine

When the news was shared with the sudden discovery and bleak prognosis of a malignant tumor in Nancy's brain, I immediately felt an enormous sense of loss for Bill and their precious family. Just months prior I traveled down that road with my mother, so I knew firsthand what the Stacey family was about to face. I knew, too, that the same God who supplied strength and grace to me during many dark days would wrap His arms around them and carry them through their valley.

I've had the privilege of serving with Bill on the Toccoa Falls Alumni Association Board of Directors for several years. He has an incredible, deep love for the Lord, exercises his faith on a daily basis, and has the gift of encouragement which he has showered upon me on many occasions.

As Bill so faithfully posted his thoughts of hope, encouragement, and feelings of despair and loneliness throughout this trial, I, like hundreds of other readers, clung to each word and shared his emotional struggle. We collectively cried, rejoiced with every tidbit of good news, embraced every sign of hope, and, like a sponge, soaked up every enlightened meaning from a Scripture verse Bill shared. It was remarkable how the Lord used this blog site to show His power, His grace, His comfort, and His healing in countless ways to countless others besides his family. Thank you, Bill, for taking us on your personal journey and for allowing us to get a glimpse of the intimate way in which the Lord spoke to you for all of us. You reminded us repeatedly that *the story is far from over,* and those words continue to provide comfort to those of us who have lost a loved one.

Sharon Sanderson
Director for Alumni and College Relations
Toccoa Falls College

Bill Stacey shares the challenge, victory, and absolute hope promised to each of us within every single page of this illuminating, heart-grabbing journal and life-changing log. Whether your own personal journey travels one day at a time, or fast forwards from cover to cover, "This Story is Far From Over" will draw you in, wrap you in the passion-filled confidence of Christ, and keep you there. With his unique gift of weaving the serious, the humorous, and the hope found only in Jesus Christ, Stacey pulls out a chair and invites the reader to the family table of real life at a time when most of us hunger for real answers and real truth; and it doesn't end there. You won't simply read these words, you will live them. You, your friends and your family will be well fed.

Greg Davidson
President & Master Illusionist
Believe Ministries

What is this thing we call Grief? Rev. Bill Stacey takes you on a journey through the pains and struggles of dealing with his wife's illness and subsequent death. I observed the strength and support he received from his three adult daughters, a caring community, and a loving church family. In reading this book you will truly find a work of hope, tender love, and deep compassion. For counselors, pastors, and lay persons dealing with grief, this book is a must.

Dr. Thomas N. Howell
Pastoral Counselor
Marriage and Family Therapist

Pastor Stacey's journal is very interesting, informative, as well as personal: all of the attributes that make up a good book. The best way I can describe it from a widow's or widower's point of view would be that it is "real life." I almost felt as if I were there with the family while they were going through the sickness and death of Nancy. My emotions were changing from laughing at the humor at times and then to sad almost to tears as he described so vividly how he and his girls cared for Nancy during those months before her passing. Even during those days, his strength and love for her was so evident. I believe this book will be a blessing to everyone who reads it.

Mrs. Merle Henry, Director
Widow's Hope Minstries

I have the privilege of knowing Bill Stacey and his family. In reading this book you will witness a man and family that truly love the Lord and are willing to serve Him in all aspects of life, regardless of situations and circumstances. This book will give you an in-depth and personal look through the struggle of illness and death, and yet through trials be able to share your faith, and at the same time give glory to God.

Rev. Nate Bunner
Associate Pastor
Indian Creek Baptist Church

This Story Is Far From Over

*T*he journey through life takes one down different and various paths. Some paths are common with the level of age or experience of the traveler. For example I remember well the day my mother registered me for kindergarten. That path opened my eyes to the beginning and ongoing journey of formal education. While I was progressing on the path of education I discovered side paths that peeked interests and helped develop maturity. One of those side paths was my introduction into Little League Baseball and learning to play organized team sports. Naturally, there were many other paths which allowed a myriad of life experiences that can be shuffled off into the good or not-so-good piles. At times the not-so-good path was soon realized and the backtracking to a better path ensued.

Life itself is a way of telling a story. As one travels through life and writes his own story, the stories of others can be helpful and beneficial in helping shape lives and follow good or better paths. Unfortunately, some paths and some stories can only be discovered by individually taking that particular journey. For sure, there will be similar paths or similar stories, but sometimes that path can seem very lonely and their outcomes seem out of control. The story of which I am writing is one that, when viewed through proper perspective, has no ending. The circumstances of the primary characters change and open the way for more paths of travel and more maturity in life so that this story is far from over.

One path with which life takes individuals is the journey of grief. Grief is masked in a cadre of forms. By definition grief is a multi-faceted response to loss, particularly to the loss of someone or something with which a bond was formed. At an early age a child learns the path of grief when her pet dies. The way in which the parent deals with such paths will often determine how the child will respond. If the parent is callused and cold to the grief often children follow in same. Likewise, if the parent is nurturing and caring during the grief process, the children often follow that path or pattern.

The first recorded human death in the Bible is that of Abel. He was the son of Adam and Eve, and his life was taken from him at the hand of his brother Cain. Genesis chapter four records the account but does not speak to the grief. I have wondered how Eve processed through the path of grief during the loss of her son. In fact, she lost two sons due to the banishment of Cain. Her heart must have broken in grief. Adam must have surely wondered how to put order back into a chaotic situation.

Abraham's story includes a full chapter concerning the death and burial of his beloved Sarah. He was a foreigner to the land in which the path of grief led him. Scripture reports several accounts of loved ones dying, and the path of grief was realized, trodden, and worn. King David faced grief on two distinct, yet specific paths of grief. His story includes the death of his son born out of wedlock as well as the account of his rebellious son, Absalom, whose life was taken from him. Other biblical stories include the miraculous work of God when a loved one was restored to life. The account of Lazarus's life being restored is duly noted, but probably the most famous story of grief being overturned is that of Jesus being resurrected. His story is far from over.

Perhaps the oldest biblical writing is that of Job. His path led him to deal with the grief of losing his children, his livestock, and wealth, as well as many of his servants. The story needs repeating as recorded in Job 1:22 "Throughout all this Job did not sin or blame God for anything." Job's story is well documented to show he was true to the Lord, and God blessed Job for his faithfulness and perseverance to endure. God prospered Job to allow him one hundred forty years following the crisis and grief.

In the pages that follow are snapshots into the life of the Stacey family as they travel the path of grief and bewilderment for 165 days during Nancy's illness. Following those riveting moments of transition from what is commonly identified as life into that of eternity; I continue walking life's paths and living the story in blocks of time which cover the next 365 days. It is a path in which the emotions are ricocheting off of life itself as adjustments are made without my soul mate.

Nancy was the fourth of six children born to Durward and Guinnell Adams in the Tom's Creek Community of northeast Georgia. During her senior year of high school at Stephens County, she met me at a Saturday night church function. Nancy and I were married September 2, 1978 and our lives were blessed with three daughters. Ashley, Jessica, and Andrea kept our lives filled with activities such as basketball, flag twirling, and playing in the band. Nancy guided them into adulthood with skills many mothers would envy because of her work ethic. Nancy was a thirty-year career teacher of health and physical education, but supplemented her income as a basketball coach for many of those years. Her skills of playing the piano were utilized by two of the four churches in which we have served. While she took her career seriously, she took the responsibility of being a wife and mother even more seriously. Her peers recognized her achievements and often called her for advice concerning motherhood or professional advancement.

The first several journal entries of this story are written through the eyes of a future son-in-law, Joshua Moore, as he observed our family in the midst of shock and bewilderment. Nancy had always been considered in good if not excellent physical condition. On January 13, 2011 I noticed Nancy was having difficulty staying focused on preparing for work. She was always a quick riser and completed the task at hand with determination, but on that day she could not get her thoughts together. We soon learned Nancy had a brain tumor.

While I have pulled the proverbial curtain back and allowed the reader to peer into the lives of what most people would consider a normal family, my goal was not to play upon the sympathies or evoke pity from the reader. The purpose of my writing is to offer encouragement to others faced with difficult challenges. Our challenge was that of a brain tumor, but others are faced with challenges in which our situation would pale beside. I have written the

CaringBridge journals as they transpired. I chose to share the emotions, confusion, and victories in a transparent way. Much of the writing was written from the waiting room of the Athens Regional Medical Center Intensive Care Unit, on the fifth-floor neurology wing, or in the guest house. We started numbering the days of our journey on day four, and I have chosen to leave the numbering of days and the dates as a way to mark our path as we journeyed along. I am not writing as an authority on the subject of grief, but rather as one that endured a difficult time on one of life's paths and continued moving forward. It is true; it is real, and because of Jesus Christ, this story is far from over!

January

- **Sunday, January 16, 2011**

Day 4

As I write this journal entry, it's Sunday afternoon around 3:15PM. The immediate family had worship service this morning in the chapel located on the first floor of Athens Regional Medical Center. Nancy was able to worship with us and she even played a few songs for us on the piano (what a blessing it was). We sang praises to God and lifted His name on high. We shared scripture with one another and then prayed for Nancy. We took her back to the room around noon. She was able to rest and nap a little this afternoon. Visitors have consistently been coming in today and throughout the weekend. We are so thankful for the abundance of love that has been shown. Please continue to pray. We can feel those prayers in a mighty way. Blessed be the name of the Lord.

- **Sunday, January 16, 2011**

Day 4

Nancy is located at Athens Regional Medical Center in Athens, Georgia. We've been told that Nancy's surgery will likely be performed sometime during the afternoon hours tomorrow. We will certainly let everyone know if that timeframe changes. The doctors want to perform a biopsy first to gain additional information about the tumor. Then they will remove as much of the tumor as possible.

- **Monday, January 17, 2011**

Day 5

We've just been told that Nancy's surgery is tentatively scheduled for 2:30 PM today. She rested pretty well last night with Bill by her side in the hospital bed. This morning she has been getting ready and playing "beauty shop" with her daughters as they helped her with her shower, hair, and getting her dressed for the day. Please keep Nancy, our family, and all medical personnel in your prayers as the surgery time nears. God bless you.

- **Monday, January 17, 2011**

Day 5

Nancy was taken back for surgery approximately 15 minutes ago. We will post updates as often as we get them. Please continue to pray. We feel your prayers.

- **Monday, January 17, 2011**

We were just informed that Nancy's surgery officially started at 3:40 PM. Please keep praying.

- **Monday, January 17, 2011**

Day 5

Nancy got out of surgery around 5:00 PM. We will post more updates later. Please keep praying.

- **Monday, January 17, 2011**

Day 5

At 8:30 PM the family was allowed to see Nancy in the ICU area. Only two people were allowed in the ICU area at a time and Bill and Ashley were the first two. The immediate family took turns seeing Nancy. Nancy greeted many of us with a "boo." She seems to be recovering well with God's help. She's awake and recognizes the family and the familiar faces. Her vitals are all doing well.

It's going to be a day-to-day journey with Nancy going forward with God dictating each and every step. The surgeon told us he was able to remove anywhere from 25 percent to 50 percent of the brain tumor. The doctor told us that visually the tumor appears to have malignant characteristics. The tumor has been classified as a grade 4 brain tumor and is also considered a primary brain tumor.

It will be 24–48 hours until we hear the results of the pathology report. This will allow us to have a lot more information to make decisions. We are currently prayerfully weighing our options and planning our next step(s) with God's help and guidance. We are unable to completely solidify a plan until we hear the full results from the pathology report.

Nancy is expected to remain in ICU for approximately 24 hours, and we've been told that she will likely remain at Athens Regional for approximately one week to recover from the surgery. Then, it's expected that Nancy will need two to three weeks for recovery from the surgery before beginning the next phase of treatments.

God is good. We appreciate so much all of your prayers. Please continue to keep praying for Nancy and our family as more information is revealed and more decisions have to be made.

May God bless you.

• Tuesday, January 18, 2011

Day 6

Nancy had a good night last night in the ICU unit. She was able to feed herself breakfast this morning. She had a good visit with her doctor this morning as well. The doctor said she is recovering from the surgery very well thus far. He said that hopefully she can be moved from ICU to a regular hospital room this afternoon. More information will be posted throughout the day. Thank you again for your prayers. Please continue to pray. We feel your prayers.

• Tuesday, January 18, 2011

Day 6

Nancy was just taken for a "Baseline MRI." The medical staff have been very pleased with how coherent Nancy has been. She is able to audibly and clearly call many of the medical staff by name (even those that aren't in the ICU unit but that assisted her in previous days). Nancy's daughters feel that she has been more like "Mom" this morning than she has in a while.

- **Tuesday, January 18, 2011**

Day 6

Nancy was moved out of ICU into a regular hospital room this afternoon. Upon arrival into her room, She requested an apple pie to eat. Her mother prepared the pie especially for her. Nancy said she wanted the pie to be "warmed just a little, but not too hot." Please continue to keep her in your prayers as well as the family.

- **Wednesday, January 19, 2011 1:28 PM, EST**

Day 7

Nancy has been able to sit up and read mail today. She appreciates all of the thoughtful cards and gifts that everyone has sent. She thought the cards and gifts from Big A elementary were very special (especially the signed gym ball).

A Physical Therapist has been working with Nancy today as well. Together they walked down the hallway and performed various exercises.

Nancy's surgeon met with her and the family this morning. Initially it was believed that 25 percent to 50 percent of the tumor was removed. However, after reviewing the MRI from yesterday he now believes that 50 percent to 60 percent of the tumor was removed...and it's even possible that they might have even removed as much as 70 percent of the tumor. Obviously, we won't know a lot more until the pathology report comes back but this is definitely a praise report! God is good.

We've been told that it will likely be tomorrow before the pathology report is made available. We will provide updates if this time frame changes.

Good help has not been in a shortage. Two of Nancy's grandchildren (Ashtin and Elliott) assisted her by placing "Dora the Explorer" and "Barbie" band-aids on her.

We want to thank you for your prayers. Please continue to pray for Nancy and the family and please praise God for the positive results He's allowed us to experience.

There has been a sign placed on Nancy's hospital room door that asks all visitors to check with the medical staff or a family member before entering. This is just to allow her to rest as much as possible right now. The family wants to stress how much they appreciate each and every visitor and they want to encourage everyone to keep coming. Your visits are uplifting and encouraging to the family.

May God bless you.

• Wednesday, January 19, 2011

Day 7

They've just removed the IVs from Nancy. Once the proper draining has completed, Nancy will be totally untethered. We will continue to post updates as we get them. Thanks again for all of your prayers. Please continue to pray. The medical staff took the drainage tube out of Nancy's incision. Please pray that she will be able to relax, rest, and get a good night of sleep.

• Wednesday, January 19, 2011

Day 7

Nancy, along with help from her daughters, was able to take her first post-surgery shower this evening.

We're still being told that we will likely speak with doctors in the morning regarding the pathology report. .

Please continue to pray.

- **Thursday, January 20, 2011**

Day 8

Good morning to all. We are praising the Lord because Nancy had a much better night as she was able to rest more than the previous night. Vital checks and bathroom breaks were the only reasons her rest was disturbed.

This morning, a week ago, at 11:00 marks the beginning of this journey. Your prayers have definitely provided great strength to Nancy and our family over the past week.

We're waiting to meet with some of Nancy's doctors and also on the pathology report. We will post more information as it becomes available.

Thank you for your prayers. Please continue to pray.

- **Thursday, January 20, 2011**

Day 8

Hi Folks...

I'm giving Josh a break and posting this little entry. He has been doing a great job hasn't he? Nancy and I are most fortunate and blessed to have such great girls. They in-turn have been blessed with wisdom in their choice of life partners. Each one has been involved this week from doing laundry and errands to being strong shoulders in which to lean upon.

A quick update is to tell you that I took one for the team today. Nancy was hungry and breakfast wasn't on the hall yet. Josh had brought me an Egg McMuffin. It was a no-brainer (pardon the pun) she would eat the Egg McMuffin and I would sacrifice for the team. Stay tuned ... hopefully I won't be admitted. Ha! Ha!

- **Thursday, January 20, 2011**

Day 8

Nancy's doctor just came by her room and said the pathology report was in. He plans on coming back by her room around 12:30 PM to discuss with the family. Please continue to pray as the time nears for the pathology discussion.

- **Thursday, January 20, 2011**

Day 8

Nancy and the family met with the surgeon to discuss the pathology report. The surgeon said Nancy was recovering very well considering what she's been through. He was also very pleased with Nancy's physical and mental capacities.

The pathology report confirmed that Nancy has a "Grade IV," malignant, primary brain tumor. The surgeon confirmed around 60 percent of the tumor was removed. He also said that a discharge from the hospital was possible by tomorrow or Saturday.

We also met with an oncologist. Positive factors that he was pleased to see were her age, stamina, physical condition, good attitude, and strong social network. In addition to those factors, we have the prayers of many brothers and sisters in Christ working in Nancy's favor as well. Based on all these factors, he suggested taking an aggressive approach to eradicating the remaining portion of the tumor.

A representative from the Loran Smith Center for Cancer Care came by to give us information on resources for support and treatment information. The representative was impressed by the amount of support Nancy has already. She stated that there are so many patients that do not have the support that Nancy has.

After all information was shared with the family and after all doctors left the hospital room, the family joined hands and prayed. We continue to process and absorb all of the information that was shared with us today and are prayerfully considering the best route to go from here.

Thank you for your prayers. Please continue to pray for Nancy and our family as we seek God's wisdom for the decisions ahead.

• **Friday, January 21, 2011**

Day 9

Good Morning Folks!!

After a busy day of consultations and doctor interviews, Nancy was ready for a good night's rest. She was rewarded with just that. By the way, for those of you who remember TV's *Hee Haw*, Nancy has her own "Nurse-Good-Bodies." Ashley, Jessica, and Andrea have been taking great care of their Mama. From my perspective —they're cute too!!!

HEEEYYY!!!!

The Doctor just came in to examine and *discharge her!!!* We will have some care-training and then be on our way home. Yes, to say the least, we are *excited!* Thanks so much for the prayers. This will close the first chapter of the journey but there is much more to come and we will equally need your prayer support.

Love Y'all!! Bill, Nancy, and Family

• **Friday, January 21, 2011**

Day 9

BREAKING NEWS!!!

Nancy is on her way home. Many, many, many of you have asked to help in some way. In fact, as I write this post there have been nearly 12,650 "visits" listed.

The purpose of this post is to share that our sister-in-law, Alisa Adams is taking charge of meal coordination. Some have asked to help so we are suggesting you contact her at XXX-XXX-XXXX and leave her a message. Nancy will probably be following a "diabetic" diet even though she does not have diabetes.

Thanks again and we will see you soon!!!

- **Saturday, January 22, 2011**

DAY 10

It was a wonderful surprise to find the *huge* banner and balloons in our carport from the teachers and staff at BIG A Elementary School when we finally arrived home Friday around 3:30 PM. My sister, Marlene, greeted us after having done some cleaning and preparation for our return. Coming home in some ways reminded me of returning from a week's vacation. There was laundry to be done, mail to sort and to which reply, phone messages to answer, and so forth.

The girl's families came over to welcome Nana home and soon it was decided that little Ashtin would require a quick visit to a walk-in clinic to examine and treat an unpleasant and painful rash that appeared on her legs. The rash was diagnosed to be SHINGLES!! What next?!?!? She is only five years old. We are determined to endure and persevere.

The family realized we were all sleep deprived so we called in re-enforcements to ensure Nancy and Ashtin would have a good night's rest. Janet, Nancy's sister, willingly came over to assist us during the night. This morning Nancy has followed her blood-sugar routine, taken her prescribed medications, eaten breakfast, given both Mamas a nightly report, and now she is resting. Ashtin, too, seems to have had a good night, and the rash seems to have subsided a little.

It is rewarding and encouraging to read the postings you have continued to send. Some are simple, well-wishing and prayerful supports while others are recalling past days of various humorous or meaningful experiences. Each is embraced as precious and helpful words. They are sent by you who are merely acquaintances or dear, dear family and friends. Some of you are co-teachers, pastors, former students, and even recent care-givers from Athens Regional Hospital. Each of you is reflecting God's love to us, and His light enables us to grow through this process.

We have the *best:* the best family, best neighbors, best friends, and certainly the BEST and ONLY God. Thanks.

• **Sunday, January 23, 2011**

DAY 11

Wow!!! Day 10 was pretty incredible. Poor ole' Mailman delivered 7 bags with a total of 32 plastic balls each being the size of a basketball. They were signed by all of Nancy's school class children and teachers from BIG A Elementary School. Thank you for such creative thoughts. I'm sure the post office enjoyed that assignment. Ha! Ha!

After the morning routine and a little rest, calls were placed, appointments made, and by 3:15 PM Nancy was sitting in a chair at Lovely Nails getting a manicure. Little Ashtin was doing the same. In fact, since that was my first visit with all the girls, I let them talk me into a pedicure at Nancy's next nail appointment ... stay tuned ... "Twinkle-Toes" Hmm ... I wonder how that will sound. One of Nancy's dear friends had already paid for her visit which was an added bonus to the day. It was another fine showing of kindness.

We checked with Nancy as we were leaving the nail place, and she assured us she felt fine enough to keep her hair appointment at Debra's Magic Mirror. That appointment provided a hair washing and styling and a little catching up of community news. Another one of our dear, dear friends had already covered the expense for that visit. We have been so blessed.

When Nancy returned home we did the medication routine, ate some supper (or dinner), and enjoyed a visit from family members, Bruce and Debbie.

This morning I am able to share that Nancy had a restful night with few interruptions. Jessica is the "Charge Nurse" but she also doubles as cook and drill sargeant! Ha! Ha! Our kids have been great, and with Jessica living at home, she has the added privilege of helping a little more.

Currently, Nancy is studying her Sunday School lesson, giving instructions for cooking, and making preparations for an afternoon visit to a family reunion.

Me??? Well, I'm trying to stay out of the way, help when I'm asked, and mostly sitting in awe of the week we've just had and thanking God for His ongoing blessings of goodness and mercy. I can't wait to see what He wants to do through us this coming week.

- **Monday, January 24, 2011**

Day 12

I know, I know. This is a little later than usual and many have said, "Where's the new update?" So here we go ...

As I mentioned yesterday, we went to the Harrison family reunion with Nancy and she ate a good lunch and enjoyed members of her mama's side of the family. We got home in the mid-afternoon and tried to regroup from the previous week. (We ain't there yet! Ha!) Between watching Barney reruns and an occasional flip of the football game, we pretty much just rested while some of the "House Medical Team" worked on reporting the times and quantities of medications and helping set up a schedule for the new week. I think their publication of "Medicine Distribution for Dummies" will be in print soon. Ha! Ha!

With the collaboration from the HMT (see above) we had a family pow-wow and decided that because Nancy's blood sugar has been so wacky, we would need to set up an appointment with the family physician to get that under control.

Nancy had another good night, and I just took her for that appointment. Our doctor adjusted the insulin quantity and hopefully, that will help. As a reminder, Nancy has not been diagnosed with diabetes but the steroid dosages she is required to take for brain swelling is playing havoc with her sugar. The doctor said everything else looked fine but did prescribe an additional med that I am going to pick up in a few minutes. Andrea and boys are here to assist while I run to town. I also want to schedule a second opinion with an oncologist tomorrow or the next day to reiterate and hear same or different options for Nancy's treatments.

In the meantime, we had a nice meal prepared for us last night and sometime around noon, some of Nancy's co-teachers are going to make a brief visit during their "free time" and bring her some lunch. You guys and gals have been great and we DO appreciate your taking time to send a humorous or encouraging note. Ashley suggested I read Romans 15:13 Now may the God of hope fill you with all joy and peace in believing, so that you may overflow with hope by the power of the Holy Spirit. I have read that and used that as my "dosage" for the day. God's Word continues to hold us up.

P.S. Alisa Adams is only coordinating meals for Nancy and the family. She said there was some confusion that people thought we wanted her to get paid to cater the meals for us. She is our sister-in-law and wants to help us by scheduling the meals.

- **Tuesday, January 25, 2011**

Day 13

There is absolutely, positively, without any question, and it is undeniably without debate—Nancy is SWEET!!! "Aw shucks, Bill we already knew that she is sweet." I'm sure you thought that I was just bragging about her demeanor and personality and many of you agreed. But, now we have documentation to prove it.

Yesterday we went to the family doctor to help get her blood sugar regulated and as many of you can share by personal experience, it can sometimes be a little tricky to get right. This morning, after the charge nurse (Jessica) got breakfast ready and all the meds in place we sat Nancy down to check her sugar. In fact, as the other girls called in to check on Nana, we decided to make a game of guessing what the number is each day. So far, Nana is keeping us guessing farther from the number we would like to reach. Yep! She is sweet alright.

Each of you has been sweet too. For lunch yesterday, Christen, Laura, Rita and Connie delivered a tasty meal and included a cash gift from some of her co-teachers. Later, a nice peace lily was sent from her two boyfriends (also, co-teachers, Eran and Keith) . The entertainment of the day was presented by Grandson Clayton, who walked around and grinned all day long. The family enjoyed an afternoon visit from Lynn, and we answered some phone calls. It's been a good 24 hours for us and for that we rejoice. Nancy and I read our devotional this morning and one of the verses was Psalm 73:23-24. I could print it out but you probably would have more enjoyment finding it for yourself. Psst—it's in the Old Testament. Ha! Ha!

Today we are going to "coast." We don't have any appointments until tomorrow. Chris P. is coming by to assist me in some "fix-it" tasks and later, Kay is coming by to assist in some insurance forms. Thanks for all the calls, cards, and various other means of communication. You are the *best!*

• Thursday, January 27, 2011

DAY 15

Check out the new pictures that have been added.

Many of you have heard the old saying, "Mama said there would be days like this." Well, yesterday (Wednesday) was one of those days. The day started rather normal for us. Up a little after six, checked the blood glucose and found it to be improving. Jessica fixed a good breakfast and we were rolling into another day. Nancy had scheduled a trip back to Debra's Magic Mirror for a hair washing and we would stop by the school for a quick visit before going to Athens for another oncology consultation.

By nine, Nancy had decided to lie down for a recharge before we went to Debra's. I was busy with laundry and returning messages. When she awoke, I felt things were a little off kilter but she said she felt fine. While walking into the beauty shop I noticed she was staggering. Always being the practical joker, I asked her if she was "playing" to which she replied, "No." I just got the door opened and grabbed Nancy as she slumped into the shop. Debra helped me get her into a chair and after a few minutes, she seemed fine. Thanks Debra.

31

I decided to stop by the school anyway to return some dishes, and Nancy was able to visit with a couple of teachers. They were kind enough to come outside to the car for their visit. We got back home and Nancy rested after lunch. Nate is our associate pastor at Indian Creek, and I contacted him to bring us the wheelchair that had been donated to the church a few years ago. He prayed with us before he left, and soon Jessica and Josh joined us so we could keep our 3:30 appointment in Athens. Andrea, Ashley and their husbands joined us at the doctor's office. I had alerted Chris to help get Nancy into the waiting room while I parked the car. Nancy succeeded in making a memorable first impression by having to sit down in the lobby floor before getting to her seat. The staff was great and welcomed Nancy and aided her to her seat. Not surprisingly, Nancy acknowledged one of the staff girls as being a former student, and they caught up on past memories.

The doctor spoke with us concerning her current condition and offered a path of treatment options for her future condition. He said because her blood pressure and other vital signs seemed well within the bounds of good health, he thought her falling was due to pressure on her brain from the tumor. Granted, the glucose situation is still wacky.

After the doctor left the examination room, the eight of us discussed possibilities and options for Nancy's treatments. We are at the mercy of calendar schedules, but as of now, we have decided to go to the Duke University Medical Center and get an evaluation from them. Depending upon their examination, we will either receive approximately 42 days of treatment there or come back to Athens for treatment. It will include both radiation and chemotherapy with another new drug running concurrently.

As we were riding home, I looked over at Nancy and told her we just heard the same sermon but from a different preacher. The reality of her condition is serious, the message has not changed, but she and the family are determined to stand together and face future days with that same peace that passes *all* understanding.

• Thursday, January 27, 2011

DAY 15a

I thought I would give a brief update. It's amazing what a little sleep and some Scripture can do to put a better perspective on the day.

Psalms 25:4-5

Make Your ways known to me, Lord; teach me Your paths. Guide me in Your truth and teach me, for You are the God of my salvation; I wait for You all day long.

Nancy slept well, well, except for the trip to the restroom at 4:15 AM and then *sneaking* into the kitchen freezer for a bite or two from a Weight-Watchers Ice Cream bar. Not to worry ... the drill sargent sprang into action! Jessica said she caught her red-handed, scolded her, and then gave her a hug. I'm telling ya, I'm gonna have to buy a cow bell for that woman. Ha!

Gotta go, as Ashley just informed me the washing machine needs some attention. Stay tuned and thanks again for the prayer support.

• Saturday, January 29, 2011

DAY 17

The last forty-eight hours, or so have been fairly quiet. Nancy's physical condition has not had any noticeable changes, and she has rested rather well. She continues to have a good, healthy appetite (including the ice cream bars Ha!) and her regular strength seems to have been maintained. The glucose numbers, well, that's still another story. They have been much like a roller coaster except the "lows" never quite get low enough. Our family doctor is helping by monitoring the recorded results. The information is gathered four-to-six times each day by the nurses ... ah-hem ... the girls. Ha! We have four scheduled appointments to various medical facilities and are in the hopes of going to Duke sometime this coming week.

That is about all I have to update on Nancy so let me turn the subject to you. You, who are the constant friends, neighbors, and family members have not forgotten us in your prayers, thoughts, or comments on CaringBridge. Isn't this a nice tool to share information about loved ones? Thanks!

Let me share some compliments about you. You have been gracious in calling or writing something at the times we needed some encouragement. I think God's switchboard forwards those messages through the various channels of media to the individuals within the family who need it. You have also provided food that has been tasty and nurturing. Amy provided a great meal topped off with sugar-free Banana pudding, Cynthia provided yummy cubed steak; Janet brought homemade vegetable soup. Julia fixed a huge pot of chili, while Mary and Geraldine followed that with meatloaf and trimmings. After prayer for Nancy with them, the doorbell rang, and in walked Leon and Eleanor with a pound cake. Are you starting to get the idea that you are genuinely appreciated? Yesterday, Nancy's principal, Mr. Sanders, came in lugging a huge, fluffy Teddy Bear adorned with a Big A Elementary tee shirt. What a great photo opportunity. Sorry, you will have to use your imagination for that one. Ha!

You have loved Nancy through thinking of our family as you have listened to songs on the radio or remembered them from times in your life that needed encouraging. You are people, such as Cyndi that sent "Under His Wings" by the Rupps and "What Faith Can Do" by Kutless or Deborah who sent "Stronger" by Mandisa. Christina encouraged us to listen to "Under Control" by the Gold City Quartet. Some of you directed us to read books or web information to consider helping the Nancy's physical condition. You are Carl, or Ken, or Jen, and you have spoken with personal experiences or that of your loved ones. These contacts have each been embraced and welcomed. Thank you for being YOU!

This morning I was reading a passage of Scripture from Isaiah 26:3 "Thou wilt keep *him* in perfect peace, *whose* mind *is* stayed *on thee:* because he trusteth in thee." As we have written before, let's see what God wants to do through us in the days ahead.

• **Saturday, January 29, 2011**

DAY 17a

Hello Again … I'm doubling up today since I didn't write anything yesterday. Actually, after the day we've had, I couldn't wait until tomorrow to post it. This morning as I was helping Nancy prepare for the day, she told me that she was planning on going to the Middle School Basketball Tournament. It is the annual, end of the season tourney and Stephens County is its host this year. Nancy coached for several years and now, for these recent past years, she has been their official scorekeeper. I nodded in agreement but in my mind, I was thinking, "Whatever, she can't even sit up for a couple of hours at a time in her chair at home, much less some bleacher seat in a gymnasium."

Have I mentioned to those of you who are merely "acquaintances" that Nancy tends to be strong-willed? I was hesitant. In fact, I thought her idea would pass once the day got going and she would realize it would be too much to attempt. Throughout our thirty-two years of marriage, I don't always like to but I will admit to being wrong. The Ole' Energizer Bunny proved me wrong again. She was determined to walk in and sit down next to Sandi at the scorer's table and she did just that. Three games later, and after having visited with several friends, she told me she was ready to return home. She didn't keep score, but she could have if they would have needed her.

We came home in time for the glucose check and the evening medications. She ate a good supper and is resting up for tomorrow. It will be Sunday, and her church attendance surpasses most people so I'm not even going to think about trying to tell her "no." Ha!

I would like to share one other thought. Many of you have lived through what we are going through now. I am aware we are not alone in any of this situation. I also acknowledge that while a family may go through a crisis, there are additional circumstances that can have an effect on the family. Yesterday, our future son-in-law, Josh, had an experience of which I am speaking. His uncle, W. C. Moore, of the Anderson, SC, area passed away and his funeral is tomorrow (Sunday). I'm told Mr. Moore was in his late eighties and had lived a good Christian testimony before his peers. Please join us in praying for the Moore family.

- **Monday, January 31, 2011**

DAY 19

Hi Folks,

I'm in a bit of a hurry but everything is going fine. We are on our way to Athens for two different routine doctor visits.

Nancy has done well the last two days, including a trip to church and a walk to the end of our long (100-yard) driveway and back. I will include more soon.

Thanks for all the encouraging posts and keep them coming.

I will write more this evening with the Good Lord Willing.

- **Monday, January 31, 2011**

DAY 19

Amazing Grace! How sweet the sound that saved a wretch like me. I once was lost but now I'm found was blind but now I see.

(Stanza 4)

Thro' many dangers, toils, and snares I have already come. 'Tis grace hath brought me safe thus far, and grace will lead me home.

As we walked into the service Sunday, the congregation was singing this great hymn of the Christian faith. I thought about the irony of escorting my lovely wife and daughter into a worship service that was proclaiming God's grace in the midst of our recent experiences. If we have learned anything through this trial, it has been all about God's grace. Nancy has shared with more than one medical staff person that if there was anything she could share about her experience that was negative, she would. However, she could not think of anything that has been negative outside of the obvious.

It is those unsolicited remarks and others that continue to strengthen the family and me as we endure this together.

We enjoyed our time of worship singing hymns, sharing testimonies, giving our tithes, and hearing from God's Word. It truly is rewarding to be one of His children. Thanks for the message, Nate.

Our jaws have fallen open numerous times, as we experience the generosity of people we love and care about and see it flooding back to us several times over. I honestly cannot estimate the numbers of you who have offered to do "anything" from cleaning toilets, running errands, preparing food, and so forth. God's grace is truly amazing.

Today Nancy was able to keep two appointments in Athens. The first was an echocardiogram followed by a lunch break at one of her favorite places. We then made our way to the radiation oncologist to discuss her projected treatments. The doctor was very transparent in relaying what could be expected given her current health make up. He inquired about our trip to Duke, and I asked him his opinion of the doctor Nancy would see by the name of Dr. Henry Friedman. His response was encouraging as he said, "There is nothing more to say except he is the best in the southeast, if not the nation." He went on to relate Dr. Friedman was the leader in understanding treatment for Nancy's type of brain tumor and cancer. Hopefully, we will meet by the end of this week or the first part of next week.

Tomorrow, (Tuesday) Nancy will have the staples removed from her scalp and a followup visit from Dr. Barnes' staff. He is the neurosurgeon whom we highly recommend. Then we travel to our family physician to examine the ongoing blood glucose battle caused by the double-edged sword of a drug called Decadron. Its purpose is to relieve the swelling in Nancy's brain. Around the house, I refer to it as Deca-Durn because the "durn" stuff is wreaking havoc on her glucose levels, and it is keeping her fatigued and seemingly weakened.

Thanks for showing interest in Nancy and her beloved family. We welcome every contact and genuinely appreciate your prayers and support.

===

February

• Wednesday, February 2, 2011

DAY 20 (23,460 Visits — 968 Posts)

My, my, my, what a day. It started early, like our usual routine, around 6:00 AM. Nancy rose slightly later to get prepared for another day of doctor visits and field trips. We left our house at 8:20 and went to the Royston Diagnostic Center where Dr. Brian Barnes has a satellite office. Today, his associate, Dr. Walpert and staff were on hand to treat patients. A nurse practitioner treated Nancy and answered our questions concerning the recovery of the surgery itself. When we questioned her concerning the Decadron she got Dr. Walpert's approval to begin reducing the amount Nancy was required to consume in an effort to bring the glucose levels closer to reasonable function. We were thrilled, and yet aware we would need to monitor Nancy's behavior in the event swelling reoccurred, causing debilitating motor skills. Nancy's progress was far enough along that the staples were removed from her scalp.

We hurried to our family doctor in the Gumlog area for the next visit. Dr. Karen Eschedor and her staff have been invaluable to this process from day one. After a report from our visit concerning the reduction of the Decadron and a thorough review of the recordings of Nancy's glucose records, she offered instructions that would further ensure better health for Nancy. She cautioned us to evaluate the glucose counts carefully as they may begin to plunge due to the reduction of Decadron.

It was nearly noon when we reached Whitlock Mortuary to visit the Sheryl Jones family. Sheryl's husband, Roger, is Nancy's third-cousin, and Sheryl had fought a fifteen-month battle of pancreatic cancer. Roger and his family members were encouraging to us.

I took Nancy for her promised hair appointment next. Debra welcomed her, and fixed her hair while I went to the pharmacy for more meds. After a quick trim for me, we left Debra's Magic Mirror and grabbed a late lunch at Los Amigos. I must admit I was getting a little anxious about our next appointment. Some of you will remember about ten days ago when I agreed to get a pedicure ... well, today was the day. Twinkle-Toes it is. Really, guys, the experience was not too girlie, and I did get to sit next to Nancy while she was getting the same treatment. Oh, the things we do for love. Ha!

By now, the afternoon time was 3:50, and I was ready to take Nancy home. That was not her plan. The Girl's Middle School Regional Championship was to tip off at 5:00 PM. We arrived at 4:00 and I demanded (yeah — right!) that we rest in the car until 4:45. Nancy rested while I returned phone messages. One of the calls was to our neighbor Sarah, who provided our supper for the evening. Thanks for understanding our tardy return home. Supper was tasty. The tournament started and Nancy took her usual seat beside Sandi, the timekeeper. During halftime of the first game, Nancy was invited to keep the official score book for the second game. Susan was kind to relinquish the position to Nancy and let her do the task she had faithfully done for all the home games before her surgery. Susan was also on hand to relieve Nancy with just over a minute left in the game while Nancy answered the call of Mother Nature. She's been calling frequently since Nancy's surgery. It must be the meds. Ha!

We returned home at 7:45 PM and *got the call!* It was that antici-pated call from Dr. Henry Friedman of the Duke University Medical Center. He said that he was extending an invitation for Nancy to come as a candidate for treatment evaluation. His office would call us soon to set the appointment. I am expecting word tomorrow. (Technically, today, Wednesday). I would encourage you to check out some websites on YouTube.com. Both of these will be found if you search under Dr. Henry Friedman. The first is: Hope for Brain Cancer Patients (CBS) and the second is: Duke Neuro-oncologist Henry Friedman. Both of these give his positive, yet realistic, approach to attacking brain cancer.

We have traveled several miles and met numerous people. Many were well-wishers, and some were carrying concerns for their family members. Roger's family is grieving, Dan is facing surgery Wednesday, and Marilyn's mother was recently diagnosed with cancer. CaringBridge unites us for a few minutes each day, but my family realizes we are not the only ones going through testing and trials. We are remembering you as well. Thanks for checking in on us again today.

• **Wednesday, February 2, 2011**

DAY 21

Hi Folks,

I wanted to give you a brief newsflash. Yesterday afternoon as we were walking into the basketball games, Nancy's head started seeping around her incision. We did not panic but we watched it at the medication times during the night and decided to call the neurologist.

We are headed back to Athens for an appointment at 1:30 PM. Again, let me say this is not an urgent or upsetting thing to us but we are going on the side of caution. Besides, Nancy wasn't scheduled to go anywhere today, and I think she was getting a little bored. Ha!

I will share more when we have more information.

P.S. Ashley called this morning to report a co-worker of Dustin's has a two year old grandson who woke up with seizures, and the doctors are trying to get him some much needed attention. Please pray for Ben.

• **Wednesday, February 2, 2011**

DAY 21a

Hi Y'all,

We are back and the Plumber—I mean the neurologist said that little leak was what he called a "Seroma." It's a fancy word as he described it, for a collection point between the skull and the scalp. It has not leaked anymore since morning but he was glad we came down so he could have a look at it. He thought it would not be a hindrance to any of Nancy's progress and the problem would be totally resolved in another two or three days.

Nancy is doing fine, and I think we are both going to try and get a nap before I go to our church gathering tonight. I still have not heard from Duke today for that final information of an appointment, but it's all in God's timing and we are fine with waiting.

- **Thursday, February 3, 2011**

DAY 22

Transparent Moments of Reflection.

I woke up this morning slightly before six and leaned over for my routine "Nancy-fix." It is a kiss and a gentle embrace. More importantly, my "Nancy-fix" includes a reaffirmation of our love by the simple declaration repeatedly stated during our two and a half years of courtship followed by thirty-two and a half years of marriage. "I Love You" is stated (with a kiss) when we leave the house or when we return. "I Love You" is stated while we are watching TV waiting for the commercial to finish, or when we end our personal phone calls. It is a great way to start each day with the one you love.

The numbers of people who have visited the CaringBridge site humbles me. I am aware other people do not have Internet access and are calling some of you to make those connections of information concerning Nancy's condition. We have interjected humor throughout the journal because, well, that is how Nancy and I have lived in our home and among our peers. Our family is strong, but we too, are vulnerable to crisis as well. Many reading the journal are seasoned veterans to what we are currently experiencing, and we continue to hear testimony of situations far worse than the one with which we are dealing.

We are merely novices to the personal health care required to attend to one with a cancerous brain tumor. We are standing upon the promises found in God's Word. We are standing on the outpouring of love, prayers, and generosity through the support group of which you have become. We are standing hand-in-hand as a family; at times, rolling our eyes when Nancy's health care or wish list has a need we are challenged to meet. It may be a moment like last week's knee buckling, yesterday's head seeping from the incision, or last night's nosebleed. That is not how we have known Nancy but we are adjusting for the days ahead. As a reader and then writer, you continue being an aid to that adjustment. Thanks for thinking about us and checking in today.

Oh yeah, and for our daily field trip, we are going to Athens for a training appointment concerning chemotherapy care. Yippee!!

• **Thursday, February 3, 2011**

DAY 22

Two steps forward, one step back. Our little field trip went kind of like that today. Nancy, Ashley, and I left our house shortly after one o'clock for an appointment, a chemotherapy training session to better inform us of what to expect once the treatments begin. As we traveled towards Athens, Ashley was insistent that we call the neurosurgeon's office (Dr. Barnes) and inform them the seeping from Nancy's incision was still an issue. Nancy and I had just let him check her yesterday (Wednesday), and he told us it would probably discharge slightly for a couple of more days. Nancy and I were resistant to bother them because they told us it would be this way. I mentioned earlier this week that I have had to admit when I was wrong, and today I was wrong again. Ashley was pesky, insistent, relentless … (Dustin could probably add a few adjectives here. Ha!) … and she was *right!*

Not wanting to call, I suggested we email the office from my phone and explain what we had observed. Well, while we were in the Cancer Center, Dr. Barnes office called and asked us to stop by for an examination. The good news is that while we were in the chemo training, Duke University Medical Center scheduled an appointment for us on Friday, February 11. That is *great* news. We were educated concerning the chemo by Charles Davis, and he took time to wrap Nancy's head because it was seeping at a faster rate.

To make a long story short, we got to Dr. Barnes office and the staff suggested we wait for him to get back from the hospital so he could do a thorough examination. He recommended we return to Athens Friday morning, and he would do a "revision" to an area around the incision and clean up the drainage. The incision itself was healing fine, but the seepage was coming from an area of weakened skin.

We agreed it was a good plan and said our goodbyes to start home. I went to get the car pulled to the door while Ashley assisted Nancy. They decided to make a potty stop. After more than enough time for them to get to the door, I saw Ashley running over and shouting that Mama was in the bathroom bleeding profusely from her head. I hurriedly reparked the car and ran into the building to see how best I could help. A quick assessment revealed I needed to run up to the second floor where Dr. Barnes office is located and get some medical staff to help us. The office was already closed but thankfully, there were some nurses finishing up their work and soon they were helping Nancy. I must interject a huge help was given by a custodial lady by the name of Mirinda. (I think that was her name.) She was sweet to help us and had a great attitude. In all, I think there were five nurses and Dr. Barnes. Soon the ambulance with three personnel loaded up Nancy and took her to Athens Regional Emergency Room. Dr. Barnes met Ashley and me and told us he would get the discharge to stop and order some CAT scans to review tomorrow. We would spend another night at the hospital. Nancy received the revision well. Well, after a couple of shots of a local anesthetic. I think she has about six or eight stitches and she is resting well.

Dr. Barnes said she could eat anything she wanted so as we were giving instructions to Andrea and Jessica, we ordered her supper. It was topped off by a McDonald's parfait. We knew the nurses would not know where to find an ice cream during Nancy's four AM prowl. Ha! Ha!

As a family, we have determined how fortunate we are to have been at the doctor's office and not on the way home. We are fortunate to be close to the neurologist who performed her surgery. As the parfaits were being handed out I told the girls we could call this a party. Andrea said, "Yes! We are celebrating that the devil didn't get us down even as much as he has tried." What a great reminder. We have been challenged again today but we are standing together and we continue to rest in God's Peace. Thanks for the prayers. We are expecting to sleep in our own beds tomorrow (Friday) night.

• Friday, February 4, 2011

Day 23

There is a passage of Scripture which states, "The Spirit is willing but the Flesh is weak." That is how the ole' CaringBridge author feels tonight. For some reason as I sit here, I can't seem to keep my eyes open. As poor a typist as I am, having my eyes closed is a really bad combination.

The short summary is that Nancy is already in bed, and I am headed that way. The girls have been bossing me (not really bossing) to go to bed. I will write a better description of our day tomorrow. All-in-all, it's been another good day.

• Saturday, February 5, 2011

DAY 24 (26,982 Visits - 1055 Posts)

"Daddy, Mama's head is leaking again." Even those words spoken with a quiet, gentle voice are not words one wants to hear when they are awakened from a restful sleep. Such was the case for me around two-thirty this morning. One may ask, "How did the situation get to this point? What happened?" The Day twenty-two journal entry gives a reasonably explained summary, but in the following paragraphs, I will attempt to bring you, the reader, up to date.

In Thursday's journal entry, we signed off with a victory celebration including dessert parfaits, and Nancy was resting well. In fact, the next twenty-four hours went rather routinely or at least as routincly as one may expect for a hospital stay. Nancy's veins have always acted like scaredy-cats when an IV needle is pointing her way. Drawing blood or giving IV medications to Nancy is the bane of any physician's visit. Not fear, but rather small, rolling veins produce the nurses' challenge. The staff at Athens Regional has been terrific in aiding her need. During the night Thursday and all day Friday, there was not a drip, drop, or trickle offering to flow from the area around Nancy's previous surgical area. Dr. Barnes suturing job performed in the Emergency Room on Thursday afternoon proved to solve the problem. Somehow, there was a slight miscommunication concerning Nancy's medicine regiment. It was lacking for about eighteen hours, but even that did not seem to cause any hindrance to her healing process. Shortly after two o'clock Friday afternoon, Dr. Barnes re-examined Nancy and found her fit and able to return home. He gave us instructions to watch for any unusual swelling or recurrence of seepage and he would see us on the fourteenth to remove the sutures. Jessica, Andrea, and I were with Nancy during his visit and after we received answers to a few related questions, Dr. Barnes left the room and we waited for the discharge papers.

By four o'clock, we were on our way home. We came straight home, well, er, ahh, a-hem, except for that fifteen or twenty minute shopping spree at Rack Room Shoes in Commerce. I do not think I need to spend a lot of time explaining this because you readers who are women understand, and you men really do not care. Nancy said she did not have any shoes to go with the outfits she was wearing to Duke University. Her outfits were Christmas gifts and she had not had a chance to match up her shoes. I did what any loving husband would do. I mumbled a few things under my breath and drove her to Rack Room. So you won't think I am totally spineless, I did charge Jessica and Andrea to be quick and to use no sudden moves. They followed orders well.

Deloris and Greg, Nancy's sister and brother-in-law who had been baby-sitting Chris and Andrea's children, welcomed us home. Also greeting us was Vernelle, Lucy, and Catie. They provided a scrumptious spaghetti pie and fresh salad. Monday the evening meal was prepared by the first-grade teachers and delivered by Terri and Christa. Tuesday's meal was from our neighbor, Sarah. Wednesday's meal was from the Colwells and Gearharts and delivered by Mallory, Miranda, and Chris. Today, Carlton delivered a chicken pie. Vicki, Joel, Kayla, and Daniel gave a "TLC" basket to us. We have not gone hungry.

Last night after a short visit, Nancy went to sleep in her own bed. I soon joined her, and we rested well until Ashley announced that Nancy's head was leaking again. We monitored her condition throughout the night and called the Neuroscience floor of the hospital to seek some guidance. At eight o'clock this morning, we decided to call the doctor's office and report her condition. We took some photos of Nancy's leaking head and (by-now) swollen forehead, eyes, and nose to send to Donna, the nurse practitioner, who responded to our call. Dr. Barnes was not on call but Dr. Walpert soon called and reassured us the swelling was not unusual given the surgery Nancy has had. She suggested a way for us to dress Nancy's head and instructed us to call her if Nancy's condition worsens.

Now it's around three o'clock Saturday afternoon. Nancy has eaten both breakfast and lunch, had a shower with shampoo and is still able to give "orders." My sister, Marlene, was on a school field trip yesterday with her daughter, Abby. They stopped at Mayfield Ice Cream along I-85 and yes, she bought Nancy a Cow Bell. I am not sure that was a good idea because I have a feeling it will ring frequently and vigorously. Don't tell Nancy, but I would not have it any other way. Ha! Ha!

• **Sunday, February 6, 2011**

DAY 25

Day twenty-four has ended. Nancy had visits from both family and friends. For now, the seepage seems to have stopped. Nancy is sporting a nice white headband made of gauze that holds a four-by-four square bandage in place. Her eyes still sag from the swelling that occurred Saturday morning, but she is determined to keep moving forward. She was able to walk to the mailbox two times Saturday afternoon while the grandchildren both cheered and challenged her to a foot race. She did not take their challenge, but I am confident that if it were necessary, she could have beaten them.

I earlier mentioned the visits from family and friends. They came by to spend a few minutes checking on Nancy after having read some of the daily journals and trying to imagine the reality. Some of you have made tangible contributions through the mail or by slipping it to us with a wink and a handshake explaining that you wanted to do something to help with gas, food, lodging, or bills. As a family we continue to be in awe of the outpouring love demonstrated to us through the gracious offers of "doing anything" to lend us a hand. The cards and posts written with words of encouragement and positive testimony through your life experiences bring extra boosts of hope.

We wade through the daily obstacles of life such as broken faucets needing repair, loads of laundry, and the occasional getting on each other's nerves. Actually, we are like many of you in that we have career jobs needing attention, schedules needing kept, or messages waiting for a reply. The difference is our star player for this team is on injured reserve and we are learning to adjust and move forward while she convalesces. The various and valued skill-sets of the daughters and sons-in-laws (Josh included) work like a woven fabric and have strengthened each other during weaker moments. Sometimes the strength comes from a gentle squeeze or hug, while at other times it may be a frank and firm conversation concerning decisions for the weeks ahead. Sometimes the strength my come from a good laugh. Late Saturday evening, Chris cut loose with some of his down-home, Hart County, humor and had all of us rolling. It capped off what had started as a rather disconcerting day. Proverbs 17:22 "A joyful heart is good medicine." We all had a good dose as we said our good nights and made plans for worship on the Lord's Day.

Keep checking in because this story is *far* from over.

• Monday, February 7, 2011

DAY 26

Okay! Okay! I get it. Suspense only works for *American Idol*'s, Ryan Seacrest or *Deal or No Deal*'s, Howie Mandell. I did not intentionally make you wait for the next installment, it just happened that way. Ha!

We are doing very well. I was going out the door yesterday on my way to church when Nancy stopped me. She pointed her finger at me and said, "You tell those people at church that I am *fine!* I am not hurting. I am not sick, but I am doing well." Therefore, I did what any loving husband would do and followed her orders. (For a change … Ha!) Indian Creek Baptist Church has exercised great patience through all of this time. I put on FaceBook that I had not preached since January 9 so when I got to the pulpit, I preached during the morning and a little during the afternoon. Aww, come on, the preaching did not last *that* far past noon. Ha! Ha!

Nancy ate good meals, welcomed visitors, and rested most of the day. Her head has had minimal discharge from the surgical area. She was able to walk to the mailbox a couple of times yesterday and then again today. Our family doctor is monitoring the glucose, and we will visit her again tomorrow morning.

I received a confirmation call today at two-thirty PM to inform me Nancy's appointment for Duke University Medical Center's Dr. Henry Friedman has been moved to Tuesday, February 15, and Wednesday 16, both at eight-thirty AM. It will not be necessary to plan for long-term treatment at the Duke hospital, but rather, they will work with one of the local oncologists in Athens. The daughters and sons-in-law, have been adjusting work schedules to be present for the appointments.

The goodness and love of you, the readers, continues to bless us with hope and encouragement. The visits are refreshing, the food has been tasty, and the various gifts are both useful and helpful. I think I am starting to get the hang of this CaringBridge tool. It seems the more I post, the more willing you are to write a sentence or two. Nancy has enjoyed all of you who have offered prayer support, and she especially smiles when she reads (or hears me read to her) those comments from past childhood days or classroom experiences whether they are meaningful or silly. Thanks again for thinking of us today. Thanks for the genuine love that we feel through your prayers and concerns.

- **Tuesday, February 8, 2011**

Bill, Nancy, Jessica, and Marlene are currently on their way to Athens due to Nancy's incision producing some additional seepage. After consulting with medical personnel, it was thought best to take Nancy to Athens this morning to help alleviate the leakage.

More information will be posted as it becomes available. Please continue to keep Nancy and the family in your prayers.

- **Tuesday, February 8, 2011**

Nancy is scheduled to have surgery this afternoon or evening to correct and repair the seepage that is occurring on her scalp. Nancy has been admitted to Athens Regional Medical Center and the family expects her to spend tonight at the hospital.

Please continue to pray for Nancy during this time of surgery.

- **Tuesday, February 8, 2011**

While the family isn't certain, it appears that possibly Nancy has encountered a stroke or a seizure. We are currently awaiting her doctor to pay a visit to assess the situation.

Please, please, pray for Nancy right now.

- **Tuesday, February 8, 2011**

We just spoke with Nancy's doctor. We've learned that the problem is *not* a stroke. However, the problem is a deep bleeding in Nancy's brain which will require immediate surgery. Nancy is being taken down for surgery right now.

Please pray for Nancy as she faces this surgery.

- **Wednesday, February 9, 2011**

Nancy's surgery is complete. Nancy's doctor said the bleeding has stopped and that the procedure clearly helped Nancy. However, the next 12 to 24 hours will be critical as far as a recurrence is concerned. While we haven't seen Nancy yet, the medical staff tells us that Nancy is responsive.

The surgeon noted that the deep brain bleeding was not related to the superficial scalp bleeding for which she initially came in today. We believe God was working to already have Nancy at the hospital in preparation for the day's events.

Thank you for your prayers and please continue to pray for Nancy and the family.

• **Wednesday, February 9, 2011**

DAY 28

I did not stay at the Holiday Inn Express, but I have learned more about brain surgery than I had planned. I have an idea I may learn even more about the human body before this situation with Nancy is resolved. The past seventy-two hours proved to have challenges, but it was the last eighteen hours which were especially overwhelming.

Late Monday evening Jessica and I were attempting to change the dressing on Nancy head. When we got to the business area of the wound, it seemed more involved than we felt equipped to handle. My brother-in-law, Andy, is a trained paramedic professional, and he and Marlene only live about six miles away from our house. We loaded Nancy up and went for a visit at 11:30 PM. He had no problem redressing Nancy's head, but noticed the area was not improving too rapidly. Nancy had an appointment with Dr. Eschedor for Tuesday morning to address a side-effect some medicine was causing her, and Andy suggested she might examine the problem. We returned home, Nancy rested throughout the night and did not "cheat" with her usual stroll to the refrigerator during the 4:00 AM potty break.

Tuesday morning started routinely with the glucose check, medicine dosages, and breakfast. Nancy returned to the couch to rest while I was preparing for the day. I was stepping out of the shower when Jessica alarmingly reported Nancy was bleeding again. I made a few quick calls to determine where we would need to take Nancy. We decided to quickly return to Athens, though Dr. Barnes was already in surgery on another patient. (Nancy's Buick handles well at high speeds. Ha!) The Emergency Room's Dr. Gowder assessed Nancy and after getting the initial bleeding to stop, called in Dr. Barnes. He took one look and said he was taking her to surgery for a complete revision of the sealing of the skull and to clean up the mess. Since Nancy had eaten a good breakfast at 8:30 AM, he was scheduling surgery for 3:00 PM It was closer to 4:00 PM before the operating room became available. Approximately sixty minutes later Dr. Barnes was explaining to us what he had done.

He had completely reopened Nancy's skull and carefully rinsed and cleansed all the area around it. The process included, as I understand it, cleaning the layers of skin or scalp and resealing (I suppose with staples) the surgical area. He was confident we would be able to keep our Tuesday, February 15, appointment at Duke University. He reported Nancy's platelet counts were diminishing, and he was unaware why. They were not to a dangerous level, but he would continue to monitor the levels. He further said he was going to get more aggressive with the glucose situation that remains since Nancy's first introduction to Decadron. Our family remains very confident with his abilities and appreciates his caring response to Nancy's well being. He said to expect to stay for three or four days while he monitored all the various concerns with which he was looking. We were satisfied with the answers to our questions, and he said he would check on Nancy Wednesday morning.

When Nancy returned around 7:00 PM, she seemed a bit more restless than three weeks ago. It was as though she was itching, and in shifts, Jessica, Marlene, Ashley, and I tried to keep her from pulling out her IVs in her arms or the drainage tube from her head. She finally began to settle down just before 10:00 PM, so Jessica decided to ride home with Josh to get some much needed rest. I escorted her to the front of the hospital so Josh could pick her up. We agreed it had been a long day and we regretted seeing Mama in her condition, but we would be strong together and get through this part.

I walked back down to where our car was parked and got an alarming call from Marlene that Nancy had just experienced a seizure. She called Jessica and they returned to the hospital. Since it was after visiting hours, we were required to enter through the Emergency Room and the three of us made our way back to the fifth floor. Josh led us in prayer as the elevator lifted us to Nancy's floor. When we walked into Nancy's room two nurses were trying to get Nancy to respond. She was breathing, but that was about her only response. Her left side especially seemed shut down, and there was no eye movement. The staff called the "Stroke Response Team" and they took Nancy down to be evaluated for a stroke. Dr. Barnes was called back to the hospital and we waited in Nancy's room until the staff could inform us our next move. By 11:00 PM we moved to the ICU, and Dr. Barnes announced Nancy was now responding with movement in both sides of her body and equal dilation or her eyes. They ordered a CT scan and once Dr. Barnes reviewed it, he was confident she was experiencing a deep bleed in her brain, and he would have to reopen her skull to address the problem. (I might remind you he had already been in surgery before Nancy's earlier surgery.) We promised we would be praying for him, and he stopped and turned around to thank us.

While we were waiting to move to the ICU we called several of our praying friends and begged them to pray for Nancy *and* Dr. Barnes. Soon the waiting room began to fill with praying support. Billy, Nate, Stanley, Andrea, Dennis, Julia, and Dustin came to join us in prayer. Many, many, many other people called, texted, or emailed promises to pray. At 1:00 AM Dr. Barnes came from surgery reporting that the bleeding was stopped. He said there was an acute arterial bleed in the tumor cavity, which is located deep within the brain. In layman's terms, he cauterized it and prescribed a drug to help prevent future bleeding. He was confident he fixed the problem, but he was unsure "why" the problem began. Though rare, he cautioned us that there is potential for a future "bleed." He said it was not uncommon for one to have a bleed after the initial surgery, but it usually occurs within the first twelve hours. Nancy's was three weeks after her initial brain surgery. That is what is disconcerting to him. He warned us these next twenty-four hours would be critical. Dr. Barnes graciously answered our questions, and we dismissed him to get some much needed and well-deserved rest.

We held hands and prayed prayers of thanksgiving. We gave God the glory and thanked Him for answered prayers. It was undoubtedly God's timing to have Nancy *in* the hospital when her deep-bleed decided to reveal itself. I am thinking it would have been fatal if we were at home. Nancy is now resting in the ICU, and we were able to visit at 2:30 AM The nurse was hoping we would cause her to respond. When we entered her room, the heart rate rose and there were other positive signs of response. We were able to get her to open her eyes and wiggle her toes. The left side responds slower than the right, but she is moving. Her vital signs are completely normal and we are greatly relieved.

I started this journal entry with a line from a TV commercial. In actuality, I have stayed at a Holiday Inn Express in the past; I just didn't know I would learn more than I really wanted to learn. Praise the Lord with us and let us see what God wants to do with this situation these next few hours. We are emotionally drained and physically fatigued, but we are standing together determined to live in God's will and rest in His peace.

• **Wednesday, February 9, 2011**

DAY 28

We have been enjoying a steady stream of visitors today. It has been a real blessing to pray and laugh together.

We were able to go and visit Nancy around 8:30 this morning. Dr. Barnes came in and gave us the encouraging report that Nancy's progress seems to be right where he expected it to be. He also stated that her vitals are good. In spite of her grogginess, Nancy was able to follow simple commands, open her eyes, and squeeze our hands (with coaxing). After Daddy got his "Nancy-fix" and we girls gave her kisses, we left the room to allow her to rest.

At 10:00 AM, Jessica and Ashley went in to see how things were going and realized that Nancy was having continuous minor seizures. Although it was quite concerning to us, the nursing staff ASSURED us that it is a common side effect to the procedure that Nancy had received. With a hand squeeze, Nancy was able to confirm that she would like for us to stay by her side. Since that time, we have been taking shifts to hold her hands and assure her that we are near.

Now her seizures have subsided and she is resting comfortably with the girls by her side.

Please continue to fervently pray that God will heal Nancy and grant the caregivers wisdom concerning her care. We have all been on this roller coaster ride for over thirty hours with no real rest. Pray that God will continue to give us peace.

We truly are blessed beyond measure to have such wonderful, caring and supportive friends. God bless you all!

• Wednesday, February 9, 2011

Nancy remains in ICU this evening. The family can definitely see God working as Nancy continues to gradually become more and more responsive. In fact, Nancy was able to say "I love you, too" back to Bill earlier this evening. Praise God for this encouraging news!

Bill is trying to get some rest this evening and will post again as soon as possible with a more detailed journal entry. Please continue to pray hard for Nancy and her recovery as well as for the family. May God bless you.

• Thursday, February 10, 2011

Bill, Ashley, and Jessica were able to rest well last night in one of Athens Regional's "Guest Houses." Nancy remains in ICU today, and the family anticipates she will continue to be in ICU for at least another day or so. It appears that Nancy is still having some mobility issues as far as her left arm not responding and moving as normal.

However, there is some encouraging news to share. Nancy is positively progressing with her verbal communication as she was able to tell Bill she loved him again today. While Ashley and Jessica were in the room with Nancy today, she was also able to verbally tell them, individually, that she loved them too. Not to leave Andrea out, Nancy furthermore said she loved Andrea, too. It's important to mention that Nancy was able to call her daughters by their names. In addition, Nancy has been able to say "good morning" and put together cohesive sentences. When asked if she's in pain, Nancy replies "no."

The medical staff gave Nancy a sponge bath in her bed today. They also put her hair up in a ponytail on the left side of her head. The family thinks that Nancy's new hair style makes her look remarkably similar to a sideline cheerleader.

Thank you so much for all of your prayers thus far. Please continue to pray. May God bless you.

P.S. Be praying for Andrea. She is working third shift this week. In addition, her son (Clayton) has been throwing up some today. All your prayers are greatly appreciated!

- **Friday, February 11, 2011**

DAY 30a (34,696 Visits - 1,252 Posts)

Here I sit while I reflect into the past four weeks and let my mind wander through the hallways of life experience. It is currently just past one o'clock in the morning, and I am sitting in a guesthouse in Athens while Nancy's broken body is held in an ICU bed across the street. I am not sitting alone because two of the three daughters Nancy has provided me are lying crossways on a pull-out sofa within reaching distance. The thought of our third daughter is just as near, while in reality, she is working third shift at a hospital in another state. In a deeper sense, I am not sitting alone because the presence of the Comforter promised by Jesus, in the sixteenth chapter of John's Gospel. It is He, who continues to fill every room in which I choose to sit. It is through His rod and His staff, the Shepherd leads His sheep away from the wiles of the world and into pastures of rest. It is in living the reality of His promise for joy, and by positioning me firmly within Christ, that I claim victory over the world and the various trials which may befall me. John's Gospel 16:33 records Jesus declaring, "I have told you these things, so that in me you may have peace. In this world you will have trouble. But take heart! I have overcome the world." Jesus said those words to the disciples who had followed His teaching for three years, and they still didn't get it. They did not quite understand what He was saying. Yet, after Jesus was ascended into heaven and after the Holy Spirit's presence dwelled within them, they were able to stand firm for Christ in the midst of the personal, physical, and emotional storms of life.

Yes, over the last couple of hours, I have reflected on some painful events. I have embraced my girls as they shed tears of sorrow and experienced anxious moments of bewilderment. I have heard the cries for relief from the helplessness of individuals who love Nancy deeply and feel as though we are being robbed of the glue which holds our immediate family together. But even through all of those tough moments, let me write a few lines of what I have observed during these last four weeks.

I was there in the chapel trying to sing through chokes of emotion as Nancy was playing the piano and a woman wandered in to listen. When I invited her to join us, she broke down and tears flowed from her eyes as she pleaded for us to pray for her husband. Those same girls mentioned in the previous paragraph engulfed her with love and hugs as we prayed.

I was there in the consultation room moments after Nancy's surgery when Dr. Barnes began to nervously share his report in which his body language beat him to the news. It was while he was searching for tactful words of an unpleasant message that I interrupted him so we could pray for him. I witnessed those girls and their husbands rising from their seats to encircle Dr. Barnes while I prayed. After I finished a brief prayer and they were seated, the atmosphere in the room changed. The Holy Spirit held us as Dr. Barnes continued his unpleasant assignment of telling us the truth of Nancy's condition.

I was there in that same chapel, and it was after Dr. Barnes graciously shared Nancy's surgical report with our family and friends, that I heard singing from those girls. They were singing praises to God in the strength of the Holy Spirit, the One who provides us joy through trials.

I have been there, in the days that have followed, as those girls and their husbands have witnessed, through lifestyle evangelism, to the myriads of people who have crossed our paths. At different times, I have been there holding hands in a circle, joined by previously unknown families who welcomed us praying for their infirmed loved ones. Those families were from Athens, Madison, Greensboro, Macon, and other locations, but they all welcomed the ministering care and genuine love from the girls.

I cannot help but mix in some wondering with my reflections. On Tuesday evening when my sister, Marlene, called me to share something was terribly wrong with Nancy, and at that time we believed it to be a stroke, I talked to the Lord. I told Him that if a debilitating step was the next path He wanted us to travel, then, I was ready to go down that road. I told God I did not understand, nor could I envision what good could come from Nancy going through a seizure or stroke, but if that was the door He placed before us, we would walk through it. Within minutes I was in Nancy's room joining the nursing staff in trying to rouse her. We were trying to get her to respond to our pleas and touches. When they took Nancy for evaluation and a CT scan, we were left with a hollow sense of hopelessness. We were calling out to God for relief and we were simultaneously calling out to friends for prayer support. I do not know how many phone calls were made in a matter of minutes, but soon all over Northeast Georgia and literally around the world, prayers were offered to God on behalf of Nancy and our family. The hour between ten and eleven that night was difficult for me. I was shaken and beaten down. I was weakening in my spirit, and I was breaking from within. Moments after the eleven o'clock hour, friends came pouring into the waiting room. They were full of compassion and equipped with the Holy Spirit's enabling to minister to us. We needed it. We joined hands to pray and God's peace engulfed me. He strengthened me through the reflecting love of His children and our friends. Wednesday's visitors were the same. Much prayer was offered and much strength was gained while Nancy continued to battle seizures and the fallout from the huge volume of anesthesia in such a short time period. The visitors filled our day from early morning until late that night. Thank you for sharing your time with us. It was so meaningful for you to drive the distances and spend those moments of encouragement.

Yesterday, (Thursday) Nancy made some physical improvements with response to vocal commands. She named and included the ages for each of the girls and the grandchildren. She made verbal declarations of love and provided me with a much needed "Nancy-fix." The doctors and nurses were pleased with Nancy's overall progress. However, there were a few hiccups in her progress.

Nancy's body shows a diminishing blood platelet count. While it can be monitored and bolstered with added units, the unknown reason is a cause for concern. Dr. Barnes' lab evaluation for infection, done Tuesday during surgery, produced affirmation Thursday that there is infection. Let me clarify the infected area is the skull and skin and not the brain. Another set-back is the fact that since her repeated surgery has placed Nancy two weeks behind schedule for recovery, the appointment with Duke University is being delayed until further notice. The problems encountered can be rectified through proper monitoring and evaluation. Dr. Barnes has ordered a PICC line and a long-term antibiotic regiment to combat the infection. Dr. Splichal is not only a first-class oncologist, but he specializes in hematology, and he will do the research in discovering and averting the platelet issue. The left arm and hand was virtually useless to Nancy on Thursday. Dr. Barnes explained in most cases, ironically, as the patient begins to awaken from an extensive surgery, like Nancy's, the body sometimes responds with neglect to certain motor skills and practices. In other words and in laymen's terms, in Nancy's case, her left arm is mobile but Nancy is neglecting to use it. Through the use of encouragement and therapy, vocal and otherwise, she should regain the use of her arm.

There is a silver lining in the cloud we observed Thursday. According to Dr. Barnes, though science has not yet proven it, many neurologists will agree if a patient with cancer has a crisis-infection (much like Nancy's head area), the immune system of that individual is ramped up considerably compared to a patient without infection. The result of the stimulated immune system is that it tends to fight off the cancer cells and extend the life of the individual.

My reflections have taken me past the four AM hour, but here are some observations of those reflections. As the Apostle Paul wrote in Philippians 1:21, "For to me to live *is* Christ, to die *is* gain." The Southern Gospel song lyric states, "I'm a winner either way, if I go or if I stay." We have committed Nancy to the Lord. She took care of that when she was eight years of age. I am not ready to give her up, but she is a winner either way. She has reared her three girls to adulthood. They are mirrors of Nancy's determinate personality, integrity, and work ethic. Her career of teaching has influenced and impacted literally thousands of students, faculty, staff, and parents. We will continue as a family to provide every means available to help Nancy fight this physical battle and defeat it. Man has already said her condition is incurable. God is still at work. He will determine when He is through using Nancy. Until that day comes, we will continue to post these journal entries because This story is far from over.

DAY 30b

Ok, new journalist ... please be patient.

After meeting with Dr. Barnes this morning, we learned that Mom has a blood disorder, which is causing the platelet issue. It is disseminated intravascular coagulation (DIC)—not sure of the correct spelling—which basically means her bone marrow "forgets" how to make platelets.

Next issue: the wound care ...The initial incision on Mom's scalp has now been "revised" due to the last surgery on Tuesday night. Unfortunately, like Dad wrote in his last entry, it is now infected and in need of serious attention. So, Mom now has a PICC line to assist in all the new medications. Later today, the "wound team" will be doing some special dressing to the incision.

The CT scan done today appears to be the same. No changes, so Praise the Lord! Mom does now have a feeding tube for nourishment; she is doing okay with that so far.

She has been sleeping most of the day; resting seems to be best right now. Jessica has been explaining all these new developments to Mom. She understands what Jessica has been sharing with her. She even told the wound specialist that she worked at "BIG A" Elementary School! She is fighting hard to be able to see her grandbabies! They are not allowed in SICU. They are very concerned and eager to see their NANA.

Thanks for the continued prayers. We feel them and definitely NEED them. We love all your encouraging words and visits. Please keep them coming.

- **Saturday, February 12, 2011**

DAY 31

My "Nancy-fix" is overdue. I walked into her room this morning with Jessica and Ashley. Nancy's nurse briefed us in the hallway and reported she had not been too responsive during the night. Nancy's platelet level was low. Her blood glucose level was up, her temperature was 103.5 degrees, and her body is in a tremendous fight against a serious infection caused at the opening of her skull. The disseminated intravascular coagulation (DIC) continues being a concern to her medical team. Seeing her weakened body with a PICC-line in her arm, a feeding tube in her nose, bandage dressing on her head, and while being restrained with two wristbands, caused me to swallow hard. The girls attempted to rouse a response from her by rubbing her chest and talking softly into her ear. I washed my hands and held her hand while the morning cleaning lady, Ms. Diane, maneuvered her way around Nancy's ICU room. The girls welcomed Diane but explained Nancy was fighting a serious infection, so they wanted her to do an especially good job for their mama. The dutiful housekeeper expertly buzzed around cleaning as one who had done it several times.

Dr. Cuff is the weekend neurologist. He acknowledged he was surprised to see Nancy because she had previously improved quickly. He had read her charts but asked us what had transpired the last few days. We related what we had observed, and he reaffirmed the information previously given by Dr. Barnes. He was encouraging by reminding us Nancy's current condition can be reversed, but she was probably exhausted from all the events of yesterday's various treatments.

This post was started at 12:30 PM, and now it is nearly 7:00 PM. Nancy's temperature has gone down to 101.3 and she has rested well. Our concerns deal especially with the infection. She did not need plasma or platelets today and for that we are grateful. The heart rate has been high but when Nancy's mama and daddy came into her room, it lowered to a better rate.

Many well-wishers have made their way to our waiting room to offer love, prayers, food, or other gifts. Each have been appreciated and welcomed. It is because of the infection concerns that we have discouraged visiting Nancy, but we are here and still welcome anyone who wants to visit. I will write a detailed post soon, but for now this will have to do. Thanks for understanding and for all the prayers. Keep Nancy on your prayer lists at church and remember.... This story is far from over.

Sunday, February 13, 2011

DAY 32

I went to bed late and arose early. It was refreshing even though I am feeling the fatigue of this family crisis. I was walking my parents down to their car last night when Marlene called me to report Andrea and Chris were taking little Jackson to the Emergency Room in Hartwell due to a severe stomach virus. I contacted Andrea at 1:30 AM, and she said they were on their way home with Jackson doing better.

The morning sun was inviting as I walked over to visit my Valentine. The nurse reported Nancy seemed to have had a restful night, and perhaps she was enjoying slight improvement. The vital signs were skewed again with the temperature, blood glucose, and heart rate above what most people consider comfortable levels. Christy, Nancy's nurse, was addressing those issues with the prescribed medicines the morning doctors have ordered.

Yesterday, the girls were singing to Nancy. I did not want to sing. I could only think of **Psalm 137** which records the broken hearts of Israel due to their bondage in Babylon. The Scripture states, "They hung their harps on the willow trees because they longed for home and could not sing." While the girls were singing, I was trying to figure out a way I could join Nancy in her ICU bed and simply hold her. It was not enough to only hold her hand. I wanted to be nearer her than a handshake. Obviously, with tubes in different parts of her body and life-recording sensors attached to her chest, I could only stand by and hope for a day she would return my embrace.

The mystery of God often challenges what is meant in some passages. The mystery stated in Genesis of a man leaving his father and mother and cleaving to his wife is one to me unexplained. The mystery goes beyond the physical joining and far into the depths of emotion that only those enjoying a God-ordained relationship can understand. While I cannot explain it, having been on life's journey of thirty-two years of marriage, I fully understand it. I suppose it is likened to the mystery of identical twins "feeling" pain from their twin though miles may separate them geographically. If the truth be known, women may be the weaker gender, but they are the stronger partner at least in our case. (On a lighter side, I have experienced childbirth four times. I experienced my own birthing, which thankfully I don't remember. Ha! And I have experienced as a spectator the birthing of our girls. Yes, ladies, you are stronger.) The bond of love which grows each day continues to add a layer of love to the mystery of leaving and cleaving. Thank you, God.

I did not let yesterday's events rob my joy completely. I had several opportunities to smile and interact with other families visiting their loved ones. I think we had either three or four group, hand-holding, prayer meetings. Those were refreshing times. I have been strengthened with the love from you who have visited, sent cards, or simply contacted through media. During our last prayer time as a group, I was able to join the singing. I certainly understand I am only reporting what some of you have lived for years. I understand these posts are reminders to those raw reflections some of you are recalling as you read. I further understand that many are reading the posts that are also on edge wondering the future outcomes for their own infirmed loved ones. I am rejoicing with those "new" friends we are meeting in the waiting room when their loved ones are either moved to a different room or completely discharged. I also understand some families have gone home saddened by the passing of their loved one. We have prayed with them as well.

Now, at nearly noon, I have spoken with Dr. Cuff (the "on-call" neurologist) and he indicated he was pleased with her improved condition. He assured me this would be a long journey but that he thought she was improving. We continue to hope for a better day today. We continue to remind you.... This story is far from over!

Monday, February 14, 2011

DAY 33

"Without Him I could do nothing. Without Him I'd surely fail. Without Him I would be drifting, like a ship without a sail. Without Him I would be dying. Without Him I'd be enslaved. Without Him life would be hopeless. But with Jesus, thank God, I'm saved.

Jesus! Oh Jesus, do you know Him today? Please don't turn Him away. Oh Jesus, Oh Jesus. Without Him how lost I would be." (words by: Mylon LeFevre)

Those are the words Nancy was singing with Andrea yesterday afternoon. She requested the song and then joined Andrea as she sang it. During good-night prayer time, Ashley, Jessica, and our friend Joanna were praying around Nancy's bed. She interrupted them to say she would pray at the end. And she did! Her prayer was, "Get well now. Get well now. Get well now." Then she asked them to sing, "I Can Sing of Your Love Forever." It seems as though Nancy is slightly more alert between the hours of 6:00 PM and midnight. All in all, Sunday was a good day for her.

When I reflect on Nancy's day yesterday, I see the testimony of what many preachers have said for years. The statement is deeply philosophical. It states, "Garbage in—transfers to Garbage out." In other words, those things with which people feed their minds are what come out when they speak. Scripture tells us to guard our minds and not be conformed to the world's way of thinking, but rather, let the Holy Spirit renew the mind (Romans 12:2). The purpose is to prove the will of God.

We are waiting to discover God's will in our situation. The obvious is that Nancy would resume her previous influence among her peers at school, church, friends from past, and especially at home. I had an in-depth discussion with a dear, dear friend in which we were discussing the relationship with God in how to pray. John 16 is one of several passages that encourage praying and believing God, and He will do what is on our hearts. However, at the same time Scriptures are prevalent to encourage praying in God's will. Passages such as Psalm 103 relay how God heals all our diseases.

In Nancy's situation, if I have a healthy interpretation of God's Word, Nancy was healed at the age of eight when she prayed to receive Jesus and begin her spiritual journey in a personal way. I am rebuking the power of Satan through the Name of Jesus Christ and claiming the saving, forgiving blood of Jesus to cover Nancy. I am comfortable living in God's presence and experiencing God's peace. I *know* about those things through the experience of our situation. I don't know the future of this event, but I am praying and encouraging others to join me in prayer that God will be glorified in everything. The song Nancy wanted to sing Sunday evening testifies her belief that without Jesus, life would be hopeless. It is by her testimony that we *have* hope.

Moments ago (noon), the wound-care nurse assessed Nancy's head and said while it does not appear the area is any worse, she did not think it was healing. Dr. Barnes has been notified and will resolve the issue this afternoon. He will trim some of the tissue around the wound and provide the healthy tissue an area to reproduce and grow. Pray that the procedure will be painless and work in Nancy's favor. Her vital signs seem to indicate her other health issues are about the same as they were yesterday.

I trust you are enjoying Valentine's Day, but keep praying and remember, this story is far from over!

Tuesday, February 15, 2011

DAY 34

Dr. Barnes strode into the waiting room to give his assessment of Nancy. The heads-up a staff worker gave us provided enough time to huddle the girls and organize a list of questions prompted from concerns observed over the weekend. Dr. Barnes got right to the point. Nancy had not progressed as he had hoped when he last saw her on Friday. His primary concern stemmed from her neglect to use her left arm. He did not seem convinced she would regain her mobility in the arm. Another concern was the deep-sleep cycle in which her body currently functions during the day was disconcerting. He had unsuccessfully attempted to rouse her. Evidently, he barely got a grunt. It was after we reported our nightly interactions that he seemed to find hope for resurgence to better health. It was after he addressed our questions that he designed the future day's agenda.

An MRI was ordered to help determine if and when Nancy suffered a stroke sometime after last Wednesday's seizure episodes. The infection around the head wound has not healed in the time allotment it should have exhibited improvement by now. A visit from a plastic surgeon has been requested to examine the head wound and offer treatment. In the immediate time frame, beauty is not the issue, but rather healing. He will provide expertise in the skin regeneration.

A huge blessing is that the disseminated intravascular coagulation (DIC) is a thing of the past for Nancy. Many people joined hands and hearts for that to be defeated. Positive reports also indicate the white blood cell level is holding steady at a healthy rate. The blood platelets have settled back into a normal pattern. We are rejoicing with those reports. Since Nancy has been in bed for four weeks, attention is now heightened for prevention of muscle atrophy. My Valentine has always had good muscle tone in her legs due in part, to the daily exercise she required from her students. Now, with all the bed rest, the prevention of bed sores is of utmost attention. The staff has kept careful watch for sores, but the potential is great. Nancy needs prayer directed towards the issue.

It is now in the early morning hours of Tuesday, and I am still reflecting on some observations of Monday. My first observation was one of irony. I was standing in the hallway next to Nancy's room and peering through the window to the outside sunshine as people were beginning their daily routines. I found it interesting that the sidewalk just off hospital grounds providing a sanctioned area for smokers was the same sidewalk others were using for their morning jog towards good exercise. Ha! I also found myself wondering about the stressors and pressures we place upon people required to perform nearly impossible tasks. My appreciation to the medical staff is great, and the huge task of meeting so many needs is duly noted. Throughout the hospital family members are constantly hoping like we are that the doctor or nurse will perform some unimaginable service to restore their loved one. On a lighter note, imagine the pressure placed upon "all the king's horses and all the king's men" when Humpty had his fall. Supposedly, they were working for the king. I am praying our staff is working for *the King*.

Finally, there was another observation I made today. My conscience urged me to travel to the church and then to the house to take care of a couple of errands. I did not stay gone too long but while I was at the house I opened the medicine cabinet in Nancy's and my bathroom. Over the years, we have written love notes and posted them on the mirror. After reading them, we would transfer them to the inside of the cabinet to keep them as reminders of our love for each other. I noticed behind the makeup remover and shaving cream was a letter I sent Nancy a couple of years ago on Valentine's Day. I won't share all of its contents because they were personal words I wrote to Nancy, but it reminded me how much I loved her when I wrote those words and how much more I love her now. I am asking you, the reader of these journals, to not quit praying for Nancy and our family. We are enduring much more than I am writing. It has now been a month since this nightmare began and we need as much or more prayer now than we did four weeks ago. Displaced families have other obstacles to overcome. Tonight, Dustin took Ashley out for a Valentine's dinner, and when she got home she was sick with what we believe is food poisoning. I can assure you we are still standing and still fighting this battle together. We have prayed for many others who have crossed our path for the first time today. I am asking you to keep holding us up in prayer because; this story is far from over.

P.S. I just woke the girls to "approve" this journal entry, and Jessica is now sick with a stomach virus. We will not give up, give in, or give out. We will stand victoriously.

Tuesday, February 15, 2011

DAY 34a

Hello dear, dear friends. We learned the report of the MRI taken this morning. Sometime around 11:30 AM our hero, Dr. Barnes gathered Andrea, Marlene, and me while Ashley listened on speaker phone. He told us news that rings loud but sounds hollow. Nancy's tumor has returned with vengeance and it appears to be larger than it was before her surgery.

I had already visited Nancy and asked her how my hair looked this morning. She said it looked fine. I told you that to let you know Nancy was as alert as she has been. In fact, Dr. Barnes said her cognition and neurological abilities seemed improved over yesterday. At this time, an attempt to remove the tumor does not seem to be beneficial to Nancy's health. Instead, we are going to meet with Dr. Barnes and the oncologist, Dr. Thomas around 4:30 PM to discuss a strategy for the upcoming weeks and months.

I will write more once we have learned more information. Thanks, in advance for your immediate prayers as we meet this afternoon. Don't forget; this story is far from over!

Wednesday, February 16, 2011

DAY 35

"There is no pit so deep, that Jesus is not deeper still." I did not cite the quote, but I think those words were stated originally from Ms. Corrie Ten Boom during the days of her confinement in a prison of war camp. I first heard them from the Commencement speaker during my high school graduation. Mr. Tom Jenkin III, related how as graduating students, we should expect difficult times in the new world voyage in which we were to soon embark. He told us to expect hardship but to rest assured Jesus would meet our needs if we would simply rely upon Him.

Tuesday my pit got deeper. In fact, I am tumbling towards its bottom in crisis while simultaneously, I am being lifted in prayer. Jesus knows all about our trials. He knows our troubles and our weaknesses. Scripture states in James 5:16, "The effectual fervent prayer of a righteous man availeth much." I suppose one may think I am presumptuous by identifying with the righteous, but even with my "warts" and imperfections, I have sensed God's presence.

I "borrowed" a wheelchair from the entrance of the hospital in order to assist Jessica to our 4:30 PM meeting. She is still attempting to conquer the twenty-four hour virus that had gripped her the night before. Dr. Barnes met us in a consultation room and laid out the whole situation. The tumor had completely regenerated itself and in actuality, it was twenty-five percent larger than it had been four weeks ago when it was removed. He reiterated Nancy's current fragile condition and answered our questions. His suggestion was to immediately begin cancer treatments for Nancy. The oncologist, Dr. Jeff Thomas, would tell us the chemotherapy path best suited for her need. It was after waiting over two hours in a small confined area, that Dr. Thomas came in to give us his assessment. He got right to the point and said he would not recommend Nancy for chemotherapy treatments. He explained she was already in a weakened condition with a diminished immune system. His fear was chemo would accelerate her demise rather than arrest it. The seven family members were not expecting to hear his assessment. But, then, name for me one instance in which any of the crisis was expected. We affirmed her desire to aggressively fight for any added length to her life, and he acknowledged her determination. However, he would not suggest treatment for even his own family member given they were in a similar situation. He reminded us radiation was a risky option but that Dr. Terry could re-examine Nancy Wednesday and perhaps try to start some treatments. I do not know when that consultation will take place.

It was after a brief family meeting of our seven that I made my way towards Nancy's room to check on her. While I was maneuvering around the crowded waiting room, Mrs. Griffith's daughter approached me to ask if I would lead another prayer meeting for her mother. We prayed with them on Monday evening. Like Nancy, Mrs. Griffith had brain surgery to remove a tumor in July and now was struggling to survive a stroke. I told her I was having another Stacey/Adams family meeting to inform the additional seven members present beyond our group of seven. Nancy's two sisters were among the other family members present. It was after I shared the news from both doctor reports that a prayer meeting broke out. We joined hands and prayed for wisdom. We prayed for healing. We prayed for strength to endure the heartaches yet ahead. The prayer meeting concluded among sniffles and hugs. Declarations of love were joined with words of encouragement and comfort. Some of the family members needed to return home to meet responsibilities and obligations. The rest of us made our way to the Griffith family. We prayed for mercy and grace. Mrs. Griffith is a believer and has led a life of influence around her siblings and children. We joined hands and prayed similar prayers to those we previously prayed for Nancy. The prayers were affirmation we were sensing the presence of the Holy Spirit. It is rewarding to know God allows us to be used in the eye of the hurricane.

Some have chuckled at the wedding vows line which states, "for richer or poorer." Newlyweds don't often think about what depth simple words may carry them later in life. It is those words, "in sickness and in health" that have recently taken on a sobering meaning. In my case, those words mean donning a pair of latex gloves and gently holding a moistened wash cloth close enough for Nancy to suck some relief into her mouth riddled with thrush. It is listening to air escaping plastic tubing, and the IV lines dripping with fluids or the feeding tube pump as it regulates a steady flow of nutrition to Nancy's body. "In sickness and in health" means observing a cooler-blanket that has been lying on Nancy for two days while it unsuccessfully attempts to lower Nancy's high temperature. The phrase means leaning over and positioning me in such a way that Nancy's restrained wrist can wriggle a caress on my face in response to my gentle caresses to her face. Sometimes it simply means getting out of the way of Hannah or one of the other ICU nurses who have offered tender care to Nancy.

Tuesday morning as Dr. Barnes was caringly reporting a hard message of her MRI results, God place two angels in my path. They stood off to the side praying while the news was being delivered. Both of God's angels have been in similar shoes as they have cared for, or continue to care for their loved ones. They were two ladies whom I have admired for their genteel spirit and their love for the Lord. Thank you Katherine and Beverly for sharing testimony and affirming what I have previously observed. I don't think anyone will convince me you were not coincidentally where I needed you.

The old cliché that God works in mysterious ways is more than cliché. It is truth. God continues to work in our family, and I am anxiously waiting to see what He next wants to do through us. I have said it before, but, this story is far from over.

Wednesday, February 16, 2011

DAY 35

Substitute journalist again…Ashley…#1 daughter…

Approximately 1 PM, we met with the radiation oncologist, Dr. Terry. He was optimistic about starting Mama on treatments immediately. Dr. Terry felt she could handle ten high dose treatments instead of the "normal" six weeks of treatments. He cautioned us that she would be extremely tired. After our consultation, our nurse, Robert informed us that Mama's first treatment would be today at 3 PM Thank you, Dr. Terry, for expediting the process! Our nurse and transporters (a.k.a. LIFT team) allowed us to follow Mama down to the treatment center. Once there, the radiation therapist prepared Mama for the treatment. She did great with her first radiation treatment, including the part about having to be squished on the elevators with us! Although the initial simulation took over an hour, the actual treatment itself was only five minutes long. She is a real trooper!

As we were waiting to see Mama, several of us began singing "Amazing Grace, My Chains Are Gone" by Chris Tomlin (Thanks, Kendra!). What an uplifting song! We definitely felt a peace about Mama's treatment, and she made sure we knew she was okay.

Thanks for all the prayers. We still need them as we continue to aggressively fight this battle with Mama. And in case you forgot … *this story is faaaar from over!*

Thursday, February 17, 2011

DAY 36

Back again…I guess my Daddy thinks he deserves a vacation!

Mama tolerated her second treatment very well. About 10 AM, Daddy, Jessica, and myself (Ashley) followed Mama, her nurse, and the Lift Team across the hospital to the treatment center. Today we encountered a small problem …we got STUCK on the elevator. All NINE of us remained calm for the seven or ten minutes until the engineer pried the door open. (Leave it to us to enjoy another "wild" turn of events in our day!) Then, we were on our way to her treatment. As we crossed the windowed walkway, she commented on the foggy weather not being too bad! We returned from treatment after taking a short detour because the elevator was still out of service! Mama was very tired. She continued to find the strength to visit with family, even though we encouraged her to rest. Mama is one tough woman. She *still* tells me she is not in any pain. I don't always believe her.

Dr. Bruner (Dr. Barnes' partner) came by to see Mama. He let us know that she seems to be handling the treatments well. He also said he was going to start weaning Mama off of the Dilantin and rely more on the Keppra, in hopes that her continued fever will drop with the change in medication. Dr. Bruner said her blood levels were good today. Please pray that continues.

Dr. Gumucio, the plastic surgeon, came by to see Mama again today. He was optimistic with the appearance of the wound. He said we might consider a skin graft in the future. For now, it is "holding its own."

Dr. Thomas, the oncologist, is still monitoring Mama's immune and blood issues. Both systems seem to be good for the moment. Pray for her heart rate, blood pressure, and temperature to *all decrease*. She is still using a cooling blanket, not her favorite!

"Thanks" continues to be an understatement around here. Our family is constantly blessed by your prayers, visits, posts, phone calls, emails, Facebook messages, and baskets of goodies. You are the best! And as always, this story is far from over!

Saturday, February 19, 2011

DAY 38

Traditions and adjustments begin with each relationship as the individuals work toward becoming one in the flesh. I have been reflecting upon some thoughts which bear out examples to which

I am speaking. I learned to tie my shoes at an early age like many of you. I did fairly well and the laces managed to stay tied in most instances. Recently, I was thinking about how Nancy introduced me to making sure the bow always crossed over the top of my shoe going east and west, versus north and south. As a guy, I was happy to keep the shoe "tied," and I was not concerned about the direction of the bow. Her instruction was reinforced as the girls grew older and the sash on their dresses needed tying. I can tell you if that bow wasn't tied going east and west it was undone and re-tied. Other reflections reminded me how I was a Miracle-Whip person when I met Nancy, but soon Duke's or Hellman's mayonnaise was what I would prefer. I was trained to replace the toilet tissue roll in such a way as to ensure the paper was dispensed over the top of the roll instead of down the back side, next to the wall. And guys, while we are in the bathroom instructions, please don't forget to put the seat back down. I would further share about how Nancy wanted the bed made up "correctly," but after all these years; I am still struggling with getting that one done just right.

Those are just a few of the many adjustments I have made since our relationship began. Some of you ladies are reading this journal entry and thinking, "Wow, I wish I could get my husband to put the seat down." Some of you gentlemen are reading this and thinking, "Wow, that Bill sure is hen-pecked." Ha! Ha! I can promise you the adjustments came because I wanted to please Nancy. She wanted the bows tied correctly because they made a better presentation. Or she wanted the bed made correctly because it was more comfortable. Let me further be fair to my own mama and suggest she probably tried to teach me those things but I didn't listen. I changed because of my love for Nancy, and I wanted to please her even in some of the smaller details of life. Nancy has adjusted to some of my wishes as well.

In the New Testament book of Hebrews the Scripture says, "Jesus Christ is the same yesterday, today, and forever" (13:8). Change is never easy. Adjustments come with challenge. If Jesus is the same (and He is), then I am going to have to make the adjustments in which He is directing. If I am going to be His servant, then I cannot say, "No, Lord." A servant cannot be in proper relationship with his master and tell the master no. If I am going to follow the leading of the Holy Spirit, I must trust Him completely and not hedge in my relationship. One may ask, "Is that done easily?" I can tell you in times like now when there is great concern for the end result of our situation—no, it is not done easily. I want Nancy restored to full health. I want to see her independently leave for work at Big A Elementary School each morning to make an impact or be a good influence to her peers or students. I want Nancy to fulfill her impact with our grandchildren and be able to interact with her other family members. I have written all of this to say, Jesus loves us greatly. I really and truly believe He does not make mistakes. Because I love him, I must be prepared for the necessary adjustments He is developing in me and the rest of you.

Nancy is reacting to the treatments with the expected results. She is extremely fatigued. I asked her Friday how she felt about the treatments, and she said she could endure them. Yes, it is that same grit and determination that has defined her all these years. She is a fighter and she continues to fight. She is able to declare love to her loved ones and welcome all of her friends and acquaintances. She continues to amaze me with her strength and persistence. Keep us in your prayers as we face seven more treatments and then await the MRI report of her health status. Until that day, always remember, this story is far from over!

Monday, February 21, 2011 5:44 AM, EST

DAY 40 (53,768 Visits - 1,677 Posts)

COLOR MY WORLD (Chicago)

As time goes on I realize
Just what you mean to me
And now, now that you're near
Promise your love
That I've waited to share
And dreams of our moments together
Color my world with hope of loving you

I know, I know. Some of you are asking, "Huh? Who is Chicago?" Ha! Ha! Recently, when I was in Nancy's room by myself, I sang to her. It was one of those moments when we were simply holding hands. She would occasionally open her eyes, but mostly, we just held hands in silence. I sang "Color My World" to her as well as another oldie, "You Are So Beautiful to Me." She would look at me through her pale blue eyes and attempt a smile. It flooded my memory of our early courting days.

I met Nancy on the last Saturday night in April, 1975. I was a member of the Toccoa Falls Academy Male Quartet, and we were invited to sing gospel music for the Tom's Creek Baptist Church Youth Group. Kathy (Britt) Penick was the part-time youth minister, and she invited us to sing for their hamburger bash and hay-ride. As Larry Munson would say before a UGA football game, "Now get this picture." Nancy was wearing a shirt with small, horizontal red-and-white stripes and blue jeans with either red or white Converse basketball shoes. I was wearing blue suede elevator shoes with blue, elephant-leg cotton slacks and a mustard yellow Mr Goodbar tee shirt. Needless to say, we caught each other's attention although we never officially dated until Saturday, May 29, 1976. We have been dating ever since that day. I will leave that picture with your imagination, and as the great philosopher, Forest Gump, said, "That's all I have to say about that."

Nancy has experienced a reasonably good Saturday and maybe even a better Sunday. She got her hair washed and cut earlier in the week thanks to Debra and Alisa. On Sunday, Nancy was able to pass a preliminary "swallow" test which rewarded her with a small portion of apple sauce. She swallowed it, though the feeding tube continues to remain in place until she convincingly proves she is able for its removal. Nancy's glucose level have finally been pulled into check and in fact, it was a tad low. Son-in-law, Chris, wisely suggested giving her a few swallows of Coca Cola. It is her beverage of choice. The nurse agreed Nancy could try a few swallows, and everybody was happy. Later, I spoon-fed her some banana pudding while Ashley took pictures. She has rested well most of the time. The radiation treatments seem to go well for her, but they leave Nancy extremely fatigued. She is getting a triple-dose each time, and she has six treatments remaining of the ten promised.

We are hopeful Nancy's condition is improving. We continue to pray for a miracle cure that man has said is incurable. Pray for Nancy. Pray for our family as we get ready to strap on another week of roller-coaster rides. The highs are fun but the lows are discouraging. We don't believe in luck. We live in peace and trust God's Word for comfort. Friends and family members continue to rally us in the lower times and help us celebrate the victories. The outpouring of love, support, and prayers are keeping us focused and centered for each day. Many families have come into the waiting room with fear in their eyes as they await doctor's reports concerning their loved ones. Pray for us as we use those many opportunities to encourage and pray for them. While you are praying, always remember; this story is far from over.

Tuesday, February 22, 2011

DAY 41

Dr. Barnes had a refreshed gait to his pace as he strode into the room. He invited me into the hallway to share his report concerning Nancy's progress. He was returning from a six-day break and looked both re-energized and excited. Dr. Barnes said he was very encouraged with Nancy's condition compared to how she was when he last saw her. He thought she would begin physical therapy today, Tuesday, and perhaps leave the ICU by the end of the week. His immediate goal is to build Nancy's health to the point she can come home to enjoy a few quality days.

Nancy endured her fifth treatment, but it has left her visibly drained and exhausted. Reghan, her day nurse, was extremely attentive to her care as she observed the swallow test, the replacement of the PICC-line, and continued to monitor the glucose levels. Nancy's temperature finally got to 98.6 for the first time in two weeks. She ate lunch and dinner while the feeding tube remained in place. If she successfully manages her breakfast, the tube may come out today. The attitude and determination Nancy models is exemplary. She

76

has never complained or noted any physical pain. She maintains a positive report when asked for suggestions of making her stay comfortable.

During Dr. Barnes assessment, I revisited the long-term projection. His response let me know he was working to get her well enough to come home and "enjoy" some quality time. When asked about the possibility of eradicating the tumor and arresting any further debilitating causes, he reminded me (in man's control) there was not a cure, but that they were trying to manage the health Nancy did have and work with treatments to which her body would respond.

Me? Well, I am trying to celebrate the good days. I have been thinking about my days as a charter member and one-time president of the Optimist Club. I recalled the creed by which the members would recite during the meetings to reinforce behavior already exhibited. The creed is as follows.

The Optimist Creed

Promise Yourself

To be so strong that nothing can disturb your peace of mind.

To talk health, happiness and prosperity to every person you meet.

To make all your friends feel that there is something in them.

To look at the sunny side of everything and make your optimism come true.

To think only of the best, to work only for the best, and to expect only the best.

To be just as enthusiastic about the success of others as you are about your own.

To forget the mistakes of the past and press on to the greater achievements of the future.

To wear a cheerful countenance at all times and give every living creature you meet a smile.

To give so much time to the improvement of yourself that you have no time to criticize others.

To be too large for worry, too noble for anger, too strong for fear, and too happy to permit the presence of trouble.

I have not been a member of the civic club for more than twenty years. While I reflect on the encouraging words of the creed, I still prefer God's Word for sustenance and spiritual nutrition. The psalmist recorded inspired words, provided by the Holy Spirit, when he wrote **Psalm 40:1-5:**

> I waited patiently for the Lord, and He turned to me and heard my cry for help. He brought me up from a desolate pit, out of the muddy clay, and set my feet on a rock, making my steps secure. He put a new song in my mouth, a hymn of praise to our God. Many will see and fear, and put their trust in the Lord. How happy is the man who has put his trust in the Lord and has not turned to the proud or to those who run after lies! LORD my God, You have done many things—Your wonderful works and Your plans for us; none can compare with You. If I were to report and speak of them, they are more than can be told.

I have needed the Lord and through many, many, prayers, I know He has heard my cry for help. I claim the promise of verse three. I am praying the joy in my spirit and the praise on my lips, will heal the brokenness of my heart in order that others will put their trust in the Lord. "Trust in the Lord." Hmm ... I continue to evaluate exactly what that means. It was quoted to me yesterday, "If we don't trust God *in* all, we don't trust God *at* all." My heart's desire is to trust God in all. I choose to remain happy in the Lord. I will continue with the song in my heart to the praise of my Lord.
And besides, this story is far from over!

Thursday, February 24, 2011

DAY 43

I was holding Nancy's hand and observing her as she slept. The last three or four days have seemed repeated. The routine of treatments and sleep with body turning and finger pricking has made the days pass. In some ways they have passed quickly, while in other ways they have dragged on and on. There has definitely been progress, but it is measured against last week and the week before. Yesterday, with permission, Nancy was able to eat Chicken Marsala from Olive Garden. It was our first date in several weeks. I might add that dating Nancy is still fun after all these years, and while the ambience of a hospital room does not quite make for a romantic setting, the company was enjoyable and we kept the conversation light. I encouraged her to feed herself while I cut her chicken and salad lettuce into manageable bites. She did well for a while before tiring and asking me to finish feeding her. The treatment she received yesterday (Wednesday) was not until the midafternoon so she had not bounced back to her perky self by the time we were eating our meal.

This morning, we have introduced ourselves to another family in the waiting room. Their elderly loved one is hampered with serious respiratory issues. One of our previous "new" friends' family members had surgery yesterday for injuries sustained in a tragic auto accident. They had not received encouraging reports when we left them to go to the guest house. This morning their news is not much better.

Nancy is expecting not one, but two super-charged treatments today. They took her to the radiation center at 7:30 AM and will again at 4:00 PM. Dr. Terry felt this would be a booster treatment to try and slow down the growth of her tumor. We are hoping for the best and feel that Nancy's physical durability will allow her to endure the treatments, but we are not expecting many visits from her because she will no doubt be wiped out. The glucose level continues to be an issue. Her other vital signs are staying within the reasonable tolerances of most healthy individuals. She interacts with me throughout our visits. When I teasingly stick my tongue out at her she responds the same. We wink at each other or pucker-up as if to kiss. Naturally, I get kisses throughout the day for my "Nancy-fix."

I am sitting in her room now. The first treatment is done. The nurse, Marcie, has evaluated her and has left to check on her other patient. Jessica has started the CD player with comforting music playing while Nancy rests between requests for her McDonald's parfait. I teasingly instructed Andrea if she wanted to continue being the "favorite" daughter, she should pick up a parfait when she comes in from her third-shift job. Marcie agreed to let Nancy enjoy one. I am writing this update and trying to get it posted before Ashley scolds me again. Ha!

How does one measure time? A quick inventory may be to answer with a clock, watch, or even calendar. In some odd ways, I suppose time can be measured by separation of loved ones due to ministry or military assignment. Maybe it is by noticing how long a family-sized bar of soap lasts in a hospital guest house. Or, for Nancy, how long it takes to drain an IV bag of antibiotic into her body. A pleasant way of measurement is to notice a candle's light during a romantic dinner as it flickers shadows around the room.

How does one measure a lifetime? The psalmist has written through the inspiration of the Holy Spirit that life is a vapor. He says men scurry about storing up riches, but someone else will own them (Psalm 39:5-6 HCSB). He even asked God to show him the end of his days and acknowledged how short life indeed is compared to eternity. The ninetieth division of the Psalms reveals God has, on average, allowed three score and ten years so we should number our days. Those days are for the development of wisdom. Are you spending your days in godly fashion? Are you developing wisdom? We are learning lessons which take us light-years beyond the class-room. God is teaching us patience and dependability upon Him. I am learning or reaffirming promises previously learned. I am taking a different look at each and every day.

My suggestion is to take an inventory of your days. While you reflect, don't forget that this story is far from over!

Friday, February 25, 2011

DAY 44

Hi Folks,

We are entering into a place of decision making. Nancy will have her last treatment of the scheduled radiation. According to the doctor, we will likely move Nancy to a step-down room today or tomorrow. The ICU staff has taken excellent care and personal attention to Nancy's every need. I suppose eighteen consecutive days in an ICU is enough for most patients, but we may need an extra day or two to ensure Nancy is fit for a regular room and the care it provides.

Today, Friday, we are hoping to meet with a Registered Nurse trained especially in the care of persons in Nancy's situation. Those persons that have not been given long-term promise of life expectation yet seem durable for extended quality for the short-term. Her training and past experience offer support in providing assistance in advance directives concerning the desires of patients who become unable to communicate with the staff due to deteriorating health. I called a family meeting last night to preview some of the questions and wishes of patients in similar conditions. Let me clarify, Nancy continues being capable of such decisions and *all* of us are together in treating Nancy's condition with the most aggressive means possible to reverse the prognosis that has been given. Nancy is not giving up on her situation and neither are the seven of us who are standing with her.

Dr. Barnes met with Jessica and me yesterday. We were the ones who were present during his afternoon rounds of checking on his patients. Two of Nancy's cousins were in the room with us when he shared his report. He was aware of our desire to have a simultaneous meeting with the oncologist, the social worker, and with him. He regretted his schedule would not permit him to meet today but assured us the near future of Nancy's condition should improve to give her some quality time at home. He is unable to state a length of time but remarked he has, in some situations, seen some patients with similar health conditions to Nancy's live three, four, or five years. He needed to tell us unfortunately, that some lived three, four, or five months. He suggested Nancy's previous good health and younger age is obviously in her favor, and he observed her recovery to better health from the previous two weeks. While his previous experiences and statistics did not give someone in Nancy's condition much hope for a full recovery, he did feel the staff could build her up for some good days ahead in the short-term. He was looking into the possibility of a rehabilitation center to assist Nancy in literally getting Nancy back on her feet after so many weeks of bed rest. The plan included strengthening the weakened left side. Nancy's left leg and arm strength is diminished since the last surgery. At this time, he did not think further surgery would be beneficial for Nancy, nor did he think her body would endure another invasive brain surgery. He reaffirmed he was impressed with how she has rallied and was expecting her to rally again once the radiation treatments concluded. Dr. Barnes has been transparent from the first time we met him. He exhibits genuine care for his patients and regretted he could not give us better news than what we were getting. After getting a hug from Jessica and a firm handshake from me, he was on his way to his next patient's care.

Our goals today are to support Nancy as she receives her last radiation treatment. We are also hoping the oncologist will give us encouraging news that would include a visit to the Duke University Medical Center for evaluation from Dr. Henry Friedman. (We were promised air travel to Duke if that is at all possible for Nancy. That is a huge offer.) We will reinvestigate the possibility of chemotherapy since Nancy has done so well with the radiation treatment.

We covet your prayers as we face this day. There are decisions, decisions, and decisions. We want what is best for Nancy. Pray with us those decisions will be met with total agreement and God's peace will be evident. Continue to pray for Nancy. She had developed a bedsore, and it is causing her considerable discomfort. Pray for the girls as they process the nightmare that has been thrust upon them. I could use a prayer or two, too. Pray that God's reshaping and remolding will make me more like him each day.

It is interesting the lessons one can learn or the observations one can make in the course of forty days. Through scripture, lives were influenced specifically with forty days. Noah watched it rain during the Flood, Moses observed God's presence in receiving the Ten Commandments, Joshua and Caleb witnessed the fruits of Canaan as they spied on God's promise. It was Elijah who ran in the strength of God's provision for forty days. Jonah gave God's warning destruction of Nineveh if they did not repent, and Jesus, Himself, fasted for forty days and nights as God's Son while He encountered the wiles of Satan. The Acts of the Apostles records the followers of Jesus waited in the upper room for forty days when fulfillment of Scripture was granted with the outpouring of the Holy Spirit. The Comforter indeed came. His presence continues dwelling within us today. Pray His leading illumines the path we must follow.

We choose to report, this story is far from over!

P.S. Pray for the Mildred Waters family as they make arrangements for her funeral.

Saturday, February 26, 2011

DAY 45

It is a beautiful day. For me, Saturday tends being a day to unwind from the activities of the week and look forward to the Lord's Day. Mine started out great. The alarm went off at 6:00 AM, and I thanked the Lord for another night's rest as I climbed out of bed. I checked my messages and returned one from a friend who has been writing every couple of days to affirm prayer support and send encouragement to Nancy and the rest of the family. I prepared for the day and nudged Jessica as I reported that I was leaving the guest house. Ashley called, requesting some items she needed because she was leaving Nancy's room to go home and keep some appointments with her church family. I got a quick hug from her as I jumped into the car to fulfill Nancy's request for coffee, an Egg McMuffin, and of course, the favored Berry Parfait. I imagine we could advertise for them, but fast food is not one of my recommendations though it is convenient for our situation. I was greeted by a cheery voice taking the order. It is always a good start to the day by being greeted with a smile.

I entered the room and discovered Nancy, Ashley, and Marlene had a long night. The short-term goal was to prepare for a rehab facility. To achieve that goal, the catheter had been removed when we moved from the ICU up to the neurosurgical floor. During the night, with Nancy's diminished muscle strength, and her regular requirement for bladder relief, the girls and staff attended to her needs five or six times. Perhaps, the more immediate issue is that Nancy has developed a soda-can sized bedsore that has been a major pain in the rear. No pun intended. Therefore, she rested little, and the girls are sleep deprived as well. Helen, the night nurse, thought the breakfast selection would not hinder Nancy's dietary regimen. In order to facilitate physical dexterity, I suggested she try to feed herself rather than to rely on me. I adjusted and readjusted her sandwich wrapping as Nancy scarfed down the Egg McMuffin. She tired after consuming nearly two-thirds of it, so I held it and encouraged her as she ate the rest of it. Now, the parfait was another story. I teased her by telling her she better eat it before the nurse took it away from her. I placed it into her weakened left hand and stuck the spoon in her right. I got back, out of the way, and watched that poor ole' parfait disappear in a flash. Ha! Ha!

Dr. Splichal made his morning rounds to check on Nancy. Upon learning of the discomforted night, especially due to the bedsore, we discussed a course of action. My fears were realized when we discussed the likelihood of disqualification for rehab due to the dependence upon a catheter. The agreement was reached to replace the Foley catheter and assign physical therapy to attempt to get Nancy's condition to at least conquer a bedside potty chair. That will be the "new" short-term goal. Pray that Nancy's physical endurance can help her recover enough strength to begin building the diminished muscle needed to obtain that goal.

Mr. Craig walked down the hall headed to his wife's room as I was visiting by phone. I hailed him down to get an update on her condition. She recently contracted a meningitis virus and was previously in a critical state while in the ICU. Our families became acquainted and prayed for each other during our extended stays in awaiting our loved ones' improvements. He came into Nancy's room to finally meet her and then he led us in prayer. Marlene and I went down to his wife's room, and I returned the favor. We have enjoyed everyone who has taken the time to come by and let us know they are thinking about us.

Family is something God ordained from the very beginning of time. He actually, instituted the healthy relationship of Him to man and then man to woman before He developed the church. I've often said one must have a healthy, reverent, and dependent relationship with God, a vertical relationship if you will, before one can enjoy the horizontal relationship with spouse, family, neighbors, co-workers, or others. In other words, one cannot expect their marriage to truly be healthy unless the relationship with God is in order. I distinctly remember times, more than a few, when Nancy and I held each other in a warm embrace, while thanking God for His divine direction in putting us together and loving us before we loved each other. Those are special times when one can hold their spouse and thank God for His love. Let me share a scripture to illustrate my thought. 1 John 4:15-19:

Whoever confesses that Jesus is the Son of God – God remains in him and he in God. And we have come to know and to believe the love that God has for us. God is love, and the one who remains in love remains in God, and God remains in him. In this, love is perfected with us so that we may have confidence in the day of judgment; for we are as He is in this world. There is no fear in love; instead, perfect love drives out fear, because fear involves punishment. So the one who fears has not reached perfection in love. We love because He first loved us.

What a great scripture! What a great promise! Some of the day-to-day experiences we are encountering are downright scary. However, with God's love, we can get past the scary parts and rest gently in His love. I do not have to worry about my standing before God or Nancy's standing before God due to our acceptance of that unconditional love God offered us when He sent Jesus to be our Savior from our sins. If one reads 1 John, he or she will learn about God's love and His view of sin. I have sinned, but God is willing, and in my case, has forgiven sin. According to the above mentioned scripture, it is not necessary to struggle with the fear of circumstances in this world when I rest in God's love. God sent Jesus. Jesus fulfilled His purpose for salvation and in return sent the Holy Spirit. The Holy Spirit drives out the fears from our circumstances.

That is an incredible promise to remember. While you are thinking, don't forget; this story is far from over!

Sunday, February 27, 2011

Day 46

The Lord's Day is drawing to a close. We have been honored and encouraged with so many churches offering prayers on behalf of Nancy and the family. We have had some good company today. To be more specific, there were family and friends, but there was also a series of doctors. There were five doctors to be exact. It started with the oncologist, and then the urologist, hospitalist, neurologist, and the infection specialist. When one adds the physical therapist's workout, one might agree Nancy has had a full day. The nursing staff, Gail, Helen, Bekah, Michelle, and Heather have taken special care to meet Nancy's every wish for comfort. To no one's surprise, she is resting.

I slept well last night if you call sleeping on a pull-out sofa a good night's sleep. However, I have been tired all day. I sent someone a text a few minutes ago and shared that the fatigue factor of our situation has taken its toll. I reminded him that my comment was coming from a former logger and sawmill operator. Join me in praying for a refreshed and renewed mind to aid in the decision making.

Tomorrow the schedule includes an early morning MRI, physical therapy, and a couple of consultation meetings with the oncologist and neurologist. We are expecting returned phone calls from Duke University and the St. Mary's rehabilitation facility. We continue to believe Nancy can gain the wanted strength to get out of bed and meet her personal hygiene needs without being dependent upon a catheter.

Scripture records the prayer of Nehemiah after the report of Jerusalem's security was broken and the city was open to the surrounding invaders. He was asking God for mercy and guidance. I want to remind you of a part of his prayer; Nehemiah 1:11:

Please, Lord, let Your ear be attentive to the prayer of Your servant and to that of Your servants who delight to revere Your name. Give Your servant success today, and have compassion on him in the presence of this man.

He was going to approach the king for help. We are praying for God's guidance as we approach the medical staff. They have been attentive to Nancy's condition and for that we are grateful. The Lord is not surprised by any of these difficult concerns our family is encountering. He knows the benefits of what we are enduring and the purpose of this whole ordeal. We are so far, clueless to the experience's purpose. In the Gospel of John, chapter nine, Jesus healed a man of blindness. The disciples were following Him and getting plenty of on the job training. They questioned Jesus as to who had sinned. Was it the man himself or was it his parents? Jesus told them that in that particular situation, no one had sinned. Rather, the man was healed to bring glory to the Father. While we have asked God's forgiveness of our sins, we, as a family, believe and pray for God to receive glory in our trials. The book of James tells us to ask God for wisdom when we lack it (1:5).

Many, many of you readers continue to pray for us. Many are praying specifically for mercy and understanding. Perhaps, all of you who are praying are asking God for healing. God healed Nancy of the eternal damnation of sin and judgment to Hell when she asked Him to forgive her of her sins. It was at eight years of age that Jesus became more to her than merely the words written in the Bible. Jesus became a real and personal friend in her relationship with Him. We are praying for God's will. Asking for God's mercy and healing is not a selfish request when we follow God's Word in Philippians, chapter four, when scripture instructs us to lift one another up in prayer. Let's see what God will do and what He will teach us during the upcoming days.

Stay tuned and remember; this story is far from over!

March

• Tuesday, March 1, 2011

DAY 48

"I'm doing good." That phrase is repeated often when Nancy is questioned concerning her condition. She has not complained one time. I am serious, not *one* time has a complaint come from her lips during her stay in the hospital. Today is the twenty-first day of our most recent hospital visit, and it is the thirtieth day out of the last forty-seven in which we have been hospital bound.

Last night Jessica and Ashley insisted I go sleep in the guest house while they took care of their mama. They contacted me when Nancy was taken for her MRI early this morning. I had gotten up and shaved but was folding some laundry when the call came for Dr. Barnes to share the finding of the MRI. I quickly and unsuccessfully hunted a hat to cover up my bed-head, but threw vanity out the window so I could jog up the hill and meet Dr. Barnes. He looked twice when he heard my heavy breathing as I came puffing down the hall. We both stepped into Nancy's room so he could relay the report. Obviously, he did not have enough time to thoroughly examine the MRI, but with a quick perusing, the MRI showed the radiation seems to have been successful and the tumor seems to have been kept in check. Her MRI was followed with an ultrasound. At 53, you can't imagine how pleased I was to hear she was not pregnant. Ha! No, the ultrasound was done to check for blood clots in her arm. It has been paining her and the doctor wanted to ensure Nancy did not have other complications.

I fully intended to post this journal entry before noon today. Now, at 11:15 PM, I want to get it posted before midnight. Nancy has had a busy day with the before-mentioned tests. She is constantly interrupted with finger pricks, blood pressure checks, body turnings, and wound care dressings. Physical therapy staff stopped in at 5:00 PM. Chantel, the therapist, spent enough time to finish wearing Nancy out as she got encouraging responses from Nancy's muscle reflexes. The storm outside has settled down, and Nancy's company has headed back to their homes. Dr. Splichal called during the late afternoon to report Nancy's opportunity for therapy at the

St. Mary's Rehab was closed. He had conferred with Dr. Morgan and one of the criterion that had to be met was the proposed survival time. If the estimated life expectancy was less than twelve months, then, they would not consider that person as a candidate for their therapy program. I was hoping to not have to share a report like that with the girls but I called them to the side of her room and told them what was explained to me. Dr. Splichal was awaiting a returned call from Dr. Henry Friedman from the Duke University Medical Center. I doubt the possibility of our being invited to Duke would be too great after the last three weeks Nancy has experienced. A plastic surgeon called on Nancy today to discuss the moving of scalp tissue into the wound area. A skin graft would be required to cover the relocated scalp and generate new skin tissue. He explained the procedure would look like a patch-work quilt but it was the best he could offer given her current wound area situation. In time, it could be improved so as not to be too noticeable, but the importance of getting the wound growing new skin was paramount.

It seems the roller coaster on which we are riding takes us swirling downward while the prayer support we receive keeps us level in our thinking and emotional stability. Our dependence upon God is the same each day, but when our lives take us to the heights of cultural success and prosperity, our human nature tends to forget about Him. Nancy and I have visited about how blessed we are and have been during these trying days. We praise the Lord that so far, she has remained relatively pain free and without the sickening nausea that often accompanies a sickness like hers. We have thanked the Lord for the prayer and love support that has been so very evident through cards, gifts, and contacts through CaringBridge. Our church family has been gracious to let me focus all my attention upon Nancy's needs. We also have agreed as a couple to keep fighting against the weakening body and discouraging doctor's reports.

We are confident God will see us through the days ahead, and we know; this story is far from over!

- **Wednesday, March 2, 2011**

DAY 49

Tuesday was a good day. Not all the news received was welcome, but there were moments of progress shining over the horizon like a new-day's sun rays beaming over a Daytona Beach lounge chair. I have watched more than a few daylight beginnings with anticipation as the sun rose over the east coast and the shrimp boats darted out of the shadows of night into perfect view of a summer morning. While I am sitting on the edge of the pull-out sofa in the guest house, my mind and imagination races forward a couple of months. Will Nancy make the annual trip to Florida this year? Our family size swells to around forty or fifty, and we will travel in an eight to ten vehicle convoy through the early morning hours of a July day towards a much-anticipated vacation period. We have fun getting ready to go. Nancy, over the years, has teasingly told her friends she has packed the "three-piece" swimming suit I got her (a pair of flip-flops and a straw hat!). Ha! Ha! I usually try to purchase a few dozen extra golf balls to feed the creeks, ponds, woods ... you get the picture. I wonder how July will pass for us this year.

Nancy has had two good mornings in a row. She seems more like the Nancy we have all grown to know and love. During the activities of being examined by four or five different doctors and then to have the vital signs monitored by not just nursing staff, but also the training staff, finally wearies her. Tuesday was the first day both the occupational and physical therapists have spent reasonable time with her. She "showed-out." Those of you readers who remember the tough extra runs in basketball training called "suicides," remember how you gave it all you had and then some. It is with that same fortitude Nancy is approaching her therapy. I am so proud of her efforts. It is all the family can do to not reach out and give her a helping hand during her exercises. I had to leave the hospital to run some errands and pay some monthly bills Tuesday. While I was gone, Jessica excitedly called me to report Nancy stood up (with help) for the first time since February eighth. We do cheer her on, and affirm the strenuous effort being exerted. I am looking forward to that family golf tournament in July.

Dr. Barnes made his afternoon visit to Nancy and shared with the girls the tumor seems to have been reduced by as much as ten-to-fifteen percent due to the radiation treatments. Praise the Lord! He regularly and guardedly cautions us, that in his experience the Grade IV glioblastoma" is not curable, but he is visibly impressed and encouraged with each visit. He does tell us there is a small percentage that has lived for four or five years with cancer similar to Nancy's, and he seems to be one of her biggest fans. He further encouraged the girls by telling them he thought Nancy's condition could be re-evaluated and perhaps she could get the needed rehabilitation.

Besides the physical therapy, the next step towards helping Nancy medically is the wound treatment. It is likely the plastic surgeon will begin work on her Thursday. The surgery will require putting her to sleep and carefully re-adjusting scalp tissue sections to cover the wound area. Without getting too graphic, Nancy has a silver-dollar sized wound which has no skin or tissue whatsoever. There is a plate screwed to the skull and the previous attempt to get the original scalp to regenerate was unsuccessful. If as a reader you are new to these previous journal entries, I would suggest you reading the later January or early February entries. They are more specific in reporting the difficulty the family had in trying to get that area to heal. It all culminated on February eighth. That day seems like a lifetime ago on so many different levels. Pray that Nancy's scalp will be malleable so the surgeon can work without difficulty.

I made a stop at our church to give our associate pastor, Nate, a night class education in "Memorial Day Weekend Gospel Singing 101." He and Heather, his wife, have been a Godsend; especially since Nancy's illness has robbed us from our regular schedule. Two of our deacons contacted us Tuesday to check on us and let us know they love us and want to help us get Nancy back to being Nancy. Dennis and Jimmy both have had family sickness of their own for which to care.

I was reading over the administrator's website for CaringBridge recently. It is humbling to observe the different people of which we have had some acquaintance or level of friendship within their social network. Granted, some may be seeking the website from a curiosity perspective. Many are wondering how to deal with their own burdens and problems. I look at the list of names and see some people who are out of work. Some are broken hearted for their own family member bound to an irrevocable terminal health condition. I notice other names on the list and recall a time when the Lord let me offer some type of encouragement or when Nancy shared a kind word to soothe an unpleasant situation. Yes, it is humbling, but I am seeing God's Word lived out in person.

The Apostle Paul wrote to a group in Galatia to help them learn how to get past a legalistic religious attitude. Paul is regarded as an excellent writer, and of course, he was inspired by the Holy Spirit. His strength in writing was to give biblical doctrine and then put application to his God-sent message. Instruction was given to, "Carry one another's burdens; in this way you will fulfill the law of Christ" (Galatians 6:2). What is the law of Christ you may ask? Jesus was asked the same question and His reply is recorded in Matthew 22:37-40:

He said to him, Love the Lord you God with all your heart, with all your soul, and with all your mind. This is the greatest and most important commandment. The second is like it: Love your neighbor as yourself. All the Law and Prophets depend on these two commandments.

Is your relationship with Jesus one in which you love Him with everything? Do you love Him with all your heart, soul, and mind? I must admit that over the years it was tempting to put Nancy ahead of my relationship with Jesus. Being a pastor often tempts me to put my church responsibilities ahead of my relationship with Jesus. In other words, people sometimes put their careers and jobs ahead of their relationship with Jesus Christ. I soon discovered when I put various things before God my relationship with other people, like Nancy, for example, suffered. We tended to have problems. God will not continue to bless a marriage that is not focused on Christ. Try it for yourself.

The Apostle Paul put further application to his thought in Galatians 6 when he wrote about burden-sharing. He said:

So we must not get tired of doing good, for we will reap at the proper time if we don't give up. Therefore, as we have opportunity, we must work for the good of all, especially for those who belong to the household of faith.

I am encouraged by the well-wishers, gift-givers, and prayer supporters who have ministered to Nancy and the family during these difficult days. By living the burden-sharing you have provided us, it makes speaking a kind word to the stranger in the hospital elevator easier. It causes me to look at the dark, cloudy days of our situation with a different perspective. Our circumstances are not hopeless. Oh, we don't like them. In fact, we seek the purpose of our trials. Scripture, such as James 1:2, reveals our trials produce a testing of our faith in order to strengthen our spiritual endurance.

While I patiently wait for an answer I am fully trusting in God's peace and resting in His love. Besides, this story is far from over!

• **Thursday, March 3, 2011**

DAY 50 (68,764 Visits — 1,876 Posts)

Wednesday has come and gone while friends, doctors, and nursing staff made their appearance in and out of Nancy's room. I forgot to mention on yesterday's journal entry that Nancy got a manicure from Marlene and Ashley. There has been a running joke about Marlene replacing Debra as Nancy's hair stylist and Debra's retaliating threat of pain if she tries to touch Nancy's hair. Marlene has provided the much needed comic relief to our situation and now has added "manicurist" to her lengthening resume'. I don't imagine Lovely Nails should feel threatened at this point. She has offered to be our laundry lady, guest housekeeper, errand runner, and patient watcher from the beginning of Nancy's illness. My brother-in-law, Andy, and their children, Abby and Micah, have unselfishly allowed her to help us.

Wednesday brought with it a change in direction for Nancy's immediate health concerns. After discussing the next step, we as a family, decided against the surgery for fixing the head wound and have taken that leap into chemotherapy. Dr. Splichal, the oncologist, has written the order for Nancy to receive Temodar. It is a special type of chemo especially for brain tumors. In Nancy's case, it will be taken by pill-form five consecutive days and do that battery once per month. He had contacted the revered Dr. Henry Friedman from Duke, and together with their discussions and results of Nancy's health exams, disqualified her for treatment at Duke's cancer center at this time. They further discouraged the use of Avastin. It is a drug specifically used to starve a tumor. Unfortunately, it is a very vascular drug, and the fears of the doctors for Nancy's use is that it could cause another deep-brain bleed. Temodar is being prescribed to slow down the growth of the tumor, but it is unlikely going to eradicate it. Usually, the side effects include nausea, but medical science has advanced its study and there are prescriptions to help make using Temodar more tolerable than in years past. We will see ...

The nursing staff here at Athens Regional has continued giving Nancy first-class care. I fear I may leave someone's name out of the list but her recent care givers include: Tammy, Carol and student Chenda, Crystal, Heather, Michelle, Whitney, and Bekah. Many other people who have previously cared for Nancy have taken moments to stop by and offer her encouragement. We understand nursing is a career profession, but Nancy and I have discussed and commended them for their caring attitude with which they perform their jobs. Thanks again folks.

Let me share a humorous reflection I had recently. I remember the first time I had flowers sent to Nancy's home. It was a few months into our courtship, and I was working third shift in a textile plant. Nancy was attending Gainesville State University, then a junior college, on a basketball scholarship. She would come home on the weekends she did not have a scheduled game. On one such Friday, I ordered flowers to be delivered before she got home, and before I came to pick her up for our Friday night date. I pulled into her parent's driveway and she bounded out the door to welcome me. (FYI for the younger readers, this was before cell phones and we didn't get to visit much during the course of the week.) Before I could get out of the car she gave me a peck of a kiss and said, "The flowers are beautiful. Who are they for?" In my confusion I asked her who she thought they were for. She replied, "Well, its Mama's birthday!" The date was November 10, 1976 and I haven't forgotten Guinnell's birthday since. Ha! Ha! I have great in-laws.

I am going to close this entry without a scriptural inclusion, but I would remind you to hold the one you love a little closer today and remember; this story is far from over!

• **Friday, March 4, 2011**

DAY 51

"How are you feeling?" Her witty response was, "With my hands; same as always." Yes, Nancy has maintained her wit while she continues to endure the physical hardships thrust upon her body. When asked if she had anything to include in the journal entry she said, "Tell them I am fine and that I plan to be back to school soon." The Nancy-fix is getting more and more like the regular schedule with which we were accustomed. For the "new" readers, the Nancy-fix is described in detail on the February 3 entry. These days, the Nancy-fix is sans the hugs, but hopefully as she progresses, the hugs will follow.

I was reflecting earlier this morning, around 3:30 AM, how the girls loved to play with their baby dolls when they were younger. Nancy has now become their baby doll. They enjoy assisting the nurses in the care of turning, bathing, and pampering their mama. I silently chuckle when I think how distressed they became as children, when Barbie's leg needed re-attaching or Ken's head somehow came off during a fashion adjustment. I would "usually" interrupt my reading or the ballgame I was watching to be their hero while putting Barbie or Ken back together so they could resume the fantasy of playing with the dolls. Now I silently sit here and silently choke back the tears of helplessness. I can't fix their baby doll this time. However, there is a vast difference between helpless and hopeless. We have hope. We find hope in the Scriptures. Our hope is encouraged with each prayer that is offered or each encouraging note you, the reader, posts on CaringBridge, FaceBook, or even the good ole' traditional card. I continue to hold out hope that the heavenly Father will interrupt His divine schedule to reach down and touch my "Barbie" to make her whole again.

God provides hope for our situation as we witness the way in which Nancy's treatments carry forward. She took her first Temodar chemotherapy treatment yesterday (Thursday). Jessica, Andrea, Kendra, Nate, and I surrounded her bed and held hands as Nate offered a petition of mercy on Nancy's behalf. He prayed the treatment would provide the necessary medicinal purpose to combat the cancer cells while the body accepted the dosage without repercussion of nausea and sickness. It gives me great delight to praise the Lord for His answered prayer. Nancy has not had one significant or notable side effect to her first treatment. The nurses have remarked more than a few times how unusual it is for one in Nancy's condition to have accepted the treatment with such grace. Now, some twenty hours later, we are all thanking the Father. PTL!!!

During lunch with only me and my parents, Mom shared how some of you, the readers, have contacted her personally to pass along testimony of how the journal has helped them in their own life challenges. It is humbling to hear such comments and I want to reassure each of you I am learning as much or more than I write. One Scripture passage that comes to mind in explaining the "hope" of our situation is found in Romans 5:1-5 which says:

Therefore, since we have been declared righteous by faith, we have peace with God through our Lord Jesus Christ. Also through Him, we have obtained access by faith into this grace in which we stand, and we rejoice in the hope of the glory of God. And not only that, but we also rejoice in our afflictions, because we know that affliction produces endurance, endurance produces proven character, and proven character produces hope. This hope docs not disappoint, because God's love has been poured out in our hearts through the Holy Spirit who was given to us.

The Apostle Paul's words were written nearly 2,000 years ago and yet, they remain applicable to our situation today. They are refreshing, like a breath of fresh air, because the same comforter (Holy Spirit) which enabled Paul to write such thoughts, enables one like me to live them. As my friend Kathryn earlier wrote in a guestbook post, "Don't give up, give out, or give in." As believers, we have that hope the scripture describes. Because of the saving grace of Jesus Christ, we can rest in God's peace by faith, while the chaos of this life hurricanes past us. I have met people here in the hospital, and know of people in our church who have gone through or are now facing extremely difficult times. They are times of which they had not previously dreamed or expected. Yet, like us, they are blindsided with unreal and unimaginable pain and fears that will swallow them and destroy them if they don't hold out and hold on to that hope in Jesus Christ.

My physical body is fatigued. The girls have commented on the gray that is beginning to sprout in my hair-sprayed locks. However, my jaw is set, and my determination to stand for Christ through these trials remains intact. Stay tuned for more of the same because; this story is far from over!

- **Monday, March 7, 2011**

DAY 54

Today starts the eighth full week of our journey. It is a journey of obstacles and barriers to which must be maneuvered before we progress forward. While I shared my turn of staying in Nancy's room with Debra, we listened anxiously as she called out numerous times in discomfort. We attempted to adjust her body for better comfort or assist in other ways, but she simply was uncomfortable. Now at 5:30 AM she is resting without turmoil. She has put in her breakfast request to which I will comply once I post this entry of our storied journey.

I remember well, how adults would explain away their happiness of a healthy marriage by stating, "Oh, it's wonderful. We love each other more than when we were dating." I continue to marvel at those friends and acquaintances whose lives have produced fifty, sixty, or even seventy years of wedded bliss. At thirty-two years of our marriage I am wondering how the next six months of completing our thirty-third year will conclude. I can assure you that I love Nancy more than when we were dating. I can further assure you of the helpless feeling I have when I cannot seem to take her pain.

When she hurts I hurt. This is a reasonably new twist to our eight-week journey. Nancy has been relatively pain free. In fact, she and I have discussed how blessed she has been to have not suffered in pain and nausea. Maybe that is what this week holds for us.

Our weekend went uneventful for the most part. With the exception of an occasional spike in blood glucose, her vital signs have been good and her appetite remains healthy. She has responded to the physical therapy (when they showed up) with the same grit and determination her former teammates witnessed her performance on the basketball floor. She has lunged towards the promise of better health at every opportunity presented her. During the weekend, we had several family members and friends stop by for a visit. They are welcomed, and Nancy can usually enjoy short visits before tiring. Yesterday (Sunday) Andrea stayed with Nancy so the rest of us could attend our church's services. I will let Ashley explain the excitement of a church-mouse in her pew. It is a funny story and Dustin is the hero. Jessica and I went to Indian Creek. It was refreshing to see our church family. Greg and Deloris sat with Andrea and Nancy while we were gone.

Today (Monday) marks another end to one of the chapters in this story as Nancy completes her final treatment of the five-day battery of treatments. We have heard differing reports on what to expect concerning the sickness and nausea. Some say the sickness follows each treatment while others say sickness comes two or three days after the last treatment. Nancy has done well to this point. We will wait and see what the doctors prescribe and the insurance requires as we make our next decisions concerning going to a rehab facility, going home, or remaining here for a few more days. I am expecting a visit from Dr. Splichal this morning, and he may have some suggestions or at least some expectations of how the next few days will be traveled.

Our cocoon is wound pretty tight. We are bound by the unknown of what lies ahead and we are not promised what the butterfly will look like once it pops out of its cocoon. We don't know what to expect. We know what the doctors expect, but we are holding with endurance to see what God's plan for this journey reveals. It is while we wait that the world continues to spin, and our friends and family deal with life beyond their control. Our heart rejoices with those experiencing joy in their lives, and our heart is saddened with the disappointing news some receive in their lives. Phil laid his father to rest, as did Rev. Jimmy Thompson in saying goodbye to his help-mate Joanne. Jeni and her husband are going thru the trauma of losing their baby at birth followed by an emergency hysterectomy. Our hearts are saddened but we move forward with the same hope mentioned in a previous journal entry.

The Bible records an inspiring letter from John's third letter to his friend Gaius. 3rd John verses 2-4:

Dear friend, I pray that you may prosper in every way and be in good health, just as your soul prospers. For I was very glad when some brothers came and testified to your faithfulness to the truth—how you are walking in the truth. I have no greater joy than this: to hear that my children are walking in the truth.

In the morning hours of another busy work week, that is my prayer for each of you. I pray God's blessing upon you, the prayer supporters of Nancy and this family. I pray that you may prosper in every way and that you will be in good health. I pray your spiritual life will take you a few steps closer to reaching the level of spiritual maturity for which God is molding you. When that happens, word will get out. News travels, and we will have joy when we know you are walking in the Truth of God's Word.

Thanks for your interest in Nancy. Remember to tell others; this story is far from over!

• **Tuesday, March 8, 2011**

DAY 55

I woke up with a pillow-head this morning. Ashley took one for the team last night. We have been having two people stay with Nancy during the night. Last night, admittedly, I was not too much help. After I looked in the mirror I realized that it was not "beauty rest" that I received either. Ha! Nancy is not totally comfortable, but I believe she is resting better than yesterday. Thanks for the prayers concerning her pain. Not to be too graphic, but her area of discomfort has been concerning constipation. She seems to have improved during the last eight hours. Our new charge nurse is a more experienced nurse who likes to use some of the proven methods of the past. Yes, Nancy just completed a warm, prune juice cocktail. I am relocating slightly farther away from the bed. Ha! Ha! Even amid the discomfort of her condition, Nancy has remained "puckish." (Thanks to Kendra, we are using the "word of the day." Ha!)

Good News. Yesterday in the journal entry I was uncertain about what to expect with the fall-out of the treatments. Nancy completed all five without any nausea. Dr. Splichal said if she was going to be sick, she would have been sick by now. He wrote orders for her to continue the nausea medicine through today. We have been blessed regarding the nausea issues others have had to experience.

Today, we met a representative from the Landmark hospital. It is located near Athens Regional but specializes in longer-term care and rehabilitation. Hopefully, they will accept Nancy as a candidate for their care, and we will begin a new chapter. Nancy works hard and is totally cooperative with the physical therapist when they have time to work with her. So hopefully, they will recognize her desire for better health and will accept her.

Twenty-four years ago today, and after having served the Lord in music ministry for nine years, I was ordained. Through the years I have observed many individuals as they dealt with a cacophony of trials. I was reading a familiar passage of Scripture this morning that I want to share with those of you experiencing extra challenges in your own personal life. Many biblical scholars believe Jeremiah, one of God's prophets, wrote these words through the inspiration of the Holy Spirit. Lamentations 3:22-24:

Because of the Lord's faithful love we do not perish, for His mercies never end. They are new every morning; great is Your faithfulness! I say: The LORD is my portion, therefore I will put my hope in Him.

Admittedly, I was defeated yesterday when I posted the journal entry. While I was not completely down and out, I was seeing the gloomier side of our situation and not trusting God. When, as Jeremiah says, "The *Lord* is my portion." I *can* put my hope in Him. As believers, we must trust the Lord and realize His mercies never end. When our strength and faith waivers, His faithfulness is *great!* Every morning is a blessing, and His love does not perish.

Now, the day is almost at its midpoint, but this story is far from over!

- **Tuesday, March 8, 2011**

DAY 55a (76,251 Visits - 1,950 Posts)

The following is the "Mouse Story" mentioned in yesterday's post. The chronological order is as close as possible without too much embellishment.

Ray Stevens wrote about the Mississippi Squirrel incident back in 1984. Although I have never personally met Mr. Stevens, his bent or twisted sense of humor brings smiles to thousands, if not millions of people. His squirrel story came rushing to the memories of more than a few people this past Sunday at a local church in Hart County, Georgia. I have heard the account a couple of different times from two different people. They both have relayed the details in similar fashion so I thought I would try and craft a humorous story in the midst of some of the more somber tales I have been reporting.

To protect the integrity of the church I must report they have been under some recent reconstruction. Everything in the service was going fine until the special music. The pastor's son was singing a favorite selection when Ashley's friend, Rosemary, leaned over to say, "There's a rat that just ran under your coat in front of you." Yikes! The girls "quietly and reverently" squealed while they pulled their legs from the floor to the pew. Ashley had just returned from taking the children to Children's Church so when she plopped down, she put her (huge) pocketbook and kid's coats in the floor. Now, in a "quiet" panic, she turned to report the news to Dustin. Except for UGA football games, he is a man of reserved nature and seldom gets too excited.

Dustin was grinning from ear to ear as he suggested Ashley reposition her legs to the other direction so he could move in for the capture. They were sitting on the fourth row from the front and people on both the third and fifth pews were privy to the dilemma. Later observations reported that section of the church looked as if they were performing "the wave" as people were up and down trying to stay out of the way of the little critter.

The poor music man was using his excellent vocal talent in trying to render spiritual stimulation for preparation of a good sermon as the carnival on the fourth row was putting together a game plan Coach Mark Richt would envy. The decision was to have Betty, who was seated a pew ahead of Ashley and Dustin, to pull the coats forward while Ashley pulled her pocketbook clear. Dustin slid over as close as he could reach and gave the signal. Swoosh, the pocketbook was pulled up and the coats were pulled forward. Dustin's foot sprang forward as quick as a cat, and the song was coming to a close.

Still grinning like a Cheshire cat, Dustin suggested he needed some paper towels to extract the wanted results. Some tissues came from the fifth row and they were rejected by Dustin because he wanted something of heftier texture for the removal. Ashley quizzed him of his certainty that he had been successful and he nodded with satisfaction and pointed to a bit of residue on the carpet. While the last chorus of the solo's song was being sung, Ashley discreetly (well, as discreetly as one who just was jumping "quietly and reverently" in a pew) slipped from the pew to retrieve some paper towels and a trash bag. When she returned the congregation was standing for the reading of the Scripture. She handed the towels to Dustin and remained standing in the aisle as the preacher continued reading. Dustin, on the other hand, reached down to remove the mouse. When he moved his foot, there was no mouse. Where was it? It was *stuck to the bottom of his shoe. Ha*! Ha! Ha!

Dustin calmly collected the remains, quickly cleaned what he could, and quietly exited the sanctuary as reverently as a conquering hero can stride with trash bag in tow. Needless to say, he has received bogus invitations to join the Mouseketeer Club or sign on as an Exterminator in his spare time. There were other remarks about the church needing revival, but they were praying for a different motivator. I don't think Ray Stevens will have any competition in trying to get something to rhyme with mouse, but then, he did do pretty well with "Pascagoula."

- **Wednesday, March 9, 2011**

DAY 56

I waited until the night nurse, Jim, and the charge nurse, Paul, finished dressing her head wound and left the room before I leaned over for my Nancy-fix. Carletta provided the personal care and all three have been carefully attentive to meeting Nancy's pain requirements due to the digestive issues. It takes special training to become a nurse. It takes a special person to provide the genuine type of care Nancy has been receiving. Yesterday (Tuesday), Amanda and Marcus were the assigned the combination of nurse and personal-care technician. They were joined by the charge nurse, Sara, and the student assistant, Heather, as they got proactive in relieving the problem of constipation and impaction. It is unfortunate for Nancy they had to manually cause some momentary pain to relieve the other, ongoing pain. Please pray that Nancy will endure the continuing process of elimination (no pun intended) due to the digestive problem that has built over the last three or four days. It is the only pain Nancy has encountered through her entire ordeal, and yet she maintains a sweet, appreciative, and pleasant demeanor. Kendra, our niece, who also happens to be an RN, has assisted Nancy with daytime care during her days off from her regular job in another hospital. She has offered some suggestions through her experiences working in the OB-GYN area and the staff here has successfully tried some of her suggestions.

Nancy, for sure, is medicated for her pain, but her verbal responses to her care is with the simple words, "I love you" or "I love y'all" if there is more than one person attending to her needs. Last night, or more accurately, early this morning, I was wondering how many times Nancy had uttered those words to me. I distinctly remember the first time they rolled from her lips. She and I were sitting in her daddy's porch swing. It was Wednesday, September 15, 1976. We had been to church and Nancy was beginning her second year at Gainesville College. We had been dating for over three months, and I wanted to be sure I really loved her before I told her something as special as a declaration of love. Too often in our current culture that phrase or those words are thrown carelessly around. I was relieved when she responded that she loved me too. Here we are many years later. Together, several challenges have been faced head-on and hand-in-hand with the same declarations of our love for each other. While I sit here watching her mama tenderly feed her lunch, I can't help but wonder how many more times Nancy will utter those same precious words to me.

The Bible tells us in James 4:13-17 to take care as to how we plan our schedules.

Come now, you who say, "Today or tomorrow we will travel to such and such a city and spend a year there and do business and make a profit." You don't even know what tomorrow will bring—what your life will be! For you are a bit of smoke that appears for a little while, then vanishes. Instead, you should say, "If the Lord wills, we will live and do this or that." But as it is, you boast in your arrogance. All such boasting is evil. So, for the person who knows to do good and doesn't do it, it is a sin.

I have preached from the pulpit how necessary it is to live from day-to-day. It is important to allow God to give the direction in life that is necessary. Too often people want to tell God what to do. They want to tell Him what *their* plans are rather than seeking what His plans for them might include. At the end of the day, it all comes back to asking yourself, "Do I trust God?" Do I trust Him with my business? Do I trust Him with my finances? Do I trust Him with my life? I suppose those are all good questions to ask. How are we supposed to answer them? We have to answer them with the faith and hope we have as believers. Nancy and I have spent the last several years trusting the Lord. We will continue, even in the face of adversity. Remaining in the center of God's will is not always the easiest place or the most relaxing place, but it brings the greatest satisfaction in the end.

The end? No, this story is far from over!

- **Thursday, March 10, 2011**

DAY 57

Yesterday was one to forget. Unfortunately, it will be indelibly marked on the memory tablets of time in stone. I thought the feeling of helplessness was bad until yesterday's events magnified it exponentially. Nancy has not only been through a physically painful event, but now the traumatic scars of knowing if her bodily functions do not properly respond, the entire nightmare could require a rerun. The good news is that she has rested well. No, I mean, extremely well. She has made it through an uneventful night except for the usual interruptions of sleep for vital sign checks and medicine dosages administered. For that, I am so grateful and appreciative. Whitney came by around 5:00 AM simply to check on us. She is one of so many care givers who have had Nancy as a patient previously, and now take their break times to visit our room to offer encouragement. Whitney brought us each a cup of coffee and while she was preparing it, Nancy and I conversely thanked the Lord for a night of rest and relief.

I previously mentioned that yesterday was one to forget. Yet, having been in ministry has given me reminders of perspective. I purposefully have not tried to keep score in that I don't keep a record of weddings, funerals, baptism, and so forth. I simply move from one assignment to the next and attempt to offer hope for the hopeless and rejoice with those celebrating. I was reminded in my reflections this morning how during one day's pastoral visiting in the same hospital I prayed with one family as their loved one closed their eyes for eternity and walked the sterile hallways to another area of the hospital to rejoice with the family of a newly born infant. So, to be fair, I know that somewhere in this world, yesterday, was the greatest day in someone's perspective. Some couple got engaged; maybe it was a track runner who beat a personal best time on the stopwatch. Someone got that promotion they have sweated and worked tirelessly to achieve. Perhaps it was the accepting of God's grace, mercy, and forgiveness the individual had previously found elusive or unattainable. Over our morning coffee, Nancy and I agreed the Lord's blessings have been immeasurable to our family.

We have a new game plan for at least the next few days. Dr. Splichal visited yesterday afternoon and agreed to let us stay here at Athens Regional until Monday. Nancy will transfer to a long-term care hospital just down the road called Landmark Hospital. They will continue to monitor the head wound area and offer some physical therapy to try and get Nancy a bit more mobile than her current condition. Dr. Caesar Gumucio is the plastic surgeon who has been summoned to evaluate Nancy's wound area for the possible correction of it. The situation is one of weighing the benefits against the possible disadvantages based upon time and possible infection. The treatments of Temedar and radiation are inhibitors to healing. The concern for Nancy's wound being corrected will require an approximately two-hour surgery. When one compounds the two hours of anesthesia and the already-present wound inhibitors, one finds himself at the crossroad of tough decisions for Nancy's best health concerns. The wound itself is a grizzly sight of bare skull at least the size of a silver dollar, with no hope of fresh tissue growth if left unattended. The decision revolves around time and the results of the previous chemotherapy. We are juggling a few options all the while Nancy's clock is ticking and the long-term prognosis is not in her favor. Needless to say, we need your prayer support in decision making. Pray that as a family we can be agreeable to do what is best for Nancy and then be committed to the end results without regret.

Yesterday proved to be another day of comfort from friends and family members. We had some of both and your visits were welcomed and encouraging. Those of you who use Facebook or texting and so forth, you continue to offer shoulders in which to lean upon. We welcome those past accounts of impish or mischievous behavior some have written about on CaringBridge. Good-natured joking always helps our family and I have received some humorous feedback from Ashley and Dustin's mouse story. We are so fortunate to not be going through these storms alone. Your contacts are refreshing moisture to a parched and desert situation. Hug your Boss today and tell him or her you are thankful for your health and for your job. Thanks…

Oh yeah, this story is far from over!

• Friday, March 11, 2011

DAY 58

Does time creep or does it fly? I guess it depends upon perspective. The Spell-Check on my Word Document suggested I use the word "flies" instead of fly. Maybe time flies during vacation or when one is ill-prepared for a homework assignment. This week is number nine for Nancy Stacey team. Much changes in a matter of a few days and even more in weeks. Clayton Segers was permitted in for a brief visit last Sunday. It had been a month since Nancy and I were able to see him. We still haven't seen his younger brother, Jackson. The kids are growing by leaps and bounds and when Ashtin, Elliott, and now, Clayton, are able to visit for a few minutes, Nancy smiles with delight. The cycle of life brings changes and adjustments. The grandchildren are growing, and we are adjusting.

Yesterday was another difficult one for Nancy with the digestive issues. The nurses and technicians, Christy, Jessica, Barbara, and Brittany were assisted by our own independent team of Marlene and Ashley as they coached, begged, cried, and pleaded. Prayers were answered with limited results. Carol and Courtney took over where they left off and our team added Nancy's sister, Deloris. The night went well and Nancy has continued in her process of elimination. The pun was intended. We can't say enough good things about the twenty-four hour care this facility has offered Nancy and spoiled us.

I went to the guest house for sleep last night. It was the first in four nights and I slept well. When I checked with Nancy's care givers this morning I learned that Nancy celebrated some of her accomplishments with a cup of ice cream and an Indian Creek Fried Apple Pie! Now, I know that some of you, the readers of this journal, have tasted what I'm reporting and now you are envious. The "pie team" is back in operation for another banner year. The Memorial

Day Weekend Gospel Singing Weekend is quickly approaching, and I've been told the kitchen is simply not the same without Nancy.

Many churches are joining us in prayer and we have been blessed with visitors throughout our stay. Yesterday, Doug came from Tennessee via Tom's Creek to get his mother, Shirley; and others from Big A Elementary School brought a huge banner stating their love for Nancy. Already this morning, the folks from Pleasant Hill have been represented. Thanks for all of your prayer and cares for Nancy and our family.

This story is far from over!

• **Sunday, March 13, 2011**

DAY 60 (81,794 Visits - 1,997 Posts)

"Show Me the Way, LORD!" is a tremendous song we needed to hear today. Crystal, one of our technicians, and four of her friends came to lift our spirits, and they were successful. So often people get overwhelmed with the situations of life and soon they are defeated and their life is ruined. In less than twenty-four hours, I have heard the heart-breaking news of one who committed suicide. Another instance of a failed relationship is leaving some in bewilderment. Someone reminded me yesterday the devil will tell lies. He will constantly and falsely accuse believers causing discouragement, depression, and defeat. He barks out falsehoods to wear people down into final destruction.

I purposefully have skipped over reading about Job until the early hours of this morning. It was then, after looking around the guest house with sleepless eyes, that I picked up my Bible and began reading Job. Chapter two records a conversation Satan was having with God. The Lord was asking the devil where he had been. Lucifer's response was that he had been roaming the earth among the believers. God's Word is true so I know we can believe the devil will work among us while trying to cause division and dissension. The devil told one more lie to someone yesterday, and they believed him. I did not know the person well, but it breaks my heart to hear such reports.

(Sunday)

I started this post yesterday (Saturday). Somewhere along the way, I either ran out of gas or got distracted. Nancy has rested well, and her childhood friend, Sherri, has stopped in for visit. In my opinion, because of the infamous drug Decadron, or as we have come to name it as Deca-durn because the durn stuff has side effects, Nancy's temperament has shifted slightly. The drug reduces the swelling in the brain and at times, Nancy gets a little louder in her personality. The doctors have begun to reduce the dosage of Decadron because a side effect is its deceleration to healing. It hinders the healing that is required for her head wound and bottom areas.

Currently, we are still on schedule to transfer to the Landmark Hospital which is the long-term care facility located down the road. The transfer should happen tomorrow before two o'clock. We have been blessed to have had the benefit of the guest house at a reasonable fee. Alice is a precious and caring lady. She is the hostess and arranges the stays for the loved ones of the patients here in the hospital. Louise and Michelle are administering care today. They got Curron to assist them in a bed transfer. Nancy has teasingly picked on all of them and declared she loved them using the same breath. Nancy's mama has supplied some pie and cookies, and my mama has just brought another batch of Nancy's requested Oatmeal cookies. Nancy has already used her persuasive skills to eat two in a row. I'm sure the glucose levels will be fine with the reduced Deadron dosages.

Continue to pray for Nancy. Pray for the family as we face the next two weeks of decision making. We anxiously await the MRI scheduled for the 25th in order to determine the activity of the tumor. We will then need to decide if another round of chemotherapy should be administered or what the next course of action should be followed. Our nurses and doctors are great. Your messages are encouraging and we enjoy every one.

Keep praying and don't forget; this story is far from over!

• **Monday, March 14, 2011**

DAY 61

What strength do I have that I should continue hope? What is my future, that I should be patient? Is my strength that of stone, or my flesh made of bronze? Since I cannot help myself, the hope for success has been banished from me.

Those are the words of Job 6:11-13 recorded from the Bible. I hesitated using such words to start another work week for many of you. The fact of the matter is that if one studies the book of Job, he or she will realize, as did Job, his life was a testing ground. God allowed him being tested to prove the love Job had for God was sincere and genuine. Forty-two chapters record the testing of Job and the misunderstanding of his friends before he declares, "I know that You can do anything and no plan of Yours can be thwarted." If Nancy and I are going through a testing, I wonder what chapter number bears our resemblance. Whether it is forty-two or eighty-two I cannot say. However, what I do understand is that Nancy calls out in discomfort when I turn her body in the bed because she is too weak to turn herself. She desires to sit up, but after short periods of time her body weakens. She would love to fix Sunday lunch, which is better described with the word feast, but she can't stand up. Together, we have endured sixty days of discovery about ourselves, our family, and our friends. What I do know, is that we love each other through the love only God can provide. What I do know, is that we have been overwhelmed with blessing upon blessing with the comforting words of encouragement from fellow believers in Jesus Christ. It is through the love *of* Christ and our reciprocated love *for* Christ that enables us to declare with assurance, "I know that You (God) can do anything and no plan of Yours can be thwarted."

One may ask, "How do you explain a statement like that when you are experiencing the challenges of life in such a way?" The best and only way to reply is to acknowledge it is through the peace that passes understanding and our abiding love for Jesus Christ. Nancy and I know without Jesus's saving grace and mercy we could not and would not endure this testing. One may say, "You are not sick,

Nancy is." I wish you could witness the singing of songs from the Christian faith Nancy was singing Sunday afternoon and evening. She tells us constantly, and I mean every five minutes or so, that she loves us. She continuously encourages her care givers as they check vital signs, draw blood samples, or redress her head wound. Her pain tolerance is admirable, and her determined grit continues to define her courage to fight. I don't like any of this circumstance. It is painful to witness a loved one bearing such a combination of ailments. Yet, as a family, we are determined to hold to God's unchanging hand and rest in His unconditional love.

Today (Monday) is going to be a busy day. Nancy is scheduled to transfer to the Landmark Hospital on Sunset road. During the last thirty-five days, we have accumulated items in the guest house that need moving. Nancy has been in this same room for seventeen days and it too, has accumulated various items to move. There is uncertainty as to what time the transfer will take place. We are also undecided as to where we will set up camp for those family members not able to stay in her room at Landmark.

Today is a new day. It is the beginning of a new work week. How will you spend your day? How will your life impact the circle of influence in which you travel. As a believer of Jesus Christ, how will you share what He has done for you? As an unbeliever of Jesus Christ, would you not like to share the same peace and joy Nancy is demonstrating to her peers?

It's just a thought ... and remember, this story is far from over!

• **Tuesday, March 15, 2011**

DAY 62

"I've never seen that before," said Corey. He is an ambulance transport attendant and was remarking about how many nurses, technicians, and other hospital staff gathered outside Nancy's door as she transferred from Athens Regional to the Landmark Hospital. It has taken some adjusting, and in fact, we are not yet adjusted to the routines of the new staff. To be sure, the ARMC staff has spoiled us. We have appreciated with fondness the kind words some of the

112

staff has taken time to write. Thirty-five days of pampering can spoil anyone, and Nancy, the girls, and I are missing them.

We have not ventured too far down the halls or made new friends with more than two or three people at Landmark. The transfer orders were carried out at 3:00 PM, and by thirty minutes later; we were in our new home away from home in room 117. I rode with Nancy while the girls finished loading the accumulation of items from her old room and sorted the items to come with us to Landmark. Duett and Barbara from the wound team got right to work on both of the areas on Nancy's body that needed attention. It was encouraging to hear their opinions of the wound areas. Dr. Butt is the attending physician for Nancy at Landmark. He got a full assessment as Jessica, Marlene, Andrea, and I gave him Nancy's previous medical history. Ashley made a brief visit but her little boy is not feeling well. It was saddening to learn later in the evening the night shift was short-staffed and extremely busy. Being proactive was necessary in getting Nancy's needs met throughout the night. I'm glad I was able to assist Nancy with her various requests … except for the one about "a million dollars." Ha!

The girls went on a scavenger hunt to find some needed items for the new location. The top priority was a bed cot. I slept well for the first two-to-three hours but Nancy's being uncomfortable has required shifting and adjusting her position to best find a restful position. My sleep was further hindered from an upset stomach. Pray with me that Nancy can find a comfortable position and that the pain medication will soothe her. She continues to declare her love to me and has sung, "Without Him," several times during the course of the night while she declares her love for the Lord.

Earlier in the evening when the girls were gone, Nancy asked me to play some music. She has worn out a Kenny G CD so I went to YouTube and when I typed in "Kenny," I went back in time to the LittleJohn Coliseum in Clemson, South Carolina. It was February, 1985. Nancy and I have always had a broad appreciation for styles of music. She and I had two beautiful daughters and while we had not told anyone, Nancy was carrying our third child. She was a terrific mother and had worked hard in meeting their needs, while teaching school, and taking care of me in such a way that many a husband would envy. It was not financially possible, and seldom easy to have a "date night," but occasionally throughout the year, we would splurge. For Valentine's Day that year I presented her with two tickets for the upcoming Dolly Parton and Kenny Rogers concert. On the night of the concert, we stopped in Seneca at a Chinese restaurant and made our way to Clemson. I could be wrong, but I think the group Sawyer Brown was just hitting their stride and opened the evening's performances followed by Dolly. When Kenny Rogers came out for his set, he entered from the cheaper seats while singing one of his signature songs, "Lady." He was in his prime and wore a white suit to match his graying hair and well-groomed beard. I know some of the guys are going to rib me about being too sappy, but it was a memorable moment as he walked down the aisle only six seats to our right and Nancy squeezed my hand as he sang.

As the YouTube version played, I couldn't help it. It is the first time I cried in front of Nancy since all of this happened. I have included the lyrics that were written by Lionel Richie for you young-sters that can't remember the music of the eighties.

Lady, I'm your knight in shining armor and I love you
You have made me what I am and I am yours
My love, there's so many ways I want to say I love you
Let me hold you in my arms forever more

You have gone and made me such a fool
I'm so lost in your love
And oh, we belong together
Won't you believe in my song?

Lady, for so many years I thought I'd never find you
You have come into my life and made me whole
Forever let me wake to see you each and every morning
Let me hear you whisper softly in my ear

In my eyes I see no one else but you
There's no other love like our love
And yes, oh yes, I'll always want you near me
I've waited for you for so long

Lady, your love's the only love I need
And beside me is where I want you to be
'Cause, my love, there's somethin' I want you to know
You're the love of my life, you're my lady!

The song plays on but, this story is far from over!
P.S. Just so you will know; Nancy said to quit crying. Ha!

• Thursday, March 17, 2011

DAY 64

"Tag! You're it," were the words daddy said as he prompted me to write today's post. We are beginning to settle in here at Landmark. Tuesday and Wednesday were both good days and similar in routine. Dr. Butt generally makes his rounds a little after 7 AM, and breakfast comes around 8am. Mama's head is redressed and ready to face the new day. Our therapy team arrives midmorning and puts mama to work right away! Pam, the physical therapist, hit it off with mama because she too was a college basketball player. Our other team members include Linda, OT, Angie, OT, Crystal, Ashton, and Sam. Just as I was making my entrance this morning, Pam, Linda, and Sam were hard at work getting mama ready to venture down to the rehab room. Each one pitched in to help mama strengthen her muscles through her new exercises. We have had three very productive days of therapy and are very pleased with Mama's progress! After therapy Mama looks forward to lunch, followed by a resting time. We try to do a few exercises on our own before supper arrives. Mama has been eating her meals from the side of the bed to help her gain "trunk control." Throughout the day the staff is in and out doing their chores of taking vital signs, blood sugar checks, medicine dispensing, and room cleaning. We have also been blessed with our visitors who stop by to check on mama and us as we continue our journey.

Since the last post, mama has developed an incessant and aggravating cough. Wednesday night she was visited by a respiratory therapist who thought she may have some fluid in her lung. A chest x-ray was done this morning, and we are waiting to hear the report.

Please pray that we can get this cleared up quickly. Her digestive system seems to be back on schedule and functioning properly. We are grateful for those answered prayers.

Thanks for the continued support and patiently waiting on the update! Hopefully Daddy will be back for the next inspirational post! And as always ...this story is far from over!

- **Friday, March 18, 2011**

DAY 65

Hi Folks,

Nancy is having a different reaction to the day than has been normal even for her. She had a reasonably good day yesterday which included physical therapy and a wheelchair ride outside for a few minutes. Janet and Ashley gave her a bath last night so she would rest better. It was with difficulty Nancy got any rest during the late night and early morning hours. She continued to have an aggravating and incessant cough. The staff medicated her so that by around 3:00 AM she was able to finally sleep. I crawled up on my cot which now includes an egg crate-like foam rubber pad. I woke for the body turning at 4:00 AM and let the staff handle it. At a little past seven the tech gave me the results of the vital signs and reported a midgrade fever of 101 degrees. Nancy was sleeping rather deeply so I tried to arose her for breakfast. I noticed her arm trembling slightly so I stepped into the hallway for the tech to come in and observe it. She said she would get the nurse and in a minute or less the nurse came in time to observe Nancy vomit. Outside of one time after her second surgery, this was the first time we have had any nausea. Rumor has it that there may be a "bug" traveling around and it's possible she has it.

The concern now, is that Nancy is despondent and less talkative. Andrea and I have tried to engage her with conversation and she seems "flat" or unresponsive. When she has opened her eyes, I have teasingly stuck out my tongue at her, and she responded with like sign. We have done that occasionally throughout her stay as a silent communication of affection. However, when Andrea has

116

asked her if she was trying to talk but couldn't, she nodded her head. A few minutes later, she would have a conversation with enough prompting to answer our questions about our concerns. Obviously, this is abnormal behavior. We have asked for a CT scan but there is not a doctor here to approve the move for going to Athens Regional to get one. I called Dr. Splichal's office to see if he would endorse a CT, and his assistant said he was out of the office and that Dr. Butt is the attending physician that would have to order it. Now, I have asked for the next highest authority to Dr. Butt to evaluate her so we can be proactive in case she has had a slight stroke.

Dr. Butt has been proactive this morning concerning getting several tests of urinalysis, blood, lung cultures, and so forth. Those immediate results can be observed but the final cultures will not be available for two or three days.

We need some medical answers and we are not getting what we are seeking.

Stay tuned ... you know the rest ...

Pray—Pray—Pray!!!

• **Friday, March 18, 2011**

DAY 65a

Andrea's afternoon update ...

The charge nurse, Lindsay, came and did a neurological assessment around 2:40 PM. Mama's pupils reacted well and the nurse was going to pass the results onto Dr. Butt. In the meantime those of us present gathered around Mama, and each said a prayer asking for God's wisdom and guidance once again. Chanda, our speech therapist, came in at 3:00 PM to reassess Mama's swallowing ability. She passed with flying colors. As Chanda was finishing up around 3:25 PM, Dr. Butt came in to assess Mama for himself. He didn't feel that Mama had sustained another bleed, but he did agree to allow Mama to go to Athens Regional for a CT scan. Corey and Abby were here in a flash and ready to transport Mama on her field trip around 3:40 PM. Daddy was able to ride along as well. They were back by 4:20 PM.

Currently, we are waiting for the results of the CT scan. Meanwhile, Nancy has once again begun to talk and has reminded us her bottom hurts. We had not heard that at all before 3:30 PM. On the way out the door to the transport ambulance, Dr. Butt told Daddy that Mama had received a shot of morphine at 4:00 AM. That would explain a lot of our concerns and Nancy's abnormal behaviors. We will post another update once we receive the news.

Thanks for the immediate prayers. It looks like this story is far from over!

• **Saturday, March 19, 2011 12:54 PM, EDT**

DAY 66 ,

It seems as though Nancy has experienced yet another downturn away from better health. The CT scan revealed no bleeding on the brain which obviously was good news. However, without speaking to a neurologist, Dr. Butt said the CT showed swelling in the brain and his feeling was the tumor was still very much active which would explain the change in behavior we have noticed in Nancy the last thirty-six hours. This morning, after an increase of the Decadron, her communications skills are beginning to improve. I asked Dr. Butt to re-explain the results of the CT from yesterday, and he said he wanted to get the scheduled March 29th MRI moved up to an earlier date. He felt the tumor has increased in size but could not determine without certainty until the MRI was utilized. He was going to confer with Dr. Splichal and make the decision together.

While it has been sixty-plus days since our discovery of the burden we would share with Nancy, it remains tender and full of raw emotion when we try to process the information given. I suppose we are processing the information in different ways as it relates to our relationship with Nancy. I observe our three daughters as they are trying to wrap their minds around the burden. I also watch Nancy's siblings and other close family members as they; too, try to make sense of which we are dealing. I have yet to find anyone who can give us an explanation or who can understand why Nancy has to endure the challenge that this life has thrust upon her.

The second letter of Corinthians records the heartache and pain the Apostle Paul was enduring. He had asked God to remove the infirmity from his body to which he was denied on at least three occasions. 2 Corinthians 12:8-10:

Concerning this, I pleaded with the Lord three times to take it away from me. But He said to me, "My grace is sufficient for you, for power is perfected in weakness." Therefore, I will most gladly boast all the more about my weaknesses, so that Christ's power may reside in me. So because of Christ, I am pleased in weaknesses, in insults, in catastrophes, in persecutions, and in pressures. For when I am weak, then I am strong.

I wonder how many prayers have been offered on Nancy's behalf. At what point does one say like Paul, "Okay, do what you want to God." I said it on the night of February eighth when the brain bleed caused Nancy to have a debilitating episode. I said "okay" then but have prayed for the "thorn to be removed" several times since that night. It's difficult to explain the peace of God until one needs it. It's hard to express the sufficiency of God's grace until one experiences that grace. I am not geographically in a position to do an in-depth word study on the passage. However, in the midst of the confusion and bewilderment of taking a perfectly healthy woman and placing a life-threatening illness that affects a minister's family and pre-occupies the regular daily agenda and schedules, God's grace is sufficient. For every believer, God's grace is sufficient. While we learn the phrase or verse from childhood, it is with experience, the sermon finds its passion, and its delivery has impact. You may not be hunting a sermon to preach, but through life's experiences, and realizing God's grace, you will have a testimony to share.

Let me share a bit of trivia before I close this journal. Nancy's parents are visiting our room today so I asked them to share a story about her. Durward said when they brought her home from the hospital, they had not decided on an official name for her. Guinnell's mother, Elizabeth Harrison, started calling her Gooly-ann. Eventually, the name Nancy Elizabeth was given her in honor of Durward's grandmothers, Mrs. Crawford and Mrs. Harrison. Some of you have known her as Nancilee or some other nickname.

The story of my "Darlin" is far from over!

• **Monday, March 21, 2011**

DAY 68

His Hand In Mine (by Mosie Lister)

You may ask me how I know my Lord is real
And you may doubt the things I say and doubt the way I feel.
But I know He's real today, He'll always be
I can feel His hand in mine and that's enough for me.
Chorus: I will never walk alone, He holds my hand
He guides each step I take and if I fall I know He understands
'Til the day He tells me why He loves me so
I can feel His hand in mine, that's all I need to know.

Sleep has eluded me once again as I take up the ole' trusty laptop and begin to write a few more words to our story. It *is* in fact, a love story. However, I don't want to label it that just because Nancy and I declare our love for one another. I cannot call it a love story solely based on the intimate or romantic times we have shared, but rather because of God's love that continues to shine on us through the crisis in which we endure. Here, in the early hours of another work week, I sit and reflect upon all the love that has been shown to our family in just the last couple of days. My, how the words of encouragement have blessed me as I read the testimonies and heart-felt feelings of you, the readers, have written on CaringBridge or the personal messages on Face Book. In only the last two days, Nancy's room door has been opened to nearly sixty individuals of well-wishers and prayer warriors. People like Kathryn or Janie are testimonies of outliving a doctor's death prognosis. God's love has shown through individuals like Roger, who less than two months ago laid his wife to rest due to cancer and yet, he wanted to encourage us. Liz was rolled into Nancy's room in a wheelchair but she had enough breath to stand and sing, "Without Him" because of God's love for her as it shines down from Him and reflects onto others. Monetary and other gifts have been given to help meet needs. Like Mosie Lister's song reminds me, I know God is real today and He will always be real. *I can feel His hand in mine and that's enough for me.*

Now, hold on just a minute. I am not Teflon or Titanium. I am not perfect. I suppose I am like the disciples in the boat with Jesus on the Sea of Galilee while the winds blew fiercely and He slept soundly. While I remain in His presence, I too, come unglued when Nancy's health takes an unexpected nosedive like it did this past Friday. I get concerned when not enough is being done to preserve what health she does still have in her body. I certainly want some sensible answers to the myriad of questions our family produces through the course of a simple room visit. However, in the realm of the "big picture" I realize God is in control and I should prioritize *my life* to *His will*. Let me explain.

In Philippians 3:18-21, the Apostle Paul is reminding his dear friends as believers of Jesus Christ to recheck their purpose and priority. In previous verses Paul said *his goal was to know Christ and the power of His resurrection* (v.10). He goes on to admit he has not yet reached his goal of spiritual maturity, but he is making every effort to bring it to fruition. In contrast to how he is striving to reach his goal, Paul observes how some are living.

For I have often told you, and now say again with tears, that many live as enemies of the cross of Christ. Their end is destruction; their god is their stomach; their glory is in their shame. They are focused on earthly things, but our citizenship is in heaven, from which we also eagerly wait for a Savior, the Lord Jesus Christ. He will transform the body of our humble condition into the likeness of His glorious body, by the power that enables Him to subject everything to Himself.

If as believers, our citizenship is in heaven, and our desire is being in the presence of Jesus, then how could we possibly have any other priority than looking for His return and living godly, Christ-honoring lives? To Paul, that meant living a testimony in front of his peers that was above reproach. He previously said as believers we should live up to what we believe (v.16). In other words, if we say that God is in control, and if we believe God is in control, then we should live as if God is in control. Sometimes for me that becomes harder in practice than it does in preaching. One might say, "Bill, you don't know what I'm going through." My response will come from personal example of how God continues being in control when our life is in chaos. As a child, our family had a major fire that nearly destroyed the family business. As a teen, I survived the Toccoa Falls flood in which thirty-nine neighbors and friends perished, and I was displaced from my immediate family. As an adult, I buried my sister only to find out six weeks later by a criminal investigator, she had been drowned for $444,000 dollars worth of life insurance but he could not prove it. Oh, there have been other general crisis such as job loss or work relationship challenges, but through all those times of despair, disillusionment, or discouragement, there has been the ongoing determination to serve Christ and live in His peace while resting in His arms. Admittedly, I needed reminding of His peace at times, but I have resolved to live for Him.

Obviously, Nancy's health care is of utmost concern. Reports from the blood, urine, and lung cultures came back negative which means no infection. That is tremendous news. The disconcerting news is Decadron dosages have increased to reduce swelling in the brain, but is causes the glucose levels to bounce around like a ping-pong ball. The difficult challenge will come later this coming week if Dr. Splichal agrees with Dr. Butt to move the MRI up and determine what the brain tumor is doing. There are very few medical options left to assist Nancy if it has grown. The decisions can be burdensome.

I have lived under pressure, but I like what the great missionary Hudson Taylor said concerning pressure.

"It doesn't matter, really, how great the pressure is; it only matters where the pressure lies. *See that it never comes between you and the Lord*—Then, the greater the pressure, the more it presses you to His breast."

Are you living life in the peace of God's rest or under pressure? Has your job caused such a pressure you hate going to work? Do financial challenges put pressure on your marriage? Or, like me, is your family dealing with a terminal health condition in which you feel the pressure of helplessness?

The Song Says: *I can feel His hand in mine and that's enough for me.*

This story may be getting longer, but it's far from over!

- **Tuesday, March 22, 2011**

DAY 69

Sugar and Spice, and everything thing nice are the ingredients of little girls according to the poem of years past. When the recipe for Nancy was created, there were a few more items added to make her the individual I found appealing. Grit and determination were qualities I was not personally requiring on my list of describing the perfect match for me, but I soon would learn that was part of Nancy's package. Often those qualities were exhibited during the competitive challenge of a ball game.

One such example was during a college basketball game between Gainesville Junior College and South DeKalb College outside of Atlanta. Nancy had been privileged to play a major portion of that particular game, and she was assigned the task of guarding the opposing team's point guard. Their player was slightly taller than Nancy and had long blonde hair which cascaded over her shoulders and down to at least the middle of her back. Unlike most girls with long hair, she chose not to keep it tied, or balled up out of the way, so it was constantly flopping loosely as the game progressed. The girl was an average-skilled player who helped keep her team close in score to that of Nancy's team. With only a few minutes remaining in the game, tension was mounting, and strategies of tougher defense were implemented. South Dekalb was bringing the ball up the court, and Gainesville was in a trap defense. The ball was fumbled and rolling across the floor with girls from both teams furiously chasing after it. For a second or two the game resembled a football pile as players were fighting for possession. Suddenly their guard came out of the pile screaming out in pain and holding her ear while declaring, "She bit my ear!" Nancy on the other hand, came out of the pile with the ball, and poker-faced as to knowing anything about that which the other player was complaining. The referees were incredulous as to what had happened and did not render any fouls or penalties of either kind.

Frankly, I don't remember who won the game, but afterwards when the players came out of the dressing room, Nancy came over and sat down beside me. I waited a few minutes and then curiously asked Nancy if she had bitten the girl's ear. She replied, "Yes I bit her! And I meant for it to hurt too!" She went on to explain the girl's hair had been a nuisance the whole game and she had said a few unkind things to Nancy. I learned then, she could settle accounts and was not afraid of anything. While I don't and can't condone biting people who have wronged us, I have had a blast retelling that story over the years. It speaks volumes to the fortitude and determination in which Nancy has engaged life itself.

Humorously, I will add that a year or more later, we were having our pre-marital counseling with the officiating minister who happened to be my dad. He used what seemed like a long list of scriptures, recommendations, and suggestions to ensure a happy marriage. As he got nearer the bottom of his checklist, he sheepishly grinned at me, looked over to Nancy and said, "Nancy, as far as spousal abuse goes, I think you can handle anything this scrawny little runt has to dish out." We all laughed, but I remembered that basketball game, and so far, my ears are unscathed. Ha! Ha!

Yesterday (Monday), my assumptions were realized during Dr. Splichal's afternoon visit. He had been informed of last Friday's episode concerning Nancy's abnormal behavior. He further had reviewed the information given through the CT scan and agreed with Dr. Butt to schedule the MRI earlier than next week. The recent scan revealed the mass of the tumor was larger than the last scan from mid-February. The Decadron will continue to reduce swelling so that Nancy's brain will respond normally, but even it has limitations if the tumor continues to grow.

The plan is to have the MRI today, Tuesday, and meet with Dr. Splichal Wednesday for the results. The last conversation we shared concerning a growing tumor did not have a favorable perspective. We fully realize the gravity of this upcoming forty-eight hours. Yet, will we trust in Christ.

The following are a few verses I have been claiming in these early hours:

Psalm 46:1 God is our refuge and strength, a very present help in trouble.

Zechariah 4:6b This is the word of the Lord… Not by might, nor by power, but by my spirit, says the Lord of hosts.

Nahum 1:7 The Lord is good, a stronghold in the day of trouble; and He knows them that trust in Him.

All I can say is if that cancerous tumor had a body, I would be gnawing on its ears. It really is. This story is far from over!

• **Tuesday, March 22, 2011**

DAY 69a

This *is* the day that the Lord hath made, let us rejoice and be glad in it…

Today has been a good day for Nancy. There has been a nice amount of company and Nancy seems to enjoy the visits.

Nancy was transported to ARMC for her MRI around 11:00 this morning. Apparently, it is not her favorite thing due to the loud noises that it makes. I imagine it to sound something like having your head in the dryer while you're drying your tennis shoes. (No, I haven't tried that)

There was plenty of excitement around Athens today. Bill was in "lock down" at ARMC and learned that someone decided to shoot two police officers. It is another reminder that none of us are promised tomorrow. We want to remind each of you to pray for the victims and their families.

There is a meeting tomorrow morning at 9:00 with Dr. Terry; he's the radiation oncologist. We expect to hear the results of today's MRI. As you can imagine, we are longing to hear some good news. Pray with us as we face whatever news that will be given to us.

Today, I was blessed to spend the day with the Nancy I have grown to love over the years. I guess I should mention that Nancy has been a part of my life since I was eight years old. Actually, I don't remember too much about life before Nancy! In case you are wondering, the author of this post is Bill's baby sister, Marlene.

I guess I'll sign off and leave the preaching to Bill. I will say that on behalf of all of the family we want to thank each one of you who have breathed a prayer on our behalf. We know that God is good, and we trust Him on the journey—especially since it is far from over!

• **Wednesday, March 23, 2011**

Day 70 (95,769 Visits—2,164 Posts)

Thanks for your concern and for patiently waiting. We received word from Dr. Terry that the tumor appears to be maintaining its size. We are hoping to hear a more detailed report from Dr. Splichal. Daddy is working on a more descriptive post. He had a minor distraction in the form of a flat tire... because as you all can imagine, This story is far from over!
The Girls

• **Thursday, March 24, 2011**

DAY 71

The roller coaster ride continues. I was going to write a detailed account of the post the girls put up yesterday. At 12:38 PM yesterday, Dr. Terry said the MRI report from the radiologist's reading was "subjective" due to the difficulty in measurement. The reports stated Nancy's tumor showed continued growth from the last picture taken. He suggested that with the ongoing use of Decadron, we could advance more days without significant changes in demeanor or health.

We were happy with that report. In fact, Nancy was able to go outside in a wheelchair, and she observed as her daddy and I changed a tire on Ashley's car. Marlene and Andrea took it for repair and brought it back with milkshakes. By 7:00 PM we had all decided Dr. Splichal had concurred with Dr. Terry, and he would not come by to examine Nancy.

Thirty minutes later, Dr. Splichal came into the room with a printed report from the radiologist. It, as you might imagine, was detailed with indication the tumor, in fact, had increased in size. (Or at least the swelling had increased causing the abnormalities we had observed last Friday.) The room was full with my mother, Marlene, Jessica, Ashley, Nancy, and me. Andrea had been earlier in the day but was home, preparing for her third-shift. I cannot say I was shocked by the news, but I was hoping for better news. Dr. Splichal explained he did not think the previous chemotherapy had been as beneficial as we had hoped. He also told us his visit with Dr. Terry suggested that more radiation was not an option. It was after Ashley reminded us of a conversation we had with Dr. Nicolakalus at Athens Regional, that it would take at least two rounds of chemotherapy before a noticeable difference was usually observed. Dr. Splichal asked what we wanted to do. The only available option towards better health was taking in more poison of the chemotherapy by using Temmadar. (Of course that statement leaves out the herbs, and other remedies mentioned but not recommended by the medical staff.)

Today (Thursday), we have been told by Dr. Butt, that we will be transferred back to Athens Regional for a five-day round of Temmadar. I can't really share more than that for now.

The transport truck is on its way to close the chapter on Landmark Hospital. However, this story is far from over!

- **Friday, March 25, 2011**

DAY 72

Do you believe in angels? I do. I believe in angels as described in the Bible, like Michael, Gabriel, or others which are mentioned but not named, but I also believe God uses people to serve Him as angels from time-to-time. Eleven weeks ago this morning God sent me one. We were in the "eye" of this turbulent storm. While trying to gain some sort of balance from the bowling over news of Nancy having a noncurable cancerous brain tumor, the custodial crew came into the room. The lady had already dumped the trash and stepped out of our room. I was in a daze but I realized I had not taken time to even speak to her. In a few moments she re-entered the room to mop the floor. I apologized for not speaking to her earlier and I asked for her name. She firmly said, "My name is Wanda Harris, but if you can't remember that, just remember J-E-S-U-S because He can take care of any problem you have." WOW! I needed to hear Jesus would take care of us. Oh, I knew it. I have studied it. As a preacher, I have even preached it. However, on Friday, January 14th, somewhere between nine and noon, I needed to be reminded of it. Today, after several weeks of unknown ends to the uncertain days we have experienced, it continues as a healing ointment to the open sore of a heart-broken body. Jesus can take care of any need we can imagine.

Yesterday (Thursday), our roller coaster would have put Six Flags's Scream Machine to shame. It started out with a routine examination from Dr. Butt, and the plan to move to Athens Regional. I was headed down the hall to re-heat Nancy's breakfast plate when I met the transport team of Abby and Ron, who by now have become family friends. I asked Abby if they were coming for Nancy because we were not packed up nor expecting them quite so quickly. She said they had another patient they could move first and then get to us about ninety minutes later. I agreed and hurried back to the room while calling Marlene to see how close to Landmark she was from her travels. She arrived and we began packing up all the pictures, posters, flowers and goodies that have accumulated in the days of recuperation. At the appointed time, the transport team came back down the hall, and this time they were intercepted by the charge nurse who informed them we had not yet received the necessary clearance to be admitted to Regional. That was disappointing after having carried all the room paraphernalia out to the cars. Even more disappointing was the cause of the issue keeping us from being admitted. (No, it didn't have anything to do with keeping Marlene off their premises. Ha!) There were two separate issues of which we were dealing. For Athens Regional, it was an insurance issue in validating a reason to be admitted for the purpose of taking a chemotherapy pill. For Landmark Hospital, it was an OSHA issue. Yep! OSHA. It was explained that their staff was not equipped to handle chemotherapy or the care for administering it to the patient.

So really, I suppose it was an insurance issue either way. Around 12:30 PM Dr. Splichal called into the room to explain the delay. He said he had called several people including administrators of each facility to try and resolve the problem. He went on to offer some alternatives that he thought might help. Evidently he rang the right phone somewhere along the way because within two hours Dr. Butt came to re-inform us that we were going to Athens Regional. Two hours after that we were rolling down Prince Avenue and headed to room 2209. The adjustment went well, and the evening passed quickly. I don't remember too much of the evening because the girls were looking after their mother, and I was looking at the backs of my eyelids.

Today (Friday), Nancy has been visited by the wound-care specialist, physical and occupational therapists, social workers, the great staff of nurses and technicians, as well as Dr. Splichal. The first dose of the second round of Temodar has been administered, and Nancy is resting well. I have had five different pastor friends visit and Nancy has had nursing staff from the fifth floor neuroscience wing of the hospital. Yes, we are loved. We have felt the love from you but we have felt the love of God through His "angels."

Our angel, Wanda Harris, just came into our room and sang, "It's A Blessing To Be Alive." It's all about Jesus and because it's about Jesus, this story is far from over!

• Monday, March 28, 2011

Day 75

Saturday was a day that will remain in my heart and mind forever. Daddy, Ashley and I stayed the night with Mama in her room Friday night. We woke up yesterday ready for a new and exciting day. Amanda came in early with breakfast from Chick-fil-A along with some much needed shampoo and conditioner for Ashley and me. (Thanks again Amanda!) Daddy, Ashley, and I began to get ready for our big appointment later in the afternoon. During the getting ready process, Mama had several visitors. Friends and family quickly filled up Mama's new room, 2209. Blake and Shellei stopped in, along with Misty, Sarah, and Jane. Needless to say, many of the visitors had the privilege of seeing Ashley and me at our finest. Matter of fact, Dr. Splichal walked in to examine Mama just in time to catch me without any make-up on and my hair up in rollers. Just as a side note, Dr. Splichal has eight children. I stepped out of the bathroom and pointed to my head and said, "Dr. Splichal if you have any girls, this is coming to your future soon!" We all chuckled and listened to the rest of his report.

Soon, Janet, Grandma and Granddaddy Adams, Mary Jo and Annie Jim came into the room. The plan was to have them take care of Mama while Daddy, Ashley, and I went to the appointment. You, the readers, are probably wondering what appointment to which I'm referring. Well, it was an appointment at David's Bridal. For those of you that do not know me or my story, I'm Jessica the *favorite* daughter … umm … I mean … I'm Jessica the middle daughter to Bill and Nancy. On December 21, 2010, I got engaged to Josh. As you all can imagine, this is a very bittersweet time in my life. I'm so excited that I have *finally* found "the *one*" the Lord has just for me; however, trying to plan a wedding while watching my Mama lie sick in a bed has been extremely tough and a bit overwhelming at times.

Ms. Alice, the sweet lady that helps with the guest house facility, and Aunt Marlene had a great idea on Friday. Since Mama is not allowed to leave the hospital for field trips, they recommended that we use Skype to help Mama feel a part of my decision making. Skype is a free way to communicate over the Internet. It allows you to hear and see the person that with which you are skyping. Using skype would allow Mama to see me try on dresses and let me know what she liked or disliked about each dress. Ms. Alice contacted David's Bridal for us and found out that they do have wireless. Friday night, Josh and I completed a few test runs to make sure we had everything ready for Saturday. Saturday afternoon came in a hurry. Mama had her breakfast, lunch, and second Temodar pill. Praise the Lord that Mama still has an appetite and no signs of nausea. What a blessing that truly is for her. After a few computer mishaps, we were able to get things up and running for our big appointment. Lucy and Jeff came at the perfect time. Their son Nick lives in Texas so they are familiar with Skype. Lucy was able to help get things going at the hospital while we headed out to the appointment.

Daddy, Ashley, and I arrived at David's Bridal around 1:00 PM. Andrea and Ms. Pam, Josh's mother, also met us there to help me choose the perfect dress. We were greeted with our consultant Shelley. She was very welcoming and helpful. After a few trials to ensure Mama could see us back at the hospital, I began the try-on process. I had a few dresses already in mind that I had tried on last weekend so Shelley pulled those dresses and a few others to get me started. Meanwhile, Ashtin, Ashley's daughter, enthusiastically arrived. Josh and I have asked Ashtin to be our flower girl, and boy is she excited. She loved getting to try on dresses with me. She was all about the accessories to go with the outfit. I'm so thankful that she was there because her sweet spirit and happy little self brought smiles to my face.

After a few shed tears, several trips in and out of the dressing room, and tips from Mama, I finally decided on my dress. Everyone agreed that dress number three was the dress for me! I'm sure some of the people in David's Bridal thought my daddy was a little strange holding his iphone up videoing through Skype, but we really didn't care. We are just so thankful for the technology of today so that Mama could be with us too. It meant the world to me to have her share this experience with me. I, too, am very thankful for my sisters, my daddy, Ms. Pam and Ashtin for making my special day extra special. I'm truly blessed to have such an amazing family.

Saturday night concluded by us returning to the hospital and hanging out with more family and friends. We spent some time looking through catalogs trying to get ideas for bridesmaid dresses and other wedding details. Now, Mama is on a mission to find her perfect dress. Please pray for Josh and me as we make plans for the wedding. Pray that the Lord gives us great wisdom and discernment with our decision making. Pray especially for Mama: that the Lord will continue to help her improve and get stronger each day.

I have definitely learned through this journey with Mama that we never know what tomorrow may bring so we must live for today. In addition, I have come to understand how God really does grant us the grace and strength that we need to get through difficult situations when we need it. He says in his word in Matthew 11: 28 -30:

Come unto me, all ye that labour and are heavy laden , and I will give you rest . Take my yoke upon you, and learn of me; for I am meek and lowly in heart: and ye shall find rest unto your souls. For my yoke is easy, and my burden is light.

He is always ready to carry our load of troubles and concerns, but we must be willing to give it all to him. While you turn your burdens over to our precious Lord and Savior, please remember ... this story is far from over!

• **Wednesday, March 30, 2011**

DAY 77

Legend records Daniel Boone, the great frontiersman, died of eating sweet potatoes. After enduring countless harsh winters, extended hunting and trapping trips, and skirmishes with Native Americans, ole' Dan'il succumbed to something as harmless as sweet potatoes. I'm guessing it was church pot-luck dinner casserole that got him.

His legend is great in the Kentucky—Tennessee areas, and the popular television show of the sixties embellished his toughness a tad, too. Something that remains true is the time he spent as a prisoner of a tribe of Indians. Part of the punishment was running through a gauntlet. He was beaten and thrashed, whipped and kicked. He survived all the punishment, and carried on his leadership position back in Boonesborough once his escape was successful.

Yesterday (Tuesday), we felt like we had been through a gauntlet. Oh, I am not bruised or scarred on the outside, but the emotional blows we received were a direct hit on the bulls-eye of reality. Nancy is in too good of physical condition to receive care provided by insurance companies, yet, she continues to be reminded she will die soon. While we were expecting a smorgasbord of options from which to choose when we were informed of our soon-coming discharge, it ended up being less than a few. Well, actually, one option but we could choose from three different hospice agencies.

There are other options, just not insurance-providing options. Out of pocket options are always available, but we are trying to decide if Nancy is truly capable or interested in some of those options. To be sure, last evening was a restless one in getting prepared for a night's sleep. It is at these crossroads I have seen families fall apart. It is on the corner of despair and discouragement, that Satan seems to show up like a con artist with an arm-full of wrist watches. He smoothly offers and begs for a decision to take something that looks appealing, while knowing it is against the will of God. Perhaps the analogy is too strong, but I think one can get the picture of the situation.

The social workers are nice ladies. However, it was difficult to keep from jumping up and throwing a two-year-old's fit as they were telling us what was going down. It was difficult to keep cool and try to believe they "really did" understand what we are going through. I affirmed yesterday, how much more sensitive I need to be when counseling or consoling a family going through trauma or crisis. Life's lessons often come in a variety of packages, and if one pays attention, he or she can increase the value of that lesson later in life when similar situations or crises arise. I hope we listened in order to put application later when needed.

After our meeting with the social workers, we had a brief family meeting and then I was "talked" out. I was saturated with information but was medically incapable of making better a situation that has become out of our control. I simply wanted to shut down and regroup. I sat and read the newest edition of the Southern Gospel Singing News magazine and tried to change the scene in my mind. It was after reading Tim Lovelace's article concerning swimming in a lake full of alligators that I got a chuckle and decided it wasn't quite that bad. Ashley needed to return to the accounting office. Andrea would soon need to head home for preparation of an early morning meeting at An-Med. Jessica and I was staying the night with Nancy. I had not eaten lunch, and it was eight o'clock in the evening so I decided to go eat and unwind from the afternoon's discussions. I made a few calls and received more than a few in offering support and concern. Before I entered the restaurant, it was nine o'clock and I needed to get back to Nancy's room. The phone calls were encouraging and informative. I have an idea there was a ton of prayers offered up due to the extended family knowing with which we were wrestling. When I returned, we agreed to think and pray about our decision before talking about it with one another Wednesday morning.

The night went without too many unexpected surprises. I fell asleep listening to the group Selah singing some old standards with contemporary musical arrangements. One song in particular pricked my interest. "It Is Well" is a song penned during a terrible crisis and yet, it has ministered to literally millions of people since it's publishing. Many of you readers are familiar with the song. As I listened, I questioned myself. Is everything "well" with my soul? Yes, my salvation is secured. I know and continue to rest in God's peace, and yet there is a storm raging. I suppose it is like the proverbial Swan gracefully gliding across a mirror-topped pond. Underneath the calm appearance of the water, are two spindly legs churning furiously. While I am in the midst of the storm, I recognize the hand of God and feel the love of family and extended family as we travel this road together. I have been feasting (literally) from reading large portions from John's gospel. I have been bathed in the comfort of God's Word and while the night's rest is short, I arise refreshed and ready to face the new day.

Nancy rested well for the biggest portion of the night. This morning, I rose at 5:30 to assist with Nancy's routine body-turning. Once she was comfortable, I was preparing for the day. I happened to hear a song from the Greater Vision Trio as they sang, "God Wants to Hear You Sing." The premise came from Paul and Silas being arrested and jailed as recorded in Acts 16. Even in the midst of turmoil and crisis as believers we are to praise the Lord. God wants to hear us sing. He loves to hear us give Him glory even in the midst of trouble while we depend upon Him.

We have interviewed two hospice agencies and will make our decision soon. I have been trying to post this journal entry since early this morning but there have been health issues to tend to and interruptions from medical staff. It looks as though this chapter at Athens Regional is drawing to a close. As we transition to the next chapter, continue to pray for us and remember, because of Jesus, this story is far from over!

- **Thursday, March 31, 2011**

Day 78

The day has arrived to go home. We are only minutes away from leaving Athens Regional Hospital and heading to our home. We feel we have contracted with an excellent care provider through the Odyessy Hospice agency. Now, the work will begin with constant hands-on care. Of course, if one had been a fly on the wall these last couple of months, one would say we have already provided constant assistance to the capable nursing staff.

The home front has been managing well with family members cleaning and re-organizing furniture, supplies, and other items in order to make "home" seem a little more like home. Our sister-in-law, Alisa is already taking names of people wanting to help, and she asked me to include her phone number again. Her number is: XXX XXX XXXX and if she is not available, she has asked that you please leave your contact information.

Our care givers on the second floor have certainly given their best, and now we would be hard-pressed to say which floor treated us the best. Let's just say the "team" at ARMC has done superb, and we will miss the pampering. As our journey continues, we welcome your visits, calls, and especially your prayers.

Your input has added to the fact that, this story is far from over!

Nancy striking a post for her 1975 senior basketball picture.

Our engagement photo for the newspaper 1978.

Working together on our wedding day proved beneficial for the next 32 years.

Silly girls having fun on Mama & Daddy's bed.

Nancy was often the ring-leader at having fun.

Our 25th wedding anniversary September 2003.

Taking a break from the 38-mile Down Hill Maui Bicycle Ride.

One of my favorite photos.

Christmas Eve 2004 with Nancy's parents and siblings.

Taking a break from crocheting to smile for a picture.

I'm getting a "Nancy-fix".

Five generations, Ashley, Ashtin, Elizabeth, Guinnell, and Nancy.

Andrea's wedding day July 1, 2006.

Nancy and Janet enjoying their friend Debra Shedd.

Nancy is teaching a bible story to some of the church children.

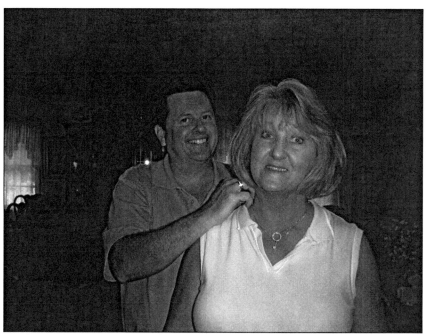

I gave Nancy a necklace for her 50th birthday. Elliott was born that day.

Nana is sharing time with Ashley, Ashtin and Elliott.

Nancy is leading the paparazzi during the annual Christmas Eve gathering.

Taking special trips was always fun and here we are in front of NYC
Rockefeller Center in December 2009.

Clayton, Ashtin, and Elliott are enjoying fun times at Papi and Nana's house.

Clayton is being held by Nana while enjoying his first snow experience.

Jessica and Nancy sharing a Mother's Day photo 2010.

Nancy's Mama and Daddy at the Indian Creek Gospel Singing.

Enjoying a day of Florida vacation at the annual golf tournament.

Nancy is holding Jackson, our youngest grandchild.

Deloris, Guinnell and Nancy December 2010.

We are clowning around in the hospital hallway a few hours before
Nancy's initial surgery.

The girls are helping me sing "What a Friend We have in Jesus" as Nancy plays the piano for her last time. We were in the chapel at ARMC.

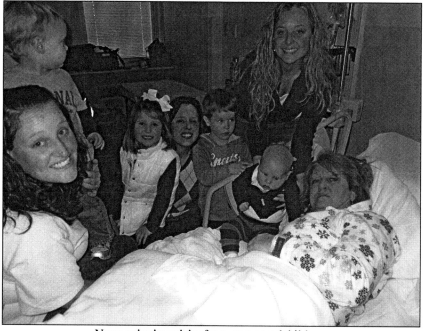

Nana enjoying visits from our grandchildren.

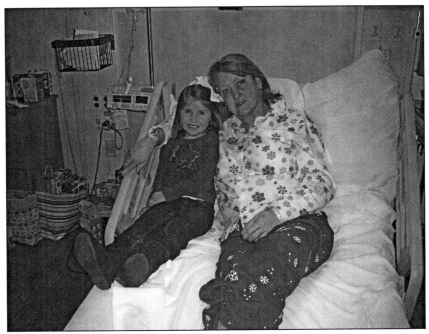
Ashtin snuggling up next to Nana.

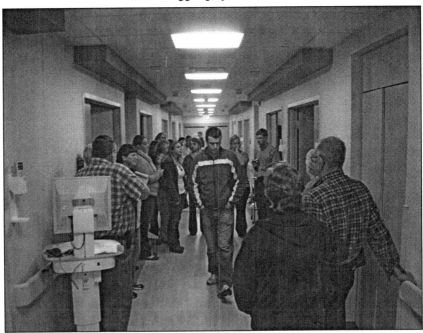
Crowded hallway supporters waiting for Nancy's transfer to surgery.

God blessed each of us with smiles moments before Nancy is taken for her initial surgery.

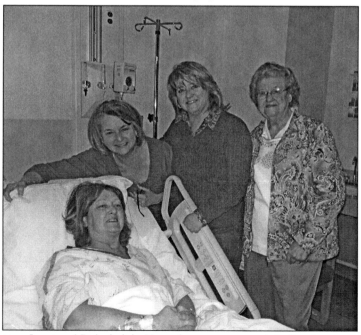

Sisters, Janet and Deloris join Nancy's mama moments before her surgery.

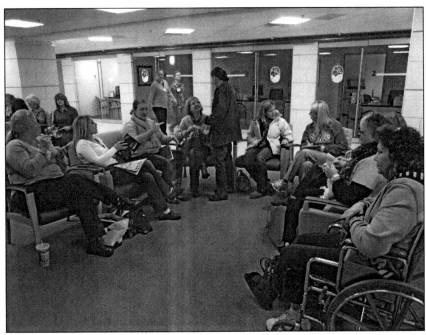

Several friends and family members awaiting Nancy's initial surgery.

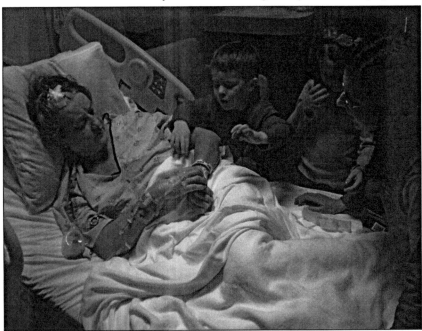

Elliott and Ashtin are tending to Nana's boo-boo's.

Our hero and neurosurgeon, Dr. Bryan Barnes with the girls.

We are still smiling as we patiently wait for the discharge papers from
Nancy's first hospital visit.

Nancy's last visit to church. She, Jessica, and I walked into the sanctuary as
the congregation was singing "Amazing Grace".

Nancy is keeping the scorebook for her last middle school game.

Third-shift Varsity workers need not worry too much from this crew of Josh,
my Mama, and Chris.

Ashley and I are taking a much needed nap while I was trying to journal another day from the ICU waiting room.

Big A Elementary school faculty and staff sharing love with us.

Marlene and Andrea are offering some much needed comic relief.

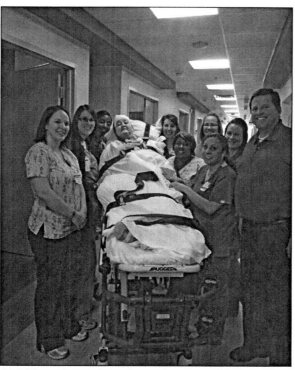

The ARMC nursing staff getting a photo opt with their "favorite"
patient moments before Nancy was transferred to the Landmark Hospital.
The transport driver remarked he had never seen so many of the staff
gathered to bid farewell to a patient.

The family is sporting their Team-Nancy shirts with "This Story is Far from Over!" printed on the back.

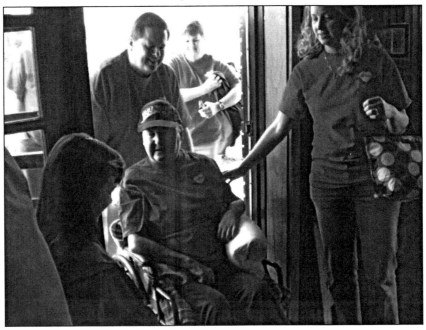

Riding into the Big A Elementary Pancake Breakfast for the Relay for Life fund raiser.

The members of the Adams family on Easter 2011.

Some of the Stacey family members Easter 2011.

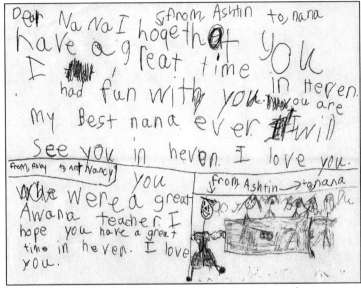

Here is a copy of the thoughts Ashtin and our niece
Abby wrote to place in Nancy's casket.

The Stacey gravestone.

164

A beautiful family photo of Jessica & Josh's wedding day taken 13 months after Nancy's death.

April

- **Saturday, April 2, 2011**

DAY 80 (109,319 Visits—2,282 Posts)

Hi Folks,

I am just checking in to let you know how things are going at the Stacey abode. We got home between two and two-thirty on Thursday afternoon. It was not long before the support troops arrived to help us get adjusted. Kenny and Mark came that morning and put up a nice privacy curtain in our living room so Nancy could be involved with the family but have privacy when she needed personal attention.

The Odyssey folks are very nice. We had to remind them of a couple of things they told us would happen but we were not getting. After that, things have gone well, and they have been extremely kind and caring for Nancy. It took a few minutes … no, it has taken more than a few minutes to adjust to being at home. I had forgotten how good a regular bed felt verses a cot. I have been enjoying even the simple things many of us take for granted during our regular routines.

Nancy seems to be doing well. Friday morning she was assisted into her wheelchair and rolled up to the breakfast table. She ate well and was having conversation with us and the hospice people, when suddenly her demeanor changed, and she could not remember what she had eaten only minutes before. We assisted her back to bed and soon she was asleep. A couple of hours later, she woke for lunch and has been fine ever since that episode. I imagine there will be more than less of those types of experiences to report. She has been up a couple of times today (Saturday), and she has been visiting with friends and family members.

I have been "privileged" to have a spring cold. I am not getting to take advantage of my Nancy-fixes because I do not want to share that with her. I am only getting around her when necessary for moving, turning, and so forth. I am trying an over-the-counter medication for now, but I may go see my doctor if it persists over the weekend.

Alisa has reported a great response to help with the meals. Amy delivered a fine presentation last night. Deloris provided lunch, and

I forgot who is preparing dinner. The washing machine has been going nearly non-stop and moment, by moment we are getting things in their proper places. Nate brought lunch yesterday and reported he has received several requests for "Team Nancy" Tee shirts. I hope that by midweek we will have contact information on how you may get some of those if you so desire. Do not call us yet. Give us a little more time to get that novelty organized.

It is *so* obvious to us that, this story is far from over!

• **Sunday, April 3, 2011**

DAY 81

Sleep has eluded me once again. Partly because I am all stopped up and cannot breathe too well, but mostly because I have been reflecting on my relationship with Jesus and His love for me. In my case, His love has had a direct correlation to my love for Nancy. It is because she loved Him that my life has been easier. We never had a quarrel about "if" we were going to church to worship Him. Nancy always was ready to go. She was always willing to see the girls were dressed impeccably and together, as a family, we would ride to church.

During these early morning hours before turning Nancy's body at 3:00 AM, I was listening to Margie's suggested song by the Whisnants entitled, "Even in the Valley."

Even in the valley, God is good
Even in the valley He is faithful and true
He carries His children like He said He would
And even in that valley, God is good.

That was an encouraging word to hear through music. It was on a YouTube clip, and I went from there to Karen Peck Gooch's song entitled, "My God Is Always Enough."

My God will always be enough
For the longings of my soul

168

He alone can fill my cup
Till my Spirit overflows

From a well of living of Water
He renews me with His love
My God! Will always be enough

Our grandfather clock just struck "five." I am no sleepier now than I was at two. I know I will need some rest, but after listening to those songs, I moved on to some praise songs such as: Here I Am to Worship, How Great Is Our God, Draw Me Close to You, I Can Only Imagine, and so forth. I am not going to enjoy the privilege of driving my family to church today. Instead, I will stay home and read with Nancy while we play some soft tunes in the background that bring praise to our Lord.

I trust each one of you will find yourselves in a place of worship today. I am praying that my pastor friends will have the freedom to deliver those messages God has laid upon their hearts. I am praying people will recognize the value of corporate worship while they are healthy.

How Great Is Our God
Sing with me How Great Is Our God.
And All Will See How Great
How Great Is Our God

It is because of our Great God that this story is far from over!

• **Monday, April 4, 2011**

DAY 82

I just returned from an early morning run to the store. It was time to assist Nancy by doing a glucose check and a routine body turning. The left side of her body continues being diminished to the point she literally cannot turn herself in bed. While I was turning her, she told me she loved me. I grinned and teased her that it certainly was comforting to know that she loved me at 3:00 AM. I jokingly suggested she was only saying she loved me because I was turning her. She smiled and said, "It worked, didn't it?" The affectionate repartee reminded me why our love has been so special to me. We have enjoyed displaying our love in various ways.

One such example is writing love notes. I have one of those special notes tucked away in my Bible. Nancy wrote it to me while were spending a weekend at the Ridgecrest Marriage retreat in 1990. Another example is the note I wrote to her on March 6, 1981. Nancy's brother, Kyle, and I were business partners in a logging and sawmill operation. The economy was terrible. It required us both taking third-shift jobs to help keep the business afloat. Nancy had recently returned to teaching at the middle school after the birth of Ashley. We barely had any time to spend with each other due to our work schedules. The routine was to sleep a little in the morning after getting home from the textile plant and then meet Kyle at the sawmill around 1:00 PM to work until around 6:00 PM. Kyle and I would eat supper, sleep a couple of hours, and repeat the previous routine. One morning while driving home, I heard the pop singer, Paul Davis, as he was singing his signature song entitled, "Sweet Life." (A version is on YouTube.) I was a new daddy with huge responsibility and a deep love for my family. I wanted to share my thoughts with Nancy and I hold those same feelings today.

March 6, 1981

Hi Darling!

I'm just writing this little note to let you know that you're the one individual that I would do anything for. You are so special to me and I love you so much.

I realize that you and I have a great deal in common—each other. Maybe someday all our dreams will come true, but for now my only dream is to have and hold you forever.

I'm sorry that our work schedules won't allow us to be together as much as we once were, but I'm so happy with the time that we do get to spend together. You make such a great wife and mother. I can't express my love for you in words, so it's always a pleasure to be able to show you.

Perhaps this note will continue to be a reminder of my love for you and also how much your love inspires me.

With Deep Loving Affection,
Bill

After writing the note, I decided against giving it to Nancy immediately. Instead, I took it to our sister-in-law, Alisa, and asked her to cross-stitch it so we could hang it up as a reminder of the difficult days with which our love sustained us. It continues to hang where we can see the reminder of my love for Nancy.

God has given us reminders of His love to us. One reminder is the rainbow that not only displays a beautiful array of eight different colors. It is a reminder of the promise He made with Noah and his family to never destroy the earth with a flood ever again. The Cross is another example of His love to us. The empty tomb is a marvelous reminder that Jesus is living and He promises to come back for us. The apostle Paul said that because Jesus claimed victory over death, we too, could claim victory and live eternally if we trusted Jesus as our Savior. Satan messed up God's perfect creation with sin through Adam and Eve. Paul wrote through the inspiration of the Holy Spirit when he penned the words of Romans 5:15-21.

But the gift is not like the trespass. For if by the one man's trespass the many died, how much more have the grace of God and the gift overflowed to the many by the grace of the one man, Jesus Christ. And the gift is not like the one man's sin, because from one sin came the judgment, resulting in condemnation, but from many trespasses came the gift, resulting in justification. Since by the one man's trespass, death reigned through that one man, how much more will those who receive the overflow of grace and the gift of righteousness reign in life through the one man, Jesus Christ.

So then, as through one trespass there is condemnation for everyone, so also through one righteous act there is life-giving justification for everyone. For just as through one man's disobedience the many were made sinners, so also through the one man's obedience the many will be made righteous. The law came along to multiply the trespass. But where sin multiplied, grace multiplied even more, so that, just as sin reigned in death, so also grace will reign through righteousness, resulting in eternal life through Jesus Christ our Lord. (from Holman Christian Standard Bible® Copyright © 1999, 2000, 2002, 2003, 2005 by Holman Bible Publishers.)

God gave us His love note when He gave us His word. I hope you will pick it up and read the reminders He has included for each of you. His Word is true and you can depend upon it—even in tough times. And it is because of the truth in His Word that this story is far from over!

• Tuesday, April 5, 2011

DAY 83

Nancy rested well last night. No, really, she did. It is rather disappointing she does not slip out of bed for that 4:00 AM ice cream any more. She has been unable to sneak anywhere since February 8, which was the day she endured two surgeries. The first surgery of the day went well. The other was totally a life-threatening, scary ordeal. I have not given up on praying for God's reversal of what seem the inevitable, yet each day the once very independent woman I married is more and more dependent. We have talked frankly concerning her condition. Ashley asked her last Wednesday evening, after our affirming and informative meeting with Dr. Barnes, if she was afraid. She said she was not. The next question was regarding sadness. She said she was a little sad but that everyone was sad. She acknowledged she was aware nothing more could be done to stop the tumor's growth, but that she trusted the Lord because He is in control.

Her days are a mix of regimented medicine dosages, satisfying her healthy appetite, and enjoying her visits with friends. Her childhood friend, Sherri, spent time Saturday and Sunday. Debra trimmed Nancy's hair to help with the head dressing. Loads of sibling families, friends, and co-teachers have made their way to visit. The meals brought in have been a huge help. The calls, cards, and other means of well-wishing are embraced and welcomed. The list of people to thank is unbelievably long, and some have helped anonymously.

When James wrote his letter to the converted and scattered Jews enduring hardship and trials, he gave some practical application concerning life in this world. The recorded writing in **James 5:7-11** instructs us how to treat one another while remembering the Lord is coming soon. Verse 11 says, "Behold, we count those blessed who endured. You have heard of the endurance of Job and have seen the outcome of the Lord's dealings that the Lord is full of compassion and is merciful." During our stay in the hospital, I visited with several people simply trying to live life. Even the hospice nurses have stories of challenges in their personal life with which they are working to overcome. To be fair to the Scripture, James was writing to ones persecuted for their faith and relationship with Jesus Christ. I do not recall any of the people to which I am referring as being troubled for that reason, but the application still remains within the context.

The comfort is in knowing the Lord is full of compassion and is merciful. In contrast, earlier this morning, I was studying a passage in Hebrews 12:18-29 concerning the holiness of God and the unshaken kingdom. Holy living leads to enjoying the compassion and mercy of God. I am resting in God's peace and reminding you, this story is far from over!

P.S. The family is gathering stories about Nancy. An easy way to share them is to post them on CaringBridge. They can be humorous, serious, or simply Nancy stories in general.

• **Wednesday, April 6, 2011**

DAY 84

Hi Folks,

I started the preparation for writing an update over sixteen hours ago. In the meantime let me assure you thing are going well. I have been distracted, busy, sleepy, and maybe even a little lazy. Nancy has had a busy day today in a good way. I will try to write more before daylight tomorrow. With overall, we are doing well.

The story has grown through these last 24 hours and it remains far from over! Thanks for the ongoing prayers. We feel each of them.

• **Friday, April 8, 2011**

DAY 86

In the early hours of Wednesday, our hospice on-call nurse answered our call for help. Nancy's catheter was malfunctioning and we have not yet learned about the proper procedures for managing it. Lisa came from Oconee County with a sweet disposition and skilled care in accessing the situation. She soon rectified the problem, monitored a couple other concerns, and was on her way. The Odyssey staff has gone the extra mile to offer Nancy the best of care. Kim is her regular nurse, and Lisha assists with cleaning and bathing. Hope and Herb have made visits to check on the social adjustments the family is making. We are well pleased.

Nancy's highlight for Wednesday was a house call from David of Lovely Nails. Her friend Harriett made the arrangement, and David was willing to pack his tools of the trade to work on Nancy's nails. I am holding off on that second pedicure. Ole Twinkle Toes can only stand so much primping in one year. The medical supply company sent someone to exchange some side rails for her bed. Therefore, Nancy had a busy day with all the extra visits, and she enjoyed every one.

Yesterday (Thursday), the routine of early rising, vital checkups, breakfast, and medicine schedules went well. The glucose level is acting up again, and the hospice doctor is offering some changes that should help get that problem under control. She seems to have had two consecutive days of reasonable comfort. (Thanks in part to some of the pain medicines.)

Hickory Knob State Park is located in McCormick, South Carolina. Nancy and I played golf there several years ago, spent the night in one of the cabins, and rose the next morning to watch the Augusta National Masters Golf Tournament practice rounds. We

174

have been there three or four times as a couple and have enjoyed seeing the beautiful flowering azaleas and dogwoods in full bloom. The golfers' skills were always amazing. Since it was the practice rounds, the atmosphere was a bit more relaxed than what they seem during the regular tournament. We have been watching bits and pieces of the hype and stories generated to project this year's winner. Who will be the new Master's Champion?

I was thinking about all the money spent in advertisements and all the business deals done over the course of a few days of wining and dining. I was emerged in thought about the coveted title of Master's Champion when I remembered a scripture acknowledging the One and only Master.

Jude's writing in verses three and four is interesting because he begins to write about the salvation through Jesus Christ but instead addresses the twisting of the Gospel. He cautions the readers to be aware of how the devil will cause men and women to lose focus of the holiness and value of their salvation.

Dear Friends, although I was eager to write you about our common salvation, I found it necessary to write and exhort you to contend for the faith that was delivered to the saints once for all. For certain men, who were designated for this judgment long ago, have come in by stealth; they are ungodly, turning the grace of our God into promiscuity and denying our only Master and Lord, Jesus Christ.

He goes on to write about the danger and doom of false teachers. He is especially speaking of those people who have twisted various doctrines to renounce the authority of Jesus and diminish His role as Savior. Jesus is God. Many have followed other masters. Many are searching for something or someone in which to believe and they pass by Jesus as Savior. The devil will cause people to chase after all sorts of false gods and false hopes to keep them from following Jesus. Be aware that Jesus is not only God's Son, but that He too, is God! Jude uses a final caution in the last couple of verses (20-21).

But you, dear friends, building yourselves up in your most holy faith and praying in the Holy Spirit, keep yourselves in the love of God, expecting the mercy of our Lord Jesus Christ for eternal life.

It is in those verses I find comfort especially in our current situation. I am staying in the center of God's love, and I am expecting the mercy from our Lord Jesus Christ for eternal life. I do not know when Nancy's life will take a different turn, but I know that based upon her testimony and the promises written in God's Word, she may close her eyes in death here, but she will open them in the eternal presence of the Almighty Master. That fact changes perspective for people like me, who live in God's peace and depend upon God's promises.

It is because of God's promises that this story is far from over!

• **Saturday, April 9, 2011**

DAY 87

What will today bring? Before sundown, someone's life will take an unexpected turn. A mother will deliver a child that will one day have immediate impact on the people around it in some way. In contrast, a family will lie to rest a precious member that has entered eternity only a few days earlier. How will you spend today?

A few moments ago, Debra and I were turning Nancy at 4:00 AM, and I questioned her about childhood Saturdays. I asked if Saturday was her piano lesson day. She said that she and Janet, her older sister, would ride with their mother to Mr. Theodore Sisk's house every Saturday at 11:00 AM. Many times, he would ask the one waiting for the next lesson to run down to the store and purchase him some Lucky Strike cigarettes. Nancy said they cost thirty cents per pack. His home was located near the old Coats & Clark building, and the store was just down the street. Nancy said she would play her assigned songs while Mr. Sisk sat nearby reading the newspaper. When he heard a misplaced chord, he would offer a different fingering position and encourage her to play it again. She received lessons between the fourth and eighth grades. Now, forty years later,

176

I sit here typing a journal post with tears running down my cheeks, wishing she could play a song for me. The last song I heard her play was in the chapel of Athens Regional Medical Center on Sunday, January 16. She played "What a Friend We Have in Jesus" as her last song that morning.

Jesus is one in whom we can befriend. He loves us with a love that never ends. I have never seen Jesus in the flesh, but I have seen the evidence of His love. I have witnessed the way in which other people have extended love to us in these last three months. I cannot say that I am shocked because I have observed kindness over the years as it related to my family through one way or another. I suppose a better description would be to use the word overwhelmed to express the feelings the family is experiencing during these days. We certainly feel loved by our friends and family members. It is encouraging to read where someone else was encouraged by a specific verse or song mentioned in the CaringBridge journal postings. It is at those times I find some sort of purpose for the journey in which we travel.

Yesterday (Friday), Nancy enjoyed visits from several people. Each has held a special place in our hearts over the years, and it was great getting to visit once again. Last night before bedtime, Josh, Jessica, and Ashtin returned from a quick trip to Athens. Josh said he waited in the car at David's Bridal Shop while the girls went to pick up Ashtin's flower-girl dress. Poor guy had to wait in the other room after they got home while Ashtin modeled it for Nana and me. She was all excited about her dress and loves dressing up to show it off. There are obvious reasons they do not yet have a wedding date, so be patient and we will let you know more when we do.

I am leaving you with the second stanza of "What a Friend We Have in Jesus."

Have we trials and temptations?
Is there trouble anywhere?
We should never be discouraged;
Take it to the Lord in prayer.
Can we find a friend so faithful?
Whom will all our sorrows share?

Jesus knows our every weakness;
Take it to the Lord in prayer.

Jesus continues being the focus because this story is far from over!

- **Monday, April 11, 2011**

DAY 89a

"Super Mom" is the title she earned back in 1987. I had been commissioned through the North American Mission Board as a "loaner" to the Billy Graham Evangelism Ministries for the special event of an itinerate evangelism conference hosted in Amsterdam, the Netherlands, during the previous July. It was while I was praying with a man inside the lobby of the Hilton hotel that God began to work. Just over six months later, I accepted a position as Associate Pastor of Music and Education. Making a longer story short, I will admit to leaving that position before I felt God was through with me in that location. However, Super Mom earned her title while we together endured.

Our routine was rather challenging but for fourteen months, we engaged it with all the passion and determination we could muster. The girls' ages were: Ashley 6, Jessica 2 1/2, and Andrea was 18 months. A typical week went as follows. I would leave for Atlanta about the same time Nancy left for her middle school teaching job each Monday. I would return late Thursday evening in order to watch the two youngest girls on Friday, my day off. Many times, a quick trip was necessary on Saturday for some church function, visitation, and so forth. On Sunday mornings, we would pack our van, load the girls, and arrive on time to Sunday School. I can only remember being tardy one Sunday even though the distance was a shade over one hundred five miles each way. On occasion, it was necessary, (not smart) to place our vehicle on cruise control and swap drivers. I do not recommend doing that trick, but we were careful, and usually traffic was not an issue in the areas we chose to swap. I drove the first part while Nancy and the girls slept. As we neared our destination, Nancy would dress herself and the girls for church, and then swap with me so I could do the same.

Many times, Maggie Campbell, a dear saint, would invite us to share a pot roast with her family. We eventually rented a house from the church for $400 a month and it became our Sunday afternoon retreat. On Sunday evenings, we would join various church families at a quick food restaurant and interact with them before making our long trip home. Monday, the cycle would regenerate.

What that meant for Super Mom was she would feed and dress three little girls each morning after getting herself prepared for the day. She would single-handedly load three little girls into our van and take them to the sitter's house on her way to school. Nancy would teach school all day and then pick the girls up while deciding what menu to fix for supper. After supper, there were baths to take, bags to prepare for the next day, and regular house chores to perform. Nancy had an added feature to her schedule because while I was in Atlanta, she was keeping the house in order so the real estate agent could show it at his beck and call. I imagine those of you with small children or lingering memories can appreciate the task Nancy accomplished while being completely supportive of my ministry. Wow! I am still in awe. Be sure to add the colds, flu, and skinned knees to the rain, sleet, and snow. Yep, Super Mom is a good title.

Hmm ... I guess after doing all of the above, is the reason Nancy gets exasperated with excuses people use for missing church. She can get a little riled when people stay home from church because their little darling needs their sleep. She can get plumb side-ways when the whole family stays home due to one member being under the weather. Nancy was a product of great parenting. She, in turn, practiced what she was taught and has modeled it for our children. If you were to ask the girls what one sermon their daddy preached more than any other, the reply is, "People will do what they *want* to do." Nancy's hearty "Amen" is affirmation to that sermon.

A man should be so fortunate to have had the encouragement and support from his wife. But then, it's only another chapter in acknowledging, this story is far from over!

P.S. Nancy continues to rest without any noticeable deterioration since arriving home a week ago. Thanks for your prayers. They are felt.

Day 89b

Hi Folks,

I have been very pleased through our situation that most of what I have heard repeated is actually true. However, as in most crises, sometimes the facts get embellished from time-to-time. To the best of my knowledge, our health insurance is very good. Naturally, we have not yet received all of our doctor or hospital bills, but we are confident the insurance will cover what is in the intended agreement.

Obviously, there are unknown expenses and other costs incurred that will need reconciling, but at this time, our insurance has not "maxed-out" its limit. Please "gently" tell the misinformed that as far as we know the insurance is still intact.

• **Monday, April 18, 2011**

DAY 96

Dear Friends,

I will attempt to get back into the practice of writing a daily journal. I have told some who have inquired that there are three other college-educated individuals that are fully capable of posting. Ha! Ha! Today, I want to share a couple of thoughts.

Saturday morning we were invited to the Pancake Breakfast sponsored by the Big A Elementary personnel and hosted at the Toccoa Applebees. I wasn't sure Nancy was ready for such an outing, but she wanted to give it a try and the Turpin's were willing to provide wheelchair transportation. Thanks, Matt and Julie. It was humbling being part of a cancer fund raising benefit in Nancy's honor. It was equally humbling to observe so many teachers scurrying around to serve tables while wearing their Team Nancy tee shirts. The visiting students and parents were a blessing with all their well-wishing and encouraging remarks. Nancy enjoyed her trip and held up well. I didn't need to ask her if she was ready to lie down when we returned home. She rested well.

In the days since her hospital stay, I don't recognize any significant diminishing health issues. She has experienced a urinary tract infection which I'm told is not uncommon for someone with a catheter. She has also been hampered with a cough, but it too, seems manageable. The Odyssey Hospice Team has served very attentively to Nancy's care, and we are pleased with the results.

The family continues being showered with expressions of love through many of your local kitchens. Some are as far away as McDonough and Helen. Each has been tasty and helpful in not having to take time to prepare food. Our schedules are almost becoming routine, but it seems odd having to provide care for Nancy. She has been a great wife, mother, and care giver all these years, so it seems unthinkable that she requires so much assistance.

There continues being generous expressions of love through financial contributions. We are determined to spend those dollars wisely while remembering the kindness of our friends and family members. The New Testament book of Acts addresses the behavior we are observing in the first churches established. Your example of sharing, encouraging, and serving are models of what God intended His church to experience through fellowship. I have been privileged to have traveled around the world, and your acts of kindness are second to none. As we continue through this coming week, be reminded of the sacrifice Jesus made for us to have a healthy relationship with Him.

I want to share one other thought for future commentary. When you find a spare five minutes, read 1 Kings 19:1-18. It is an interesting account of Elijah's despair after having claimed victory over the prophets of Baal recorded in chapter 18. There is an interesting process of events leading to a great personal discovery. Are you lingering at the mouth of the cave?

For sure, Elijah's story is interesting, but this story is far from over!

- **Tuesday, April 19, 2011**

DAY 97

It does not take anyone as old as me to know life has its ups and downs. Life begins at conception and goes from the cradle to the grave with pitfalls, obstacles, and challenges. Nancy and I have shared our life with each other while leaning upon the other to get us through those times.

Nancy was completing her teaching degree the fall we were married. She commuted to North Georgia College for the fall quarter and then did her student teaching at Banks County High School the following spring. I was working at a local sawmill and served as a bi-vocational music minister for Tom's Creek Baptist Church. As the old saying says, "We were living on love," because there was not a surplus of money. She graduated in the spring of '79 but could not find a teaching position near enough our home to accept a job. Wrights or Oxford Wear hired her until she could begin her teaching career. The sawmill burned to the ground on Nancy's birthday, July 3, and the economy was bearing the burden during the Carter administration. Times were tough. I would come home from the sawmill exhausted, and Nancy would report my 1971 SuperBeetle Volkswagen was making a "funny" sound when she drove it to Banks County. I would tell her to turn up the volume on the radio and keep driving. It sounds like a typical husband, huh? Ha! During those early days, we determined to trust God with everything. Hubert Sosby served as an elderly deacon and shared his testimony concerning living through the "Hoover Days" and trusting God even with his tithing. Nancy and I committed to trusting God with that same passion. We continued having obstacles and challenges because we continued living life, but we trusted God and He made the difference.

Now, here we are nearly one hundred days into a major challenge to our relationship. 1 Kings 19:1-18 records an interesting story of Elijah. The previous chapter reports two tremendous visuals of God's power through the "Fire falling from Heaven," and the "Return of rain" after a three-year drought. Elijah was the key prophet at the time and obviously had an open communication and relationship with God. To me, it seems odd that only a day later from his mountain-top experience of God's power, wicked Jezebel could strike such a fear and dread upon his life. He ran for his life in verse three and prayed to die in verse four. Verses eight and nine report Elijah took a forty-day hike into the barren wilderness until he came to a cave and camped out there.

What do you suppose Elijah thought about while he was traveling to his refuge? Do you think he questioned God concerning the turn of events? Like so many others, do you think he felt alone? Scripture says he thought he was the only one willing to serve God (v.10). Why is it the devil causes one to forget the almighty, sovereign power of God?

Thankfully, when one reads farther into chapter 19, he or she will read that God cares. God sent an angel to feed Elijah on two different occasions. God is concerned for us, and He was for Elijah. He questioned Elijah why he was in a cave. God cares for us. He really and truly does care, and He is concerned, even when we feel alone or defeated. The story reveals God was not through with Elijah. Elijah had a purpose. He had a task to carry forth. When people feel worthless or without purpose, the devil will cause them to doubt. He will accuse them of their inadequacies and failures. The devil often uses those down times, like he did with Job, to make one second-guess one's actions or even attitude towards God.

I must admit over the years, there has been a time when I was traveling that same dusty road to barrenness. I have been lingering at the mouth of the cave while trying to make sense out of a particular situation. Even in our current situation, it seems there have been those darts of indecision or second-guessing; the devil has flung in my direction. I know he has attempted to cause me to challenge God's purpose in allowing this situation to happen to us. Nancy and I trust the Lord. It's just like the early days of our relationship except there is more on the line with this challenge. We will not give up, we will not give out, nor will we give in to the wiles of deception.

We will trust God and watch what happens because; this story is far from over!

• Thursday, April 21, 2011

DAY 99

Where does the time go? It has been my observation that the window for opportunity to write a journal is between four and seven in the morning. My difficulty with such scheduling is that I am usually either busy attending to Nancy or falling asleep in my computer chair while trying to keep the readers informed of Nancy's condition.

This morning, I got Nancy to sit up on the bedside in order to transition to a wheelchair and then roll up to the table for breakfast. Nancy often reminds me her name changes from Nancy-to-Eileen when she sits up. In Nancy's words, "*I-lean* to the left or *I-lean* to the right" while trying to maintain her balance. Ha! She has a good appetite and often asks for something extra besides what is presented for her to eat. She gobbled her egg omelet and toast, took her medicine, and was working on her yogurt when I noticed she was sleepier than usual. She slept well last night, but when I got her back into her bed, she has not budged since. It is challenging to watch Nancy as she clumsily negotiates her spoon through a bowl of milk trying to chase a wayward Cheerio or trying to get the kernel of granola to stay in her cup of yogurt.

(Four hours later than the previous paragraph)

Nancy has eaten a good lunch and seems slightly more alert than earlier this morning. I do not understand the issue causing her lethargy, but it is rather disconcerting. It is comforting to hear her utter affectionate phrases of her declaration of love to me or her promises to get better. She definitely continues to battle each day.

My agenda has been full with deciding the best approach for Nancy's future days. I have had several well-meaning people "tell" me what I ought to do concerning her health. Weighing that opinion (which usually includes, "Don't trust the doctors.") with what her doctors have shared, causes a good deal of confusion for my miniature mind. I am confident that in a couple of years, I will be capable of expounding great ideas and opinions upon those with lesser experience. I pray those thoughts are God-directed.

It is true there are several topics in which I simply do not have a clue. However, on this date in 1963, I learned of something in which I can depend. I trusted the simple gospel message presented to me at that young age. The Holy Spirit drew me to the altar, and I told Rev. Bill Carey I wanted to go to Heaven and that I wanted to ask for forgiveness of my sin. He was a kind and gentle man. He took time with me to make sure I understood for which I was asking. Now, forty-eight years later, I shudder thinking about the ministry opportunities in which I have failed, but I also rejoice at the ones in which I was faithful. I am well aware of those times, in which I was nudged by the Holy Spirit to share a brief testimony, but instead shied away and neglected the opportunity. I am encouraged and affirmed when I step through those doors of opportunity and know I did what I was instructed.

I cannot help but think about the servanthood Jesus modeled as recorded in the gospel of John 13:13-15 literally hours before His betrayal and crucifixion. He washed the feet of His disciples while giving them an example of humility.

You call Me Teacher and Lord. This is well said, for I am. So if I, your Lord and Teacher, have washed your feet, you also ought to wash one another's feet. For I have given you an example that you also should do just as I have done for you.

Jesus gave an example of humility. It was not about hygiene. God's Word reports time and again how those with proud attitudes will be humbled, and those living in humility will be exalted. He further gave an example of how to treat others and especially more concerning the attitude Christian leaders should example before their peers.

Nancy, the family, and I have been shown a great deal of kindness these last fourteen weeks. We have been the recipients of fervent prayers, tasty meals, generous contributions, and Christian love. We are blessed beyond measure, and because of God's love, this story is far from over!

• **Saturday, April 23, 2011**

DAY 101 (125,713 Visits - 2,416 Posts)

Hi Friends,

Nancy is up and at-em' this morning. She rested well yesterday and last night. After her adjustment and body-turn at 5:00 AM, I took a casual ride to Wal-Mart to get some needed items. One of which was a different toaster oven. We received one as a wedding gift, and it lasted about twenty-five years. The replacement only lasted about seven. Hmm ... looks like China won again. I breezed by Mickey-D's for a change of pace to get the oatmeal and Egg McMuffins. I accidently-on-purpose forgot the parfait. When I got home, I did not mention it, and she forgot to ask for one. We are trying to cut back on some of the sweets.

Yesterday was full with the regular routine of care giving and making some health care decisions. We are not sure how everything will play out, but it looks like I will take Nancy to Athens Regional on Tuesday for an MRI and then, again on Wednesday for a follow-up visit in preparation of another round of chemotherapy. To do that, we will need to temporarily discontinue our agreement with hospice for a few days. I have been told it is not a big deal, but I do not like all the paperwork and juggling. Again, insurance rules the world on stuff like this situation. Join us in praying for smooth transitions, a favorable MRI report, and a plan for Nancy's improved health. I am concerned two trips in two days may be more taxing than she needs. However, she is a tough ole' bird and will probably do better than me. Ha!

Since our marriage, we have celebrated every Easter together except one. That particular year, I was stuck at the Lima, Peru airport with Hulyn Kight from Rome, Georgia. We made an advanced mission trip to Bolivia and had an unscheduled, two-day layover in Lima. I think Hulyn and I are still friends, but he has not offered going back to Bolivia with me. Ha!

Tomorrow, I am not sure Nancy will get to the service with me. I am planning on preaching for the first time since February 6. After the Easter celebration at church, our families are coming to our

186

house for additional celebration and photos. I cannot tell you how enjoyable it is to host our families at Christmas Eve each year. This is the first Easter we will host, and there is plenty of preparation to do before tomorrow.

Now, about tomorrow, I want to encourage each of you to find a place of worship in which Jesus is glorified. Jesus is celebrated at Easter, but He rightfully deserves daily praise. His sacrificial and selfless love enabled Nancy being healed. It is that same love in which we are healed. The Old Testament writing of Isaiah, chapter 53, records a thought-provoking testimony of Jesus's love and the world's reactions.

53 Who has believed what we have heard?
And who has the arm of the LORD been revealed to?
2 He grew up before Him like a young plant
and like a root out of dry ground.
He had no form or splendor that we should look at Him,
no appearance that we should desire Him.
3 He was despised and rejected by men,
a man of suffering who knew what sickness was.
He was like one people turned away from;
He was despised, and we didn't value Him.
4 Yet He Himself bore our sicknesses,
and He carried our pains;
but we in turn regarded Him stricken,
struck down by God, and afflicted.
5 But He was pierced because of our transgressions,
crushed because of our iniquities;
punishment for our peace was on Him,
and *we are healed by His wounds*.
6 We all went astray like sheep;
we all have turned to our own way;
and the LORD has punished Him
for the iniquity of us all.
7 He was oppressed and afflicted,
yet He did not open His mouth.
Like a lamb led to the slaughter

and like a sheep silent before her shearers,
He did not open His mouth.
8 He was taken away because of oppression and judgment;
and who considered His fate?
For He was cut off from the land of the living;
He was struck because of My people's rebellion.
9 They made His grave with the wicked,
and with a rich man at His death,
although He had done no violence
and had not spoken deceitfully.
10 Yet the LORD was pleased to crush Him,
and He made Him sick.
When You make Him a <u>restitution offering</u>,
He will see *His* <u>seed</u>, He will prolong His days,
and the will of the LORD will succeed by His hand.
11 He will see *it* out of His anguish,
and He will be satisfied with His knowledge.
My righteous servant will justify many,
and He will carry their iniquities.
12 Therefore I will give Him the many as a portion,
and He will receive the mighty as spoil,
because He submitted Himself to death,
and was counted among the rebels;
yet He bore the sin of many
and interceded for the rebels.

Verses 4-6 are the verses addressing the eternal healing Jesus provides for each and every one that asks for forgiveness from sin. Sin separates, but the acceptance of Jesus' blood generates new creatures. Like spring flowers, those new creatures blossom into full bloom of spiritual maturity and reflect God's love to others who have not yet, understood their need of a Savior. My prayer is that you will discover that eternal healing.

It is because of such healing; this story is far from over!

- **Monday, April 25, 2011**

DAY 103

Enjoy the new pictures!

Hi Friends and Family,

This is a quick note to say we had a great day Easter Sunday. It was refreshing to celebrate the Resurrection of Jesus with our various churches. I enjoyed the opportunity to preach for the first time since February 6. Indian Creek Baptist Church continues being very supportive of our situation. Nancy was disappointed she could not go to church, but with all of the people coming Sunday afternoon, we thought it was better for her to rest. Debra came over to "fix" Nancy up for some photo shots with the family. After the pictures were snapped, a huge lunch was enjoyed. The Adams/Stacey families are blessed with wonderful cooks.

After lunch, Nancy laid down for an afternoon nap while all the children enjoyed the traditional Easter egg hunt. The adults caught up with all the latest news or swapped stories from the past. The Lord has blessed us with a place suitable to host the family. There is no place like home.

Enjoy the pictures. Our niece April, provided the photos for the CaringBridge site. We are preparing for our trip to Athens tomorrow. Pray with us that everything goes well and that a good report is given.

This story is far from over!

- **Wednesday, April 27, 2011**

DAY 105

I'll bet you have been wondering what is happening with Nancy aren't you? Plans changed since the last post, and I will try to give you a brief update. No great words of wisdom and no fun stories of the past, but at least you won't have to wonder anymore!

Today we went to Athens to have a MRI and see if we will be able to take some more chemo. While in Athens, we also wanted to have her head wound cleaned again.

We will have to wait until the Oncologist comes to find out what the MRI will reveal.

NEWS FLASH... NEWS FLASH...

The MRI results show that there has been *no change* in the size of the tumor. We are very excited!

We will be staying in Athens for the five days of chemo and then return home.

Please continue to pray as Nancy endures the chemo and has her head wound debrided tomorrow.

I'm sure Bill will give you a better update ... but not any better news!

Thank you for your love and prayers,

......Bill's baby sister (and Mom's favorite) hahaha

• **Thursday, April 28, 2011**

DAY 106

Yesterday was definitely a day of praise for Team Nancy! We were so thankful to receive such great news regarding Mama's MRI results. Praise the Lord for the wonderful blessings He continually provides!

Last night Daddy and Ashley stayed with Mama at the hospital while Andrea headed to work and Marlene and I headed to her house. Daddy called this morning to chat with Marlene and me. He first asked us if we survived all the storms, winds, and rain. After informing him that we slept right through them, he went on to share with us that they had to make a trip to the hallway around 2:30 AM. He said that they remained in the hallway for about 45 minutes...and that was the *good* news. We said, "oh no...what's the *bad* news?!?" He proceeded to tell us that Dr. Splichal came by early this morning with some discouraging news. Dr. Splichal shared that the hospital's pharmacy informed him that they would not be able to get the Temodar (chemo pill) until Monday. At this time, Mama doesn't really have additional ailments that will allow for her to stay in the hospital until Monday; therefore, we will have to go home and do the chemo there.

I spoke with Daddy around 1:00 PM, and he said that right now they are just waiting on the plastic surgeon to come by to debride Mama's head. They are not real sure what time this will take place. After Mama's head wound is treated, the plan is to sign back in with Odyssey, the hospice group, and head to Herron Road. The Temodar should arrive at Jerry White's Pharmacy sometime in the morning. Mama will begin her third round of chemo tomorrow. Just like the last two rounds, the treatment will last for five days and will be in the form of a pill. The only difference is the nausea medicine will be given to her orally instead of intravenously. Please pray with us that Mama will have another successful round of chemo and refrain from any sickness. In addition, pray that all the little kinks get ironed out, and Mama has a safe transport back home.

Stay tuned for the next update, and in the meantime remember ... this story is far from over!

P.S.
Roses are red,
Violets are blue,
I picked up my wedding dress yesterday,
*So....**WOO HOO!***

• Friday, April 29, 2011

DAY 107

Peeking out over the top of the sheets enabled me seeing who it was interrupting my sleep. Standing at the foot of my cot, looking rather dapper, and ready to start another day, was Dr. Splichal. Less than twelve hours earlier, he shared the uplifting news, the tumor had not increased in size according the radiologist's report of the

MRI. While it was undeniably encouraging news, I was waiting for the "but" that often accompanies news of which I was receiving. He was not sharing that information at 6:45 AM. It would come in the afternoon. The morning report informed us that we had another snag with which to deal. It seems the pharmacy was unable to obtain the necessary chemotherapy medicine until Monday. Twelve hours earlier, we were high-fiving, and preparing for five additional days in the hospital in order to receive the chemo. Now, he was telling us that he was not sure how we would get the treatment. His previous experience with hospice caused concern whether or not they would service our home while we were administering chemotherapy. A second concern, was whether or not his office or our family pharmacy could obtain the medicine. He promised to call us once he had an answer.

Making a longer story short, many of you have already read Jessica's journal entry and know that we are now home and we will administer the chemo ourselves. Hospice (Odyssey), has agreed to continue service to Nancy and it looks like soon we will all be back on schedule. Dr. Splichal announced the change in plans during the afternoon. He admitted he was impressed with Nancy's condition. Personally, I think he was surprised she was doing as well as she is. He told us we have had a great April, and that we would continue with the pattern for future treatment. His plan is to do the Temodar, wait four weeks, and get blood samples. Then, if the blood work came back in a positive report, the plan was to do Temodar for a fourth time, wait four more weeks and then go back to Athens for a comparative MRI to the one taken Wednesday, April 27. Dr. Splichal once again affirmed us for the good care obviously recognized which was given to Nancy and then, we got the "but" I was expecting on Wednesday. It was while he observed her condition did not seem to diminish this past month, he did not expect her condition to stay in a plateaued condition. He felt if we were able to enjoy her company until August, we would be most fortunate.

Riding home and following the nonemergency transport carrying Nancy allowed me time to reflect. Well, at least in between phone calls. I thought of one of our first dates, when as we were nearing a stop sign, Nancy reached over and grabbed my head. I looked at her in bewilderment, and she said, "That sign back there said 'Stop Ahead' and I thought I would stop yours." Remembering insignificant moment's like that one, flash through my mind like lightning. I catch myself dwelling on best ways to spend future days. We have been offered a condo in Hilton Head, but I don't think Nancy could actually endure the trip to or from that distance. Right now, it is a pretty big trip from the bed to the wheelchair and from the wheelchair to the dinner table. It is hard thinking that about Nancy, but the reality bears out its truth.

Being home allows us to get back into some type of regular schedule. The kindness and generosity of our friends and acquaintances continue to overwhelm us. Nancy and I realize how blessed we are as a family. It is humbling to hear remarks concerning how fortunate we are to have a family kinship like ours. I can assure you, we are ordinary people with ordinary problems, but we serve an extraordinary God. His love and care is reflected through the countless messages of encouragement left for us to absorb.

My heart goes out to those people left strewn from the turbulence of the recent storms. Having gone through similar crises, and seeing it lived out through some of our church families a few years ago, makes me hurt for those trying to wrap their mind around what has happened. The heartache of losing a loved one in such a tragic event is one mostly unexplainable. We have been reassured of many prayers offered on our behalf, but I want to encourage a few prayers sent to those unfortunate people as well.

They will have their own stories, but this story is far from over!

May

• **Wednesday, May 4, 2011**

DAY 112 (134,915 Visits - 2,477 Posts)

Good Morning,

I'm taking pity on all the folks that are feeling uninformed. Someone, I won't mention who, is looking tired and acting too busy to type.

Yesterday Nancy took her last chemo pill for this round. She has been very tired since she started the treatments. Thankfully, she has not been nauseated and has been able to eat her normal foods.

The daily "grind" has taken its toll on all of us. Many days I get home and realize that I didn't sit down all day! Today will be different … thanks to your inquiring minds! I am not a great typist, and I certainly wouldn't attempt it standing up!

Lisha, our hospice tech, is here giving Nancy a bath and brightening our day again. Please pray for her dear friends who lost their seventeen year old daughter in a car accident yesterday.

Kim, our hospice nurse, will be here shortly to tend to Nancy's head wound and make sure she is responding well to her medications. We have been blessed with people who genuinely care about her.

Most of you probably know that Indian Creek Baptist Church hosts a gospel sing every year. Please pray that the details will fall together and that God will be honored in the planning and completion of this event.

We have been blessed with another beautiful day today so be sure you enjoy it and remember to thank God for your many blessings.

I'll sign off until they trust me to do this again, and remember.... This story is faaaar from over!

PS This is Bill's baby sister and Mom's favorite…in case you were wondering, tee hee.

• Thursday, May 5, 2011

DAY 113

I suppose rhetorical questions have their place, but how did May get here so quickly? The month of May has a few dates of significance for Nancy and me. One such date is May 2, 1976. Okay, I will be honest about this date, because it was about girls. My friend, Larry Salzman, reminded me about "that girl from Stephens County which played basketball so well." He was always thinking about basketball at the time, and we were both thinking about,… girls. I had met Nancy a year earlier, but because of logistics, and me not having "wheels," I did not pursue her. Larry had heard me talk of Nancy several times and encouraged me to see if she was interested in dating me. We talked my older brother, Tom, into taking us to church the next Sunday which was May 2. When Sunday rolled around, Tom and I got into his vintage 1941 Chevrolet pick-up truck and drove to get Larry. For sure, Tom's truck was a classic that most teenage boys would envy. It had loud mufflers, a 283 cubic inch engine that would fly, and a radio. In reality, it didn't look too appealing with its two-tone primer paint and two tattered seats, but Tom was willing to drive, and we needed a ride.

We were seated in the sanctuary of Tom's Creek Baptist Church just before the Sunday School classes had been dismissed. I was a little nervous as I looked around trying to notice some familiar faces from a previous trip to the church when my quartet sang for their youth group. I spotted a couple of kids I recognized, but I did not see Nancy. The choir entered the sanctuary and I noticed a girl who resembled Nancy playing the organ , but it was not Nancy. In fact, it was her sister Janet. When the service started, we were invited to stand and sing a hymn. I had searched from pew-to-pew, and from front-to-back, but I did not see Nancy. The special music was sung as a duet from a woman and man that I would later learn as Guinnell Adams, Nancy's mama, and Bruce Leverette. They sang, "If That Isn't Love." Rev. Michael Dellinger was the pastor, but at the time, my mind was whirling in wonder as to where I might find Nancy.

After the service, we spoke to a few of the acquaintances of which I had met previously. When I inquired about Nancy's absence, I was told she had gone to Tennessee with her college roommate for the Olympic basketball tryouts. Nancy's roommate, Donna Wilson, was from Monroe, and she eventually played professional basketball. Naturally, Larry was impressed with that information. I was disappointed that I did not get to see Nancy. Only a few days passed before I was surprised with a letter from Nancy. She told me she regretted not being at church but that if I wanted, I could call her, and she left me her phone number. She shared her school schedule so I would know when she was going to be home. I was elated and soon we were visiting by phone. I will share a few more significant dates for May in the days ahead.

Now, here I sit thirty-five years later. I reflect on those days passed with fond memories and yet, earlier in the week I was having a little pity party. I became a bit overwhelmed while assisting Nancy. Physically lifting her from bed to chair, to the potty, and so forth affects more than muscle for me. It is sobering to see how healthy people take their health for granted. It is challenging to observe Nancy attempt lifting a cup of coffee to her lips without spilling it. It saddens me to leave her in her bed while I try to squeeze a few winks of sleep in our bed without her. Believe me; I have tried lying with her only to discover there was more room in the cab of Tom's '41 Chevy truck for three guys than there is in her bed for just the two of us. I will settle for the regular Nancy-fix and the half a hug she offers with her diminished left side. I continue to affirm how proud I am of her for not giving up. I have told her I am impressed with her determination to get well.

I have learned God wants to affirm us. He wants us to know He loves us even if we don't love ourselves. His love is unconditional, and He keeps His promise to those who trust in Him. King Solomon declared as much, as he was praying the dedicatory prayer for the new temple as recorded in 1 Kings 8:23:
and he prayed,

"O LORD, God of Israel, there is no God like you in all of heaven above or on the earth below. You keep your covenant and show unfailing love to all who walk before you in wholehearted devotion.

The challenge rests firmly upon our shoulders. We should walk before Him in wholehearted devotion. We will always live in God's love when we rest upon His promises and strive to live a life of holiness. No doubt, I have disappointed God during times I have chosen my way of doing things instead of trusting His way. Yet, He loves me and affirms me.

We are only bit-players in this story; but this story is far from over!

• Saturday, May 7, 2011

DAY 115

Nancy continues with her lack of complaining and maintains her sense of humor. Her face, head, and shoulders show the side effects of the various medicines she is taking. Sleep has been her best friend this week as she moves past the recent chemotherapy treatment. I try to get her to feed herself, but she welcomes assistance after she eats half of what has been on her plate. Our "code" word is "bird." She often sits with her eyes closed while she eats. When she is ready for the next bite, she opens her mouth and says, "bird" so I will know to poke more food in her mouth. I love helping her.

When one starts asking around concerning Nancy's childhood, it is refreshing to hear the tales. Friday I was greeted with more than one such story. I saw many friends and acquaintances, and each asked about her. Wesley Kellar said he remembers the competitive spirit Nancy had in every aspect. He especially remembers the contest Nancy and Kathy Walters Crawford held to see who could do one thousand sit-ups the fastest. Jean Sheriff Poole recalled the time Nancy's mom was bringing the girls home from a ballgame, and a cow jumped into the path of Guinnell's Ford LTD. Sherri Lane Cauthen reported the time that she and Nancy were bored one Sunday evening before the service. Nancy suggested they squeeze a glob of Avon hand cream on the window fans before they were turned on. They went inside the sanctuary and strategically chose a pew that was not directly in front of a fan. When the fans were turned on, the girls were disappointed to realize the fans blew in the opposite direction so the hand cream did not splatter on anyone. After the service they went outside and noticed the globs of cream splattered in the parking lot. (Another example of preacher's kids playing with the deacon's kids. Ha!)

In my travels yesterday (Friday), several people assured me they were praying for us. Harry said his Sunday School class has prayed for us every Sunday since the news of Nancy's condition was known. Cathey Cobb shared some special thoughts and commented on the way CaringBridge journals were having a positive impact on people. Teresa and Mike made similar comments when I visited with them in Lavonia. Remarks regarding the journals are humbling. Nancy and I realize we are not the only ones dealing with difficult situations. We also realize how comforting it is to have the prayer support and concern from so many people in Stephens, Franklin, Hart, and other counties. The website is read in probably a dozen different countries of which I am aware.

The news is full of reports concerning high fuel prices or the death of Osama. Often the challenges of motherhood are taken for granted. Often the task of working a job, caring for children, and volunteering for P.T.O. or the church's nursery go unnoticed. It is only through a positive mother's role model that younger moms continue to endure the challenges. I remember sitting in a restaurant with our "three little darlings," when an older lady, a complete stranger, approached our table to encourage Nancy and me. She had observed us as we attempted to meet the menu desires of the kids and get them fed without too much difficulty. She affirmed us and told us that in time, things will get easier. They did. In fact, now in recent years, Nancy and I have "enjoyed" watching younger parents negotiate with their children at restaurants.

Nancy and I are both the benefactors of loving and caring parents. Our mothers came from different geographical regions, and yet, they taught us kids the values of life. There were six children at Nancy's home and five at our home. I continue to reflect on how we managed to get by with one car, while dad worked a second-shift job, and we kids got to all the places we were scheduled. Our moms were the taxi drivers, the nurses, the financial stretchers, and were many other role players. Our dads came from a generation in which the ladies did all the housework and kid-nurturing, while they worked to provide food, clothing, and shelter. The best thing our dads did was to love our mothers. Love was modeled in our homes. Nancy and I have, in turn, modeled that love. In return, it brings us joy to watch our daughters and sons-in-law as they exhibit that same love in their children.

The Apostle Paul wrote a letter to one of his preacher-boys. His message was concerning consistency and sound, doctrinal teaching. Titus 2:1-5 says

But you must speak what is consistent with sound teaching. Older men are to be self-controlled, worthy of respect, sensible, and sound in faith, love, and endurance. In the same way, older women are to be reverent in behavior, not slanderers, not addicted to much wine. *They are* to teach what is good, so that they may encourage the young women to love their husbands and children, to be sensible, pure, good homemakers, and submissive to their husbands, so that God's message will not be slandered.

from Holman Christian Standard Bible® Copyright © 1999, 2000, 2002, 2003, 2005 by Holman Bible Publishers.)

The verses 3 thru 5 speak to the importance of being respectable role models as women. It is important for them to live life in such a way that younger women would want to be mentored by the older ladies. I can say that while Nancy would not claim "perfection," she would admit to having a positive impact on our girls. While we were in the hospital, a younger lady and her husband visited us. She thanked Nancy for some wisdom Nancy had shared with her concerning married life. It was a precious and genuine testimony of what Paul was suggesting as responsible behavior for the people in Titus's church. Motherhood truly is an honorable position. A godly mother is one for which to be thankful.

Happy Mother's Day—this story is far from over!

• Wednesday, May 11, 2011

DAY 119

Nancy actually opened her eyes to eat last night. She has not done that in about three days. She simply has not felt like opening them. Tuesday morning, Jessica, Andrea, and I were turning her when we noticed a discharge coming from the sacral wound. A closer investigation revealed her bedsore was back with vengeance. Monday, Nancy simply could not get up to eat, and we let her lie in the bed for her lunch and dinner meals. We have allowed her to stay on her back for meal times to keep from getting choked when she swallows her food. However, we have also monitored her body-turnings to prevent bedsores. Evidently, with the combination of a lowered immune system due to the chemotherapy and our allowing her to lie on her back for meals has aggravated the bedsore and it is causing us sadness and Nancy soreness. We contacted Dustin, Kendra, and our hospice nurse, Kim, and soon had good suggestions to better the situation. Kim came in the afternoon and we conversed with Dustin by phone to get in agreement of the best solution. Kendra came last night, once she was off work, and she shared some ideas given her that would help Nancy get better sooner. Nancy rarely says anything about her discomfort. Lately, she has attempted several times, and successfully achieved a few times, the removing of the head-dressing for the head wound. We have put a sock on her hand and have tried to monitor her even closer than previously, but sometimes she wins that contest.

The dining room table is adorned with some beautiful flowers. Saturday, Carla sent some azaleas and then, our niece and nephew, Siara and Silas, along with Courtney, his fiancée, brought Nancy some yellow roses. Sunday, Nancy's aunt and uncle, Annie Jim and

James Ayers brought some red and white roses left over from Tom's Creek. Monday, Nancy's cousins, James and Nancy Segars brought her some pink roses.

In one of the earlier journal entries, I wrote May has dates of significance for Nancy and me. Well, today, the eleventh is another one of those days. On this date in 1976, I rode home elated from Gainesville Junior College with my track team. Although I had worked hard to prepare for the region track meet, and in fact, I did win the mile, two-mile, and the mile relay races that day, my elation was stemming from something else. You may remember the earlier journal entry concerning getting Nancy's phone number and calling her. During that conversation, she shared that she was playing in a tennis tournament at Gainesville College, and it so happened that I would be running the same day. "Maybe" we could see each other. And we did. Now, I don't believe in luck, but that day before the race, Dale Poser and I were running some warm-up laps when I looked down alongside the track and saw a four-leaf clover. I told Dale I saw one, but he didn't believe me, so the next time we circled, I bent down and picked it up without hardly breaking stride. I probably should confess I was at least a hundred pounds lighter at the time. Somehow, I was able to keep my mind on the races, and it was not until after the track meet that I saw Nancy. She had won her tournament and came down to the track area. There was a chain-link fence separating us, but we got to visit for probably fifteen or twenty minutes before I had to get in the team van and return home. It was a couple of more weeks before we would see each other again, but I was elated.

Another significance for this date happened in 2002. Our oldest daughter, Ashley, married Dustin. The wedding was beautiful, and it has not only produced a great life-partner for Ashley, but it has also produced a beautiful granddaughter and handsome grandson. Just be careful not to tell Elliott he is handsome. He takes offence to the title. Ha! Ha!

We have had a challenging few days, but we will continue moving forward. We can move forward because of the prayers of so many. It is fun reflecting on the past, but I look forward to the future because, this story is far from over!

- **Friday, May 13, 2011**

DAY 121 (141,365 Visits - 2,526 Posts)

Superior Vena Cava Syndrome. That is my new medical term of the week. Some of you were unaware our bodies even had a superior vena cava, but you do! Ha! In Nancy's situation, the SVC seems to have an obstruction. It is the main channel for blood flow to return from the area above the heart, including the head. Dr. Klassen, our hospice physician, made a house call on Wednesday and noticed the extensive swelling in Nancy's face, neck, and shoulders. He believes it is caused from an agitated lymph node, and that it may have swelled next to the superior vena cava, causing the obstruction of blood flowing back through her heart.

Obviously, I was aware of the swelling, but I dismissed it as a side effect of some of the medicines. Nancy does continue to take the steroid, Decadron, a.k.a. Deca-Durn! So I thought it was the culprit. While it appears very uncomfortable, Ole' tough Nancy does not complain, and she says it does not cause her pain. Dr. Klassen said in his thirty-five years of practice, he thinks this is only the fourth time he has observed the condition. (Way to go, Nancy, do something different. Ha!) For now, the hospice staff does not suggest any treatment, but they will continue to monitor the situation in case it worsens.

I mentioned previously, Nancy has been pulling at her head dressing and successfully removed it a few times. Wednesday's review further indicated Nancy is having an allergic reaction to the tape used to secure the bandage. In fact, it was being used in three separate areas of Nancy's body. The areas included her head, the sacral wound (bedsore), and the PICC-line. In layman's terms, the PICC-line was inserted in Nancy's left arm and is a tube going from her arm to her heart. It was for the purpose of IV use as well as drawing blood for lab cultures. While it was used extensively during her stay in the hospital, it has not been used for any purpose at home. Kim, our hospice nurse, noticed the skin irritation around the PICC-line and suggested its removal. I agreed, and it was soon removed. Dustin was doing research on superior vena cava syndrome Wednesday evening and said according to some of his research, the PICC-line may have been an accelerant for the SVC syndrome because the PICC-line flows into the superior vena cava. We are not saying the PICC-line has caused the swelling, but we are waiting to see if within the next week or two, we notice a change for the better.

Yesterday morning, (Thursday), I helped Nancy to the breakfast table for some of her mama's biscuits and my scrambled eggs. She ate well and was conversing with us fine. I left her visiting with her daddy and the girls so I could prepare for a missions board meeting followed by a radio interview. While I was at my desk studying, perhaps fifteen minutes later, Ashley came in and announced I needed to come and help Nancy. She had suddenly switched to a blank-stare, and nearly non-responsive state. I rushed in to examine her and found that she could utter a grunted yes or no when questioned about her condition. The girls assisted me putting her back to bed and we let her sleep. At 1:30 PM when I returned from my meetings, I found her sitting up eating a late lunch and talking like she usually does. Marlene's husband, Andy, is a paramedic and he suggested Nancy may be experiencing some mini strokes. His suggestion seems reasonable to me, and I suppose they may come more and more as time progresses.

Zane and Cathy stopped in for a visit. It was good to sit down for a few minutes to chat with them before I rushed to Cornelia, Toccoa, and Lavonia for more appointments. The Eleventh Annual Indian Creek Baptist Church Memorial Day Weekend Gospel Singing is only two weeks away. (Try saying that sentence three times at a fast pace. Ha!) The girls have been stepping up even more than they were to enable me make some needed appointments in preparation of the singing. I would appreciate specific prayer concerning Nancy's condition and the simultaneous requirements and responsibilities of the singing. The church has been so gracious in allowing me to take care of Nancy, but I feel the responsibility of meeting the needs of the singing.

Jean Poole and Sherri Turpin, some of Nancy's childhood classmates, along with Henry Watkins and Amy McCollum delivering food filled Nancy's afternoon. Visitors continue to be welcome. I had someone in Carnesville, and a couple of people in Toccoa, specifically tell me they appreciated the journal entries. I have received emails and Facebook postings telling me the same. It is humbling and encouraging to hear that our story is touching others with a positive impact.

Today is a new day. It is Friday, the 13th. I believe God made this day slightly different than yesterday or the day before. I am committing my time to Him regardless of the circumstances. I hope you, too, will be able to embrace the day and face the challenges you will meet in your path today with the same enthusiasm as I feel. Let's see what God is going to do through us today and keep looking up because He *really is* coming back soon. Don't forget to tell the story because this story is far from over!

P.S. Please add Tracy Stuffle to the prayer list. He is the owner and bass singer of the Perry's singing group. He has had health concerns especially with his heart all year, but today is in bed with a fever.

• **Saturday, May 14, 2011**

DAY 122

Nancy's uncle James, her oldest brother, Bruce, and my oldest brother, Tom, all share birthdays today. Happy Birthday, men. However, May 14, 1977 holds significance for Nancy and me. It was a day in which I had been planning for a while, but at the same time, I decided to low-key the event. That won't seem too romantic but hear me out, and remember we are still together.

It was another one of those spring Saturdays in which the Dean's Grocery softball team had entered a tournament. I did not go to every game, but I went to several so I could catch up on the local news with Clifford Allen, Ronnie Yearwood, Roger Shedd, or others. Nancy and I had been dating for almost a year and I enjoyed spending time with her even if it meant sitting in the bleachers of the old cotton mill field or some other place. I was on the Tom's Creek team so Nancy came to my games for the same reason.

Nancy and I had talked about getting married for a couple of months, but I was too poor to provide the ring, so we had never made our engagement official. On May 14, I had been thinking about how to give her the ring I purchased earlier in the week. Bobby Carter was a student at Toccoa Falls, but he also had been working in a local jewelry store and I trusted him to be fair with me. I had plenty of time to think about it that day because I was working on my 1971 VW Super Beetle. It had some electrical problems and Bobby Sellers suggested I replace the voltage regulator.

I decided to present the ring to Nancy after her ball game. I was living in the lower trailer park at Toccoa Falls, and I had told Nancy I would see her at the game. After fixing the car, I stuck her ring box inside the discarded voltage regulator box, stuffed it with a clean shop rag, and tossed it in the floor of the car. (I told you this wouldn't seem too romantic. Ha!)

Some have teased me for remembering what we were wearing when we met, and I will have to confess, I don't remember what I was wearing. Nancy had on her yellow Dean's Grocery uniform that Carlos had provided for his players. The tournament was played at the old Coats & Clark ballfield, and Nancy's game was the last one of the evening. She was playing first base and the last play of the game was a grounder hit to the shortstop that happened to be Nancy's sister, Janet. In one fluid motion, Janet fielded the ball and tossed a strike to Nancy which ended the game. They won that game but would need to return Sunday afternoon to determine the winner of the tournament. Betty Jean Sheriff was one of Nancy's team members, and she lived a short distance from Nancy's house. She had ridden to the game with her husband, Clinon, so I asked her if she minded driving Nancy's car home so Nancy could ride with me. Betty Jean was happy to do us the favor, and soon we were sitting in my car. I was nervous even though we had discussed our future on more than a few occasions. I started the car and Nancy asked what "that box" was doing in the floor cluttering up her foot room. I told her I wanted to keep the contents of that box in my car the rest of my life. She was puzzled at what I meant so I told her again. I wanted to keep the contents by my side the rest of my life. She did not understand why I wanted a voltage regulator by my side for the rest of my life, so as I put the car in gear to leave the ball field, I suggested she open the box. She reached in and pulled out the shop rag and threw it at me. She asked why I wanted a shop rag next to me. I laughed and told her to look a little deeper in the box. She looked again and discovered the ring box. Knowing that it was not her birthday or any other holiday, she asked what was in the box. I told her a third time to open it up because I wanted to keep the contents by my side the rest of my life. If memory serves me correctly, I think she actually was a little surprised as she leaned over the gear stick to give me a "Nancy-fix" just as I was turning left onto Hwy 145, and headed for her house. I might add here that Nancy was pleasantly surprised with an upgraded ring for our twenty-fifth anniversary, but I didn't throw that one in a voltage regulator box. Ha!

In the months previous to May 14, I shared with Nancy how the Lord had called me into some type of ministry as a tenth grader. At the time, I had no idea of knowing what that meant, but I wanted Nancy to agree she would follow me wherever the Lord directed me. We discussed the possibility of moving away from her roots. It was not merely a fifteen minute conversation, nor was it a begging or pleading in anguish. Instead, it was a period of time in which we talked on numerous occasions about serving the Lord at some point in the future. The Lord was gracious in giving us time to adjust our lives to follow His leading.

It would be naïve to think our marriage has endured without challenges. I am confident Nancy could report more than a few things I have done over the years that annoyed her. There were times I did not understand what she was thinking or doing. However, we have purposefully tried to keep Jesus Christ in the center of our focus. We have worked to protect our marriage and keep it from being a failed statistic. When we married in September of 1978, we said some wedding vows. We were giddy and excited on our wedding day, but when we said those vows, we were made to understand that we were not simply saying them to each other, but also before Almighty God.

I have discovered through our current situation, that because I chose to be true to my wedding vows earlier in my marriage, it is not a "chore" to care for Nancy now. I love taking care of her. It is because I love her so much that I get a bit overwhelmed and sad realizing she is not the independent woman I married. She is totally dependent upon one of the family members for her care now. Nancy has not stopped declaring her love to me as I am turning her, feeding her, or meeting other needs. I am confident she loves me and would gladly attend to my needs if the roles were reversed.

Well, that is the testimony part. Now, let me preach to you for a moment. The only way to have a healthy relationship in your marriage, at your workplace, or with your neighbors, and so forth is to first have a healthy relationship with Jesus Christ. Matthew 22:37-40 commands us how to live.

> He said to him, "Love the Lord your God with all your heart, with all your soul, and with all your mind. This is the greatest and most important commandment. The second is like it: Love your neighbor as yourself. All the Law and the Prophets depend on these two commandments." (from Holman Christian Standard Bible® Copyright © 1999, 2000, 2002, 2003, 2005 by Holman Bible Publishers.)

If each of you will get the relationship with the Lord right, the relationship with each other will improve. Selfishness is a destroyer of relationships. It will especially destroy a marriage. If a marriage partner constantly "takes from" and never "gives to" the relationship, it will fail. Let me encourage you to give to your relationship so that when the dark days of terminal illness, financial crisis, or some other tragedy occurs, your relationship will be so tightly woven with the love of God, His love will be reflected into your love for each other.

Well, that is our engagement story for another significant day in May, but it is only one of many stories, because this story is far from over!

• **Tuesday, May 17, 2011**

DAY 125

"Oh me... Oh my... The Ref's done told a lie!"

It's well documented by now that I have known Nancy a long time. However, recently, I learned a chant from her I do not ever remember hearing uttered from her lips. Ha! Ha! You must know I have done my share of hollering at the referees in the past, but that chant was a new one to me. Nancy introduced it to me as we were transferring her back into the bed. The process moves her from the wheelchair to the edge of the bed. Then I place her into a hug and gently lay her down as an assistant simultaneously moves her legs into a comfortable position. She usually groans during the process. Nancy said she used to chant it as a child during her big brother, Bruce's, basketball games. It is difficult to imagine either of her parents shouting it, but I am confident, there were other, more experienced, "referee criticizers" who taught her.

Sunday night into early Monday morning provided a new wrinkle in the care giving story for Nancy. It was shortly after midnight when Jessica and I had turned her and were giving her the required late night meds. It's hard to guess what triggered it, but Nancy went into a seizure. There was not the wild thrashing of arms and legs, but one eye blinked while the other one starred and her head quivered. Jessica and I urgently and unsuccessfully tried to get Nancy to speak to us and tell us how to help her. After calling several people from two counties, Kenny and Janet appeared with Andy closely following. Andrea was at work, but Ashley rushed back after getting to her home in Royston only minutes earlier. A local emergency crew arrived too, but Nancy was already breathing normally and she seemed to be back to her ole' self again. Yes, seizures are scary for those of us who have not had to experience them. A hospice nurse came to affirm the care givers and assess the situation. George made some helpful suggestions and agreed Nancy was as normal as she could be given her situation. I finally lay down around 3:30 AM. (I know, I know, that would have been a good time to write a post. Ha!)

Thanks go to the "Williams" sisters for the BBQ Saturday followed by Rodney and Betsy for the tasty meal Sunday. Some of the family attended and was able to enjoy time at the Dooley reunion Sunday. Nancy enjoyed her visits on Monday, starting with her Daddy delivering some fresh-baked sausage and butter biscuits. Carla, Misty, and Susan came by for an update on the annual field day activities. Other teachers, Amy, Tracy, Julie, and Matt came with kids in tow. The sixth-grade teacher's group provided supper.

John and Jan visited yesterday evening along with Nancy's family members, starting with Janet and followed by Deloris, Greg, Alisa, and Mark.

I started writing the above entry early this morning. Now its 10:30 PM, and I need to go turn Nancy again and do the night meds. It's been a busy day and I have some more news to share soon. I will try to add more tomorrow. Nancy has had another seizure this morning but it was not as pronounced as the one mentioned above. (Thank the Lord!)

There is definitely more to the story because this story is far from over!

Please add Debra Shedd to the prayer list. She is our friend and hair-dresser and is recovering from knee replacement surgery.

• **Wednesday, May 25, 2011**

DAY 133

Hmmm ... It's been over a week since I last posted on this journal. A myriad of world and national events has transpired these last seven days. Mr. Harold Camping told the world he knew when Jesus was returning, President Barack Obama took a political swipe at Israel, and Joplin, Missouri discovered a small, and I mean incremental portion of, the forces of nature even though it was displayed in a magnitude previously not experienced. Debaters could converse on which event has the larger repercussions for future days. The Bible gives perspective thought to each. The gospel of Mark 13:31 "Heaven and earth will pass away, but My words will never pass away." The first three gospels record verses in which Jesus tells of all nations being against Israel. They also warn of catastrophic disasters which will occur before the return of Christ. Scripture is crystal clear in warning that people should be ready because no man knows the day of hour of Christ's return.

So, how has the last seven days effected your life? Do you have compassion for the homeless and bereaved in Missouri? Do you have enough compassion to do something about it, or will the tragedy become merely a memory of historical account and you let it pass without personal input? Will Mr. Camping's failed projection of Jesus Christ's return become only fodder for the news media, or will you capitalize on the recent awareness to drive home the point that while we don't know when, Jesus is coming again, we are told to be ready for His return. With as much damage as has been caused by one storm, pause for a moment and realize the fury and wrath of God is yet to be experienced by those who chose not to bring glory and praise to His Son, Jesus.

So, how has the last seven days effected the Stacey household? Nancy continues being the center of attention and requires twenty-four hour care. We have not noticed the seizures experienced last week although there have been times I have wondered what was going on behind the blank stare of her blue eyes. The routine of her care is constant in that she needs personal attention every two hours for adjusting her position in an effort to make her comfortable and prevent her from having bedsores. Her face, neck, and shoulders are extremely swollen, and while she does not complain, it seems she would be terribly uncomfortable. She has been able to sit in the wheelchair for most of her meals, but it is with diminished help on her part and reliance upon the care giver to see she is transferred from place to place. She is less able to help with her arms as we move her, and even rolling from one side of the bed to the other is a chore. I do not regret one minute of offering care, but it is taking an emotional toll on me as I perform needed care on such a previously independent Nancy. Certainly, I am not in this alone. The girls, sisters, and other family members make sure she is getting the best of attention. Her father comes nearly every morning around 7:30 to bring a few of her mom's homemade biscuits before he goes about his day. It is touching to see the care offered. Mostly, I do well in keeping the emotions in check. However, there are times the situation is overwhelming, and I sense a stage of anger brewing from within. The anger is not directed to any individual or even to God. It is merely an understanding of how Genesis chapter three forever changed a perfect world for mankind. Recorded in Psalm 38 is a transparent view into David's life. There are thoughts and emotions within it that mirror some of my feelings. Verse nine says, "Lord, my every desire is to know you; my sighing is not hidden from you."

As I write this post, I think of the verses of the hymn entitled, "No, Not One!"

There's not a friend like the lowly Jesus—No, not one! No, not one!
None else could heal all our soul's diseases—No, not one! No, not one!
There's not an hour that He is not near us—No, not one! No, not one!
No night so dark but His love can cheer us—No, not one! No, not one!
Jesus knows all about our struggles; He will guide till the day is done.
There's not a friend like the lowly Jesus—No, not one! No, not one!

The psalmist finishes with a plea in verses 21 and 22. "Lord, do not abandon me; my God, do not be far from me. Hurry to help me, Lord, my Savior."

I know God is with us and that He will continue to reveal Himself to Nancy and me as we travel the road together. Our love for each other is sweeter and our times together are special.

Yesterday (Tuesday), was a bitter-sweet day. Stephens County retired teachers hosted a reception for the soon retiring educators for this year. Nancy was hired by then, middle school principal, Jim Bellamy. He remarked how his hiring of Nancy was a wise decision and how the children of Stephens County benefited from that decision. Her current principal, George Sanders, at Big A Elementary School, conveyed to the attendees how Nancy was not only professional in her classroom, but also personable to her co-workers. He too, told of her humorous injections to long, hot days that would help keep the attitudes light and the work easier. He further shared how Nancy had the uncanny ability to memorize the vehicles of the children's parents who were picking the children up after school. When there were pauses in the car line, Nancy would call out names of celebrities with which the children were oblivious and the teacher's found humorous. Thank you Stephens County Educators, for recognizing the thirty-year career of my Nancy.

As long as there are people with which Nancy has known, there will be stories how she has influenced many; but this story is far from over!

P.S. Please remember my brother-in-law's family. Kenny, and his brothers, Curtis and Jerry. They buried their mother in March, and now their youngest brother, Bruce Waters will be buried tomorrow.

• Sunday, May 29, 2011

DAY 137

Wow! What a weekend! I have only a couple of minutes to share an update but wanted to post it today. Many of you know I have been busy with our annual Indian Creek Baptist Church Memorial Day Weekend Gospel Singing. Each year my family knows my priority, time, and attention is consumed with the singing. Nancy has been completely supportive of the ministry time over the years. Let me interject, that she has not always been "happy" with the amount of time, but she has volunteered her own time to join me in going from Spartanburg to Atlanta in helping promote the singing.

This year obviously has been more challenging. It was emotionally difficult for me to leave her Saturday morning to meet the challenges of the day. I got a couple of catch-up "Nancy-Fixes" to get me started, and she told me she would love to be at the singing too. She is a wonderful support to the ministry God has given us. Nancy's health continues to weaken. She has developed an eye situation in which eye drops are required. Turning her is painful for her body as we move her. Yet, she does not complain, and she continues to declare her love for whoever happens to be the care giver at the moment.

While Nancy's body is weakening, God's love, grace and peace is strengthening. He continues to hold the family up, and we are leaning heavily upon Him during our storm. There is comfort in knowing He holds us, and we can depend upon Him.

This is, as mentioned, a brief update. God has provided amazingly this weekend and I will share more soon because this story is far from over!

This Memorial Day Weekend, Don't forget to thank a veteran ...

* **Sunday, May 29, 2011**

Day 137 Second Story

I am writing this in the last hour of the 29th day of May, 2011. It was thirty-five years ago today, that I graduated from the Toccoa Falls Academy. I suppose an odd little bit of trivia would include that my classmates and I graduated in the First Baptist Church in Toccoa because our high school gymnasium had been flooded the night before in one of those good ole' Georgia frog stranglers. It was the last official day of the Toccoa Falls Academy due to the financial strain it placed upon the college, but that is a story for another time.

I had a double-date that night. Dean Bogert and Beth Poole were going to a graduation party hosted by Debbie Watson Holland's mother. I was taking Nancy. It was our first "official" date. I did not yet have a vehicle so Dean picked me up, and we three went to Tom's Creek to pick up Nancy. The first person I met at her house was her dad. He had been reclining on his couch without wearing a shirt, and when I came to the door he stuck out his hand, and said, "D.C. Adams. Come on in and have a seat." I had barely seated myself, when Nancy strode confidently into the living room and announced she was ready to go.

The four of us went to Debbie's house which was a short distance from the National Guard's Armory in Toccoa. The party was probably better described as a reception and it was nice of Ms Lillian to host us. Nancy knew the guys from our male quartet but did not know anyone else. So, she was rather quiet. I suppose I should mention there were thirty-seven or thirty-eight graduates and only about a third of them lived in the Toccoa area. Dean and Beth wanted to visit another family at Toccoa Falls, so we left the party and while they briefly visited their friends; Nancy and I waited in the car and got better acquainted. I apologize for letting the readers down by not remembering what we were wearing for our date. I asked Nancy this evening if she remembered, and she said she did not.

The next part of our story is a bit perplexing as I report it one way and Nancy defensively remembers it another. While we were taking the girls to their respective residences, we were traveling up Tugalo Street in Toccoa. My story is that somewhere around the First Baptist Church, Nancy leaned over and kissed me. Now, she continues (even earlier tonight in front of the girls) to deny it happened quite that way. She argumentatively claims I kissed her. Either way, yes, we kissed on our first date.

Tonight we celebrated the thirty-fifth anniversary of our first date with another kiss. It was not in front of the First Baptist Church, it was in front of our three lovely daughters. I also brought a "Mr. Goodbar" candy bar to enjoy as a reminder of our first introduction to each other thirteen months earlier.

It is all part of this story that is far from over!

June

- **Wednesday, June 1, 2011**

DAY 140 (153,766 Visits - 2,582 Posts)

Dear Family, Friends and Prayer Partners,

It is with a saddened heart I report that Nancy's condition continues to weaken with noticeable acceleration. Yesterday (Tuesday), Kim, our hospice nurse came for a routine visit after a five-day scheduled time off. We had been in touch through the mode of texting and asked her to contact the hospice doctor for some direction on any treatment that might reduce the swelling caused by the combination of the steroid, Decadron, and the Superior Vena Cava issue previously reported shortly after Mother's Day. Kim was shocked to hear his response when he asked, "You mean she is still living?" He obviously had not previously encountered the down-n-gritty determination of those "Tom's Creek Girls."

Since it had been five days since she had been here, Kim was able to reassess Nancy more readily than if she had been coming each day. Nancy's condition was much more obvious, and she gently told us. One has to remember, being a care giver or hospice worker takes its toll on individuals. Without getting too personal, let me explain Nancy has once again wrapped her personality around the hearts of her care givers. Kim shared that from the first day of meeting us, she knew there would be tender moments and floods of memories from her own life. While she is not yet forty years of age, her mother was a school teacher and her father is a pastor. She was at her mother's bedside five years ago, when she saw cancer win another brave battle.

Marlene was with me, and Andrea was asleep in the other room, when Kim began to gently point out indicators of Nancy's worsened condition we had overlooked. I asked her to wait until I could get the girls all on the same page together. I awakened Andrea and called Ashley, then Jessica to stop their work so we could discuss Nancy's condition together through a conference call. Nancy's mama came by for her afternoon visit and sat with Nancy while we gathered in our sunroom to plan a strategy. Kim was checking on the doctor's recommendations and suggestions. The hospice house and hospital are both available options for us, but we have, as a family, agreed to stay home. Kim reassured us we were providing excellent care. She said there isn't much more that either the hospice house or hospital could offer that we that were not already doing. After getting through the shock of placing Nancy's current situation on high alert, we decided to stay home because of Nancy's wishes and for convenience to the other family members.

We are doing well as we trust the Lord through these challenging days. We are leaning upon the uplifted prayers of you, our faithful prayer supporters, and the strength only God can give. As I was writing this journal entry, I couldn't get the Stephen Curtis Chapman song out of my head... I think the Holy Spirit put it in there as a reminder. I googled the lyrics so you, too, could find encouragement.

Lyrics to "His Strength Is Perfect":
His strength is perfect , so perfect

I can do all things through Christ who gives me strength
But sometimes I wonder what he can do for me
No great success to show
No glory of my own
yet in my weakness he is there to let me know

(chorus)
His strength is perfect when our strength is gone
He'll carry us when we can't carry on
Raised in his power the weak becomes strong
His strength is perfect
His strength is perfect

We can only know that power that he holds
When we truly see how deep our weakness goes
His strength it must begin
When ours comes to an end
He hears our humble cry and proves again
Chorus Repeats Twice:

We love each of you and the love of Jesus Christ that you have reflected upon our family through the various caring ways. We continue to stand and face this because we are standing in *His* strength, and because or your shoulders in which we lean upon from time-to-time.

Always remember: this story is far from over!

• Wednesday, June 8, 2011

DAY 147

Last night was better. Well, better for the care givers at least. The night before last, one of the girls and I were taking our turn of caring for Nancy. It includes turning her every two hours and meeting any other need she may encounter. Neither of us woke when the alarm(s) went off. At 6:30 AM I was awakened and asked to assist in turning Nancy. With tears in our eyes, the two of us turned Nancy knowing she was probably stiff and sore from our error chalked up to fatigue. The other two girls were supportive in agreeing they, too, in the past had overslept, but that one of the other four of us had wakened them to assist. I was disappointed that Nancy was dependent upon me, and I had let her down. Truth be known, if that is the worst thing done to her in these last 147 days, we are doing pretty well. Last night the same daughter and I had "duty," and we responded in a timelier manner. Nancy seems to rest well and for that, we are grateful.

Since the last journal posting there have been numerous crises that have happened to our extended family and friends. The youth from Indian Creek took a mission trip to Ohio and encountered everything from a water-pump failure, and equipment trailer tire blow-out, to hitting a deer and knocking out a headlight. No injuries reported and everyone is fine. My brother, Tom, drives a truck rig with dual trailers across the state of Texas nearly every day. Last week, a wheel bearing went bad causing the trailer to catch fire and he lost both of the loaded trailers, sparing only the tractor. No injuries were reported and everyone is fine. A family friend's father had a heart attack but reports he is in rehab and doing much better.

Yesterday (Tuesday), our nephew, Nathan, and his wife Loren, lost all of their earthly possessions to a house fire. No injuries were reported, and everyone is fine. Here at the house, the basement air conditioner went out, a light fixture required replacement ballast, the toilet valve has failed, the living room television picture tube is going bad, and the fuse from the main power line left us without electricity for a brief time. No injuries were reported, and everyone is fine.

Life certainly has it challenges. In the midst of one battle, ours being cancer, we hear of the heartaches and crisis met by our extended family and friends. While we sympathize and regret the things happening to others, we recognize the "blip" it represents on the radar of eternity. We constantly need the reminder that life with all of its challenges is merely a passing moment when compared to eternity. For sure, some will argue their "blip" has more bumps and potholes than others, but they can't argue long when they compare it to eternity. Sometimes seeing Nancy endure through the day-by-day weakening, it seems like eternity. Fortunately for us, she endures without many groans or complaints. She makes few demands and is understanding when we forget something or oversleep.

Since the last posting, hospice supplied continuous care nurses for a twenty-four hour period. Nancy seemed to be going into a valley of weakening health, and hospice sent assistance to us. In the meantime, Nancy rallied once again. When the nurse entered the house, she observed Jessica on one side of Nancy feeding her a bowl of fresh-cut fruit. I was on the other side of Nancy feeding her some of her aunt Annie Jim's pecan pie fresh out of the oven. Later the nurse called all of us aside for a conference. She said when she is dispatched to a home for continuous care, she observes the patient with a fixed stare, set jaw, and no communication with anyone. I shrugged my shoulders and told her that Nancy had rallied once again. Earlier, we had witnessed a steep decline, but she rebounded. She truly is much weaker than even a week ago, but she continues to battle. Nancy sleeps most of each day and has not been strong enough to get out of bed since last week. While she rests, we go on with "normal" activities throughout the house. I verbally check on her often, and she will grunt a response or declaration of love. She has not lost her cognitive skills or her sense of humor even though her strength is diminished.

Yesterday (Tuesday), began with the routine of getting the girls off to work and discussing the agendas or plans for the day. Nancy's daddy brought biscuits while I fixed her some scrambled eggs. We were cleaning the kitchen when the phone rang. Mr. Sanders, Nancy's principal at Big A Elementary, called to say he had a special gift to deliver. I told him to bring it when he was ready, and he said he was on his way. What he did not mention was that several of the teachers were coming with him. We must have had forty teachers and staff workers stop in to offer us well-wishes and present us with a park bench as appreciation of Nancy's teaching time at Big A. A clever craftsman welded the steel bench together and added a plate with the greeting Nancy shared each day as she entered the school. "Greetings, Salutations, and Hallucinations!" We have been blessed by the love and concern from so many. Each day brings hugs, smiles, food, or gifts from people we have known for years or from acquaintances briefly known. The mail continues to produce cards and letters declaring prayers for Nancy and the family. Yesterday alone, we benefited from Denise and Linda's visit to 211 Restaurant in Lavonia, and I received three cards from various church congregations. Two were from churches that learned of Nancy's condition during the recent Gospel Singing at Indian Creek. Visitors are welcome to come anytime and spend a few minutes with Nancy. We appreciate each visit. Yesterday afternoon, she had a visit from the longest distance so far. My brother, Steve, and his wife, Penny, came from Taiwan. Their daughter Siara joined them as they spent the afternoon with us. They will be stateside for two months before returning to their mission responsibilities at Morrison Academy in Tai-Chung. Last evening, Lucy and Vernelle brought a meal along with hugs and smiles of encouragement while Wendell brought a flat of eggs. We are so blessed.

The psalmist recounts the difficult days of Israel in the 126 division of the Psalms. Verse 3 says, "The LORD hath done great things for us; whereof we are glad." Yes, our road is rough. It is totally unexpected. We are bruised by the results of what has been discovered and projected. Yet, as with the thoughts of the psalmist, we, as a family, recognize the Lord's hand upon us. We feel His love through the touch of other believers that love Nancy and care for us. We sense His presence even in the depths of the sorrow we are enduring. Our grief is kept in check by the outpouring of prayer support and love from people we don't even know. I recognize the strength is of *the Lord*. He is the one who has done great things. We are the recipients of His love and we are glad.

Well, I better sign off for now. Nancy needs turning and breakfast, and the toilet needs that valve fixed. In the meantime, while you, too, go through the challenges of life, trust Jesus for your strength, and always remember that because of Him, this story is far from over!

- **Thursday, June 9, 2011**

DAY 148

Twenty-seven years ago today was a Saturday. I remember well, how life for Nancy and me was to a point we felt more children would be a blessing. In September, 1983, I was full-time minister at Tom's Creek Baptist Church and was enrolling into Truett-McConnell College for a music degree. Nancy was beginning her third year as a teacher to Stephens County Middle School, and little Ashley needed a sibling. Nine months later, Jessica arrived.

Nancy had chosen a group of obstetricians in Anderson, SC. Outside of the usual morning sickness and a few headaches, she had a routine pregnancy. When she delivered Ashley in December, 1980, she played the piano for the morning church service, went to a Sunday School lunch/party after the service, and told me around 2:00 PM we needed to go to the hospital. Ashley was born at 4:20 PM and all was well. There is nothing like getting down to business. Ha! Ha!

On June 9, 1984, sometime after 7:30 AM she told me it was time to go to the hospital. Knowing she delivered quickly with Ashley and knowing we had a little farther to travel to get to the hospital, I was a little more anxious to get the trip started. As we were nearing the I-85 on-ramp in Lavonia, she suggested we stop at Hardee's and get a biscuit. Her experience told her she may not get a meal for a while so she wanted to get a biscuit. I offered a brief hesitation, but soon realized a "happier" trip (Ha! Ha!) would require a Hardee's biscuit. When we got close to the hospital, she suggested we stop by the doctor's office for a quick examination just in case she was having false labor pains. Again, with the knowledge of the expediency of the first delivery, and the ongoing contractions coming closer and closer, I hesitated anxiously. She calmly but firmly won again. However, I negotiated for her to get examined while I turned the car around in the doctor's parking lot. I put the car in "park" and was reaching for the ignition keys, when I looked up and saw her lumbering down the sidewalk towards the car. When she got into the car I asked how the examination went and she grinned as she reported, "The doctor said to get to the hospital immediately and don't stop at Bojangle's on the way!" I was thinking, "I told you so!" but knew that was the wrong response, so we raced a couple of hundred yards to the emergency room door. Some nurses and attendants came out to assist her and I suggested they hurry because of her previous delivery. They looked at me like I was just an anxious father-in-waiting and told me to park the car and go up to the delivery floor. When I got off the elevator, I urgently encouraged the people at the nurse's desk to let me back to be with her. They told me there would be plenty of time, so I needed to go down the hall to the Father's Waiting Room and they would call me. I felt defeated and unheard, but I made my way to the waiting room. I barely had time to sit down with a Sports Illustrated magazine in my hand, when I heard someone running down the hall towards me. A nurse, in full delivery apparel, stuck her head in the doorway and asked me if I was Mr. Stacey. I said that I was and she said, "Come on! You're going to miss it!" Again, the thought, "I told you so!" went through my mind, but I hurried to Nancy's side in time to watch her deliver Jessica. It was just over three hours since she told me she was ready to go to the hospital. Jessica weighed 7lbs 4oz, and at birth, she was a clone to Ashley. She looked so much like Ashley when she was born.

Now, twenty-seven years later, I reflect with joy the decision Nancy and I made to have more children. Jessica has brought much happiness into our home and her outgoing personality has been embraced by her peers. She has been teased about being a drill sergeant during Nancy's illness, but in reality, she has attended to Nancy with love and tenderness. Fourteen months after Jessica was born, Andrea came on the scene. That's another story for another post, but I will say there was a tuxedo involved with that delivery. Ha! Ha!

Two years ago today was a Tuesday. Andrea and Chris presented us with their first child and our third grandchild. Clayton John was born and he continues to bring joy into the Segers/Stacey families. God sends us reminders of His love through the gift of life. Childbirth is a miracle to behold. I can only imagine what was going through Joseph's mind when Mary told him she was about to deliver Jesus. The Bible does not mention tuxedos, Bojangle's, or Hardee's but it does mention the miracle of Jesus's birth. It is because of His birth, life, death, and resurrection that we are able to rejoice through the trials of this life.

It is because of His story that this story is far from over!

Happy Birthday, Jessica and Clayton

• Saturday, June 11, 2011

DAY 150 (162,139 Visits—2,688 Posts)

Nancy continues to battle the beast that has robbed her of her strength. Her sleeping has increased, and her appetite has decreased slightly. She is surrounded with the love of her family and friends and continues being alert and witty when she is awake. The doormat with "Welcome" greets those who have chosen to visit. Thanks for the kindness many have shared with our family. It is overwhelming, but in a positive way.

There is excitement in the air concerning a birthday party for our two-year-old grandson, Clayton. The girls have worked on gift wrapping, toy assembling, and house straightening in order to host a gazillion children (give or take a million or two) at our house. Thirty-three years ago, I attended my future father-in-law's fiftieth birthday party and marveled how healthy the "old" man was. Today, Saturday, he turns eighty-three and can still outwork most people.

With the recent celebrations of Jessica, Clayton, and Durward's birthdays, I thought about some of the past birthday parties or celebrations I shared with Nancy. I remember the very first birthday gift I purchased for her. We had only been dating for about six weeks, and since my funds were limited, I did not exactly go "all out" and spend a wad of money. I bought her an earring and necklace set with her birthstone, rubies, in the settings. Now don't get too excited about the purchase because it was the cosmetic, cheap stuff, and probably only cost about twenty-five or thirty bucks. She acted like she appreciated it, and wore it several times during the first months of our courtship. I suppose she has it somewhere in her collection, but I cannot remember seeing it in the last several years.

As I reminisce celebrating July 3 over the last thirty-five years, I chuckle at some of the impromptu gatherings we have enjoyed. There have been the usual parties with family and friends here at the house. The girls and I surprised her with a party while in Pigeon Forge one year. We were staying at a motel with a pool, and she loved to tan by the pool so I kept the children in the room and made some make-shift decorations. The kids enjoyed the surprise more than Nancy but she played along well. One year I made reservations to the Sundial Restaurant at the top of the Peachtree Plaza in Atlanta. The restaurant is famous for revolving, and those dinning can enjoy a picturesque view of the Atlanta skyline. Well ... unless like Nancy, one has a fear of heights and gets dizzy up that high. Ha! Ha! I had to request a table positioned near the center of the room. However, we were able to enjoy a fabulous fireworks display that night as our view went over the Fulton County Stadium after the Braves game. One year, Nancy and I celebrated her birthday with church friends while traveling on a mission trip to El Salvador. Four years ago, we celebrated with Ashley and Dustin as they presented us with our second grandchild, Elliott. It was Nancy's fiftieth birthday, and I tried to convince her Dustin and I planned something extra special for the occasion by presenting her with a grandson but she did not believe us so I went ahead and bought her a necklace. (There is a photo of me placing it around her neck in the CaringBridge photo gallery.) For the record, it was a lot nicer than the first necklace I got her.

I would say the best surprise party she had was for her thirty-fifth birthday in 1992. Mr. Yarborough was a friendly acquaintance that had invited us to swim or fish off of his lakeside dock. His house was located close to Charlie Holcomb's landing which happened to be a place Nancy and I frequented over the years during the hot summers. Mr. Yarborough agreed to let me host a family-and-friends gathering, and the guest list swelled to well over fifty people. I bought beef steaks for everyone, and John Thurmond and Kenny Waters agreed to grill them while other friends supplied salad, potatoes, drinks, and so forth.

The plan was for Greg and Deloris to invite Nancy, the girls, and me to go water skiing. My siblings were visiting from Texas and Malaysia so my mother suggested we all eat together. She just didn't tell Nancy "where" we would eat together. I wanted to keep it a surprise, so I did not tell the girls just in case they slipped up and told Nancy. Because my side of the family was not familiar with Holcomb's landing, I drew maps and copied enough for the family. (Ask Marlene how the map thing worked out for her. That's another story. Ha!)

When we got to the lake with Greg and Deloris, I had Greg pull me skiing first, and he took me down the lake to Mr. Yarborough's house to make sure everyone was ready for the surprise. We then went back to Holcomb's landing to let Nancy ski but when we returned, she had changed her mind. It was a cloudy day, she didn't want to get her hair wet, and we were supposed to eat supper with my parents. I had to do some quick thinking and fast talking. I scolded her to shame by telling her Greg had gone out and bought a new battery for his boat just so they could take us skiing. I further pointed out that since she was a good skier, I doubted if her hair would get wet because I was sure she wouldn't even fall. We went back and forth for a couple of minutes, and finally Nancy gave in to give the skis a try. As expected, she got up on the first try and Greg took her the opposite way from Mr. Yarborough's so I would have time to get the girls loaded into the car and surprise Nancy at his dock. As soon as Greg, Deloris, and Nancy got out of sight, I announced the plans of a birthday party to the girls. They immediately thought I was joking with them since they didn't see any evidence of party stuff.

I finally convinced them to get into the car, and we tore off for Mr. Yarborough's house. We waited for the boat to come up to the dock and then we would run down and surprise Nancy. It worked great. Nancy's story is that as soon as she got up on the skis, Greg and Deloris would not look back at her. She kept trying to get their attention because she was getting tired, but they would not look. Finally, she had to drop and yes, her hair got wet. Ha! Once the boat pulled up to the dock and we surprised Nancy, her concern to me was, "Did you bring me any dry clothes?" I had in fact planned for that as well. We had a great time and built some great memories. With the exception of one sibling's family being out of town, her side of the family was all present and I think Nancy was truly surprised.

I don't have any idea how many more birthdays Nancy will share with our family, but we have enjoyed the years that have passed quickly. She and I were able to water ski last summer and to the best of our memories it was the first time since her birthday party. Yep, we both got our hair wet, and we were more than a little sore the next day.

This story is simply another example of our ongoing love we have shared with each other. However, it is only part of the story because this story is far from over!

• Sunday, June 12, 2011

DAY 151

Turning from night into morning has also rearranged the plans for the day. I was planning to preach this morning. I was able to meet the schedule nearly every Sunday in May and enjoyed sharing God's Word with the church family. This morning around 4:15 AM the girls awakened me with the concern of Nancy's breathing. They had been monitoring it closely for the previous hour and decided to share their concerns with me. Dustin recently purchased a gizmo to measure oxygen in one's system, and Nancy seemed to be well within the parameters of normalcy. Her frequency of breathing seemed diminished but when the hospice on-call nurse was summoned she reassured us that while Nancy's condition was weakening, she did not think we should be overly alarmed yet. Nancy, not surprisingly, claimed she was fine.

One of the girls called another family friend, who is well acquainted with comforting the sick, and she too agreed the numbers we reported seemed acceptable given Nancy's current condition. Dustin, the girls, and I visited the situation for a few more minutes, and I came into my study for more sermon preparation. Around 6:00 AM I walked passed Nancy's bed, and we exchanged whispered declarations of our love. She told me she was comfortable and did not need anything so I went back to my computer desk. Earlier in the week I told our associate pastor, Nate, that I was planning on preaching, but that he would be wise in having a sermon prepared in the event I was unable to preach. It was after I shaved and showered that I went to check on Nancy again. She requested I stay with her this morning. Throughout my ministry, she has understood the odd hours and time requirements of being a pastor's wife. When she asked me to stay home, I checked the time, and at just a few minutes past seven o'clock I placed a call to Nate. He and his wife Heather are not only capable, but also generously willing to step up and move forward without hesitation.

After my phone conversation with Nate, I decided a Nancy-fix was in order so I went back to her bedside and leaned in for a kiss. I asked her if she thought there was enough room in her bed for me to join her and she agreed a hug would be appreciated. We snuggled up together for a few minutes and I held her while she slept. Andrea came walking through the house a few minutes later while meeting the needs of little Jackson. I told her I could hold him while she checked on things. My perspective scripture passage for the morning sermon continued flashing through my mind.

Second Corinthians 4:7-12 speaks to the tremendous treasure believers possess within their bodies. Earlier, Jesus told His disciples that He was the Light of the world. John's gospel records how Jesus, being the light, outshines the darkness of the world. He overshadows the darkness of sin. Later, when the Holy Spirit dwelled within the believer, in essence, the believer reflected God's light to others. The apostle Paul wrote to the Corinthians for the purpose of reminding them of the treasure and value of our salvation through Jesus Christ. He reminds us the treasure is powerful and extraordinary but that it is from God and not from our own power. In fact, as humans, we are powerless in the face of adversity and trials. It is only through the saving blood of Jesus and the power of His resurrection that we are enabled to stand in the midst of turmoil. The devil is a thief, and he wants only to kill and destroy. Death seems so final for the unbeliever, but through the resurrection of Jesus, as a believer, we too, have power over even death. Paul through the inspiration of the Holy Spirit further iterates his point of victory (v.16-18).

2 Corinthians 4:16-18

Therefore we do not give up; even though our outer person is being destroyed, our inner person is being renewed day by day. For our momentary light affliction is producing for us an absolutely incomparable eternal weight of glory. So we do not focus on what is seen, but on what is unseen; for what is seen is temporary, but what is unseen is eternal. (from Holman Christian Standard Bible® Copyright © 1999, 2000, 2002, 2003, 2005 by Holman Bible Publishers.)

There is no reason to give up. Even when our world is crashing around us, the Holy Spirit enables us to be refreshed daily. I needed to hear that today. I needed to share that today. I know some people are going through what seems like unbearable, unthinkable, excruciating pain. Sometimes it is not even physical pain, but pain of brokenness and heartache due to circumstances beyond the individual's control. Yet, like Paul, the believer must be reminded those trials are only temporary. For some, temporary may seem like a lifetime, but when it is laid beside the measurement of eternity, it becomes manageable.

I held my infant grandson close this morning. I held Nancy even closer. However, as I try to imagine what is in store for that little guy, I am comforted in knowing God is in control of everything. This old body may be broken down, and Nancy's life on earth may be fleeting, but new life is being born every day that will carry on the legacy of those believers who trusted God with everything. With God being in control, I KNOW—this story is far from over!

• **Friday, June 24, 2011**

DAY 163

Six years ago yesterday I was stopped by a Commerce City Policeman for speeding. I was on HWY 441 headed back towards I-85 and on to our house. As we pulled over at the new Tractor Supply Store, Nancy asked me what I was going to tell him. When he approached the car he asked me what my hurry was and if I knew how fast I was going. I told him I thought I was probably doing about ten miles per hour over the speed limit and that I was not in any particular hurry. I went on to explain our first grandchild, Ashtin, had been born earlier in the day at Athens, and I did not have my mind on anything to do with driving. He took my license and insurance card and told me he would be back in a minute. He returned in a minute or two and said, "Grandpaw, I'm going to let you go with a warning to slow down." I grinned and agreed I would pay a little closer attention to what I was supposed to do.

My, how those six years have passed quickly. Nana and I have loved every minute of being grandparent,s and we are four-time participants. It is refreshing to watch the interaction with my children as they interact with their own. It is a bit humbling to hear the same phrases used to correct or instruct their children that was used on them only a matter of a few years earlier. As our parents admitted they were not perfect parents but did what they thought was best for us at the time, Nancy and I can say the same.

I remember several of the "firsts" that happened as our children and grandchildren developed. We were all excited to see the child take her first steps. We teasingly argued whether or not the first words uttered were Nana or Papi. I remember the first Sunday they attended Indian Creek Baptist Church and how proud I was being a grandparent. The children and grandchildren continue setting markers in life that have a determining factor upon their future days.

Now, in her last days, I sit and think about Nancy. I reflect about the last Christmas we spent together. I think about the last New Year's Day as well as other celebratory times we shared as a couple. Yes, those are fond memories which I embrace with the filters of memory which allow capturing those moments through the use of the five senses being sight, sound, hearing, tasting, and touching. Those memories are not limited to only the last days or last times, but they include the youthful, playful times of a newly married couple, throwing cold water over the top of the shower curtain to the one taking a shower and hearing the screams of surprise or remembering the shock of cold water when she did it to me. I will forever cherish the love notes that are tucked away in a box or drawer somewhere that will be searched for later during a more personal time for reflections.

Yes, Nancy is experiencing what the family believes are her last days and hours. She is resting and seemingly in little or no pain. We do supplement the times of turning her body with medicine to help allow her ongoing rest. Nancy remains quite aware of her situation and continues offering suggestions when she is awake, to assist us in her care.

In our backyard is the Big-Ten. In actuality it is a 1979 Chevrolet Bonanza model pickup truck that we bought from Nancy's brother, Mark, several years ago. It was handy for several purposes but especially as a less-expensive insurance vehicle for the girls to drive as beginners. One of the girls didn't want to be seen in the same county with it because of its poorly maintained paint and its constant, but distinct squeaks and creaks that accompanied a ride to town. Another one of the girls loved it for the same exact reasons. That old truck let me down one day, and Roger Shedd helped me discover that the gas gauge was faulty. Of course, we discovered the problem after we tried a few other options, including putting on a new fuel pump. I don't think any of the girls ever ran it out of gas, but there were at least two times that it happened to me. On both of those occasions, I coasted into the gas station without having to walk an extra step.

I remember coasting into the station while the gas gauge reported I still had fuel in the tank. It was a surreal feeling of riding without the sound of the engine and yet powered by the force of fuel already spent. Psalm 90:10 "Our lives last seventy years, or if we are strong, eighty years. Even the best of them are struggle and sorrow; indeed they pass quickly and we fly away." According to that, Nancy's fuel gauge says she has another sixteen or so years, but in reality she is coasting into the station. I believe she is gliding in the power of the fuel already spent, and she will soon come to rest into the station of eternity. The psalmist goes on to ask God to "Teach us to number our days carefully so that we may develop wisdom in our hearts" (v. 12). I cannot think of any regrets Nancy has had during her life. She has not mentioned anything she wanted to do or see. She seems content. I am now asking God, as the psalmist did in verse 16, "Let Your work be seen by Your servants and Your splendor by their children." May it ever be so.

This story is far from over!

• Sunday, June 26, 2011

DAY 165

Dear Family, Friends, and Prayer Partners,

Nancy is currently in a final approach to her landing into heaven's reception. She has run the gamut of scenarios, and we are witnessing God's mercy and grace as she restfully continues drawing breath. In the late hours of yesterday, when I thought she was closer gone than with us, I leaned over and whispered, "You're sweet." To which she replied, "I know it." We all had a chuckle and agreed she still had her sense of humor even in the transition of her passing.

I gave in to rest around 3:30 AM and arose a little after 5:00 AM. Nancy's heartbeat continues at a high rate, but shortly after 6:00 AM there was a noticeable change in the respiration rate. As a family, we feel she is moments away from entering the presence of the Lord. My, how grateful we are for all the texts, emails, Facebook postings, and phone calls giving us affirmation of your love for Nancy and the rest of us. We are surrounded with family members and friends and have encouraged Nancy to take God's rest. We will post more information as we have opportunity.

Even in the shadow of death, because of Jesus, this story Is f-a-a-a-r from over!

P.S. I encourage you to pray especially for the Adams/Harrison families as they memorialize the nineteenth anniversary of the death of Nancy's Uncle Billy Harrison today.

• **Sunday, June 26, 2011**

DAY 165 Second Entry (175,446 Visits - 2,814 Posts)

The Story Is Far From Over!!! However, the earthly, central figure has gone to be with Jesus. Our family was gathered since early morning to observe the transition of Nancy's life into eternity. It has been a long and grueling day for us, the bystanders, but Nancy has fared rather well. During countless times of the day we sang numerous hymns of faith or other Christian songs.

She told the girls and me at 6:45 AM that she loved us and as far as I know, that was the last vocal communication Nancy shared with anyone. Twelve hours later we found ourselves closely holding our breath as we were watching her draw hers. At 7:00 PM or very nearly so, she drew her last breath and entered into eternity to the presence of the Lord based upon the promises of His Word. There were probably forty family members present as we shed tears, hugs, and grief. Then we circled Nancy as we held hands and offered prayers of thanksgiving for the answered prayers of allowing God's mercy take Nancy from us in a peaceful and graceful manner.

God's goodness is everlasting and we are finding strength through the peace that passes understanding. Naturally, we are grieving. The ladies are preparing her body for removal even as I type this journal. While I don't have full disclosure on the arrangements, I will tell you this much. Nancy's body will be at the Whitlock Mortuary in Toccoa, Georgia. Her funeral will be held in Martin, Georgia at Tom's Creek Baptist Church. Times and dates are yet to be determined.

You have continued to shower us with the reflection of God's love through your caring and generous ways. While we can never repay fully the kindness shown, we will continue to remember what you have done. Because of Jesus, this story *remains* far from over! Stay tuned to see what God chooses to do through the lives who meant the most to Nancy.

P.S. I am Bill, not Josh Moore. The CaringBridge website changed some templates and we have not changed our log-in information.

- **Monday, June 27, 2011**

The family wishes to share the visitation and funeral arrangements for Nancy. Whitlock Mortuary in Toccoa, Georgia is in charge of the arrangements. Their address can be found below.

Whitlock Mortuary, Inc.
120 Rose Lane
Toccoa, Georgia 30577
706.886.9411

The family will receive friends at the mortuary from 2:00–4:00 PM and 6:00–9:00 PM Tuesday (6/28/2011) afternoon and evening. Funeral services will be held at four o'clock Wednesday (6/29/2011) from Tom's Creek Baptist Church with the Rev. Bill Stacey officiating. Burial will follow in the Tom's Creek Baptist Church Cemetery. The address for the church can be found below.

Tom's Creek Baptist Church
3604 Georgia 145
Martin, GA 30557

July – June
2011 – 2012

• Sunday, July 3, 2011

Isn't it interesting how a week can seem like a lifetime? In reflection, it has been a week of decisions and adjustments. I have an idea that the upcoming week will continue the trend. Most of the CaringBridge readers are aware that my sweet Nancy has died.

It truly is a surreal feeling to hear one's spouse's name and obituary on the radio. It is odd to pick up the local newspaper and read about her life printed in only a few lines of ink. Certainly, it happens every day of the week, every week of the month, and every month of the year again and again. How was this week different?

It was different this week because of the personal relationship we each had with Nancy. It was obvious to me after having stood by her during visitation Tuesday at how she had influenced so many. When has anyone in our area had a continuous line of guests flowing by for ten hours? That, in and of itself, was a great tribute to Nancy and the impact she has had upon others. The family and I wanted to make her send-off as special and as memorable as possible. The only way for it to have been complete was for the community to attend and experience it with us. If one can have a "good" experience at a funeral, I felt the opportunity provided had ensured one.

Now the odd adjustments ensue. Nancy and I have told each other we loved each other numerous times throughout each day. As we have gotten older, and trips to the restroom during the night were required, there was always a warm embrace and a whispered, "I love you" when one of us returned to bed. Already, on two specific occasions, I have turned in search of a kiss and to tell Nancy where I was going, to realize my Nancy-fix is forever reduced to only a memory. For me, that is an odd and empty adjustment. By walking through the living room and dodging all the Peace Lilies and other beautiful plants sent to us, I am reminded of those special trips to the Opryland Hotel for our romantic getaways that now are reduced to memories. Throughout our marriage, we have done goofy stuff to keep our relationship fresh and not one taken for granted. Since we were married on the second day of the month of September, each month on the "second" Nancy and I would compete to see who could say, "Happy Anniversary" to the other first. Now remember, Nancy was extremely competitive, so we would have to keep score by writing it on the calendar and by October it was usually determined that Nancy had won again. Yesterday, I went to bed in the early hours of July second wishing I could tell her, "Happy Anniversary." Yes, there are many odd and empty adjustments in which I am making.

Today, (Sunday) is the date on which Nancy was born. She was one week shy of her fifty-fourth birthday when she died. There is a birthday party planned, but it is for our grandson Elliott because God sent him to us on Nancy's fiftieth birthday. It has been a pleasure to know Nancy for these last thirty-five years and to have her as the center of my affection. I have been embraced and held up through the love of her family. I am determined to get through these ongoing odd and empty adjustments.

Indian Creek Baptist Church is truly phenomenal in their care for us. I have spoken with the leadership and asked for a few more weeks to get through some of the adjustments and get my head back in order for ministry. Sometimes one needs ministering before he can minister. I am currently in that mode. I continue to welcome your calls, texts, emails, and so forth, and know that with God's help I will continue in a God-honoring way. I plan to write from time-to-time either in CaringBridge or a website yet to be announced in order to stay in touch with those of you who have embraced us during these days of trial.

At the funeral Wednesday I forgot to make the statement, so I will remind you now … This story is far from over!

• **Sunday, July 10, 2011**

Two weeks ago today, Nancy died. I am adjusting, or at least trying to make the adjustment from becoming "One Flesh" on Saturday, September 2, 1978 to simply living without a part of me. I had my gallbladder removed in March of 1997. There was a part of me removed. It had become unresponsive and useless, causing me discomfort and pain. The doctor properly diagnosed the situation and scheduled a date for me to have it removed. There was initial pain the first couple of days after the surgery, but after a couple of weeks I was back to normal. Now, there is another part of me that has been removed. Obviously, it is not a major organ of my body. I am able to eat, sleep, and move through life as any other person my age, but something is missing. It is difficult to explain the mystery of God and His putting couples together. I truly believe God gave me Nancy, and our relationship was a healthy, loving, and caring one in which we enjoyed each other's presence. I wanted to come home at the end of the day. I looked forward to her return when she had been somewhere for a few hours. We knew the other was waiting with a kiss and embrace when we got to our home. I don't want this to sound sloppy or ridiculous, but we needed and wanted each other. We depended upon that love to get us through the rough edges of life, and we thanked the Lord audibly and often, together, for making us one.

What does it mean to become one? As I reflect upon that question, I look back to our premarital days and remember thinking that becoming one had to do with the physical act of consummating our relationship once we were married. I have learned since then, that becoming one is much more than a physical encounter. In fact, there are many who abuse the privilege of something very beautiful and special with only the physical rendezvous. There is never a lasting connection or a meaningful relationship when God has not sanctioned and blessed the joining of two-becoming-one.

No, Nancy and I became one in more ways. We became one in our love but we became one in our work. I supported her teaching skills and abilities while she supported me in logging, textiles, and ministry. We did not always need the smallest of details to know and support the occupation of the other. Sometimes we needed all the details to best know about the other. We became one in our family. When Ashley, our first child, was born, Nancy and I became closer and one in our relationship. Our responsibilities began to change and our love drew us closer together in the support to the other as we became parents. Jessica's and Andrea's births simply cemented those feelings, emotions, and responsibilities even more. We became one in our worship. Nancy and I had an equal desire to attend worship services together. I loved the privilege of driving the family to our church. Even when the girls were old enough to drive themselves, I enjoyed the oneness of going to church as a family. We had no problem knowing where we would be on a given Sunday. We did not have a problem debating or scheduling our calendar when it came to Sundays. Nancy and I were one in our understanding of ministry, and though we had different roles, we supported the other and because of that support we became closer together and one.

While I have studied and read about becoming one, I now am trying to learn about the coming apart as one. I am sitting on the shores of Daytona Beach watching the sunrise. This is one of Nancy's favorite places in the world. She loved the beach and the whole experience of getting things together and going to Florida each year to spend time relaxing. She was patient with me in knowing I would rather play golf than bake in the sun. She loved me and would always have my beach chair and umbrella set up so that when I finally came out of the room and down to the beach my place was ready. I was patient with her in allowing her to spend as much time as she desired at the beach each day. Often, she would play golf with me in the morning and then spend the afternoon at the beach. Most of the time we would be the last of our extended family to leave the shores and breaking waves to make our way back to our room.

This year was different as I packed the car. I only needed to include one beach chair and one set of golf clubs. I am with the extended family and Jessica has joined me for a few days. I miss Nancy and the part of me that made us one. Certainly, Jesus was truthful as John recorded His promise of sending the Comforter — the Holy Spirit. This adjustment is so new that I am numb to Nancy's passing. It still does not yet seem real. I am trying to get my mind adjusted to knowing that a part of me is no longer one with me. I will forever carry her memories. I even brought her picture with me, but it is still not her. It is neither her tender touch nor her hilarious humor. It is not her careful attention to detail in caring for the needs and inventories of spending time at the beach. Yet, I am comfortable in knowing I will get through this chapter in my life. I am confident in knowing God's promises are true and I have experienced first-hand His comfort during these last days.

Many of you have shared concerns and prayers for my well-being. I have answered several text messages or responded to the FaceBook postings and I have been honest with each of you. Today,

I am doing okay. I am living in the "today" every day and trying to make the adjustments for that particular day. I have learned a great deal about reaching, looking, or listening for Nancy only to realize she is gone from my presence. Yet, I see her through our daughters or other family members. I chuckle at the stories others continue to share in fond memory of a certain time Nancy did a certain thing. While I am aware the best part of me is gone, I recognize her ongoing influence which continues revealing her to me and the memories for which I will always have.

Yes, Nancy is gone. I am coming to grips with the reality and yet I know this story is far from over!

• Wednesday, July 20, 2011

I am back at home with a head full of reflections. The time at the beach without Nancy was, well, weird. Oh, I had a good time, and the family was helpful in keeping me involved with golf and the dinner schedule. I even had the privilege to do some fishing in the Atlantic, boating and alligator watching on the St. Johns River, and shrimping in the Halifax River. I especially enjoyed the shrimping because it was a totally new experience and we caught some pretty nice ones. Of course being one of the "swamp people" for an afternoon while scoping out the gators ranked close to the top. Mike and Ruth Moore, along with their daughter, Laurel, hosted Jessica and me for the boat stuff. We visited their church last Sunday (July 10) too.

I was fine as long as I was busy and had my mind occupied. During one afternoon of relaxation, I watched the forty-year old Paul Newman classic, "Cool Hand Luke." Ole small-town Lucas Jackson had been bored to the point of drinking, and then whacking the tops of the parking meters to steal the change. That act of boredom won him the privilege of spending two years in a Florida work camp. It was after his second unsuccessful run from the law, that the Captain of the camp explained to Luke he was going to have to get his mind right. I began to think about what it meant to get one's mind right.

I did a little word search to find some of the scripture passages which speak to getting one's mind right. (The previous paragraphs were written Saturday, July 16.)

Psalm 26:2 Test me, Lord, and try me; examine my heart and mind.

Proverbs 23:19 Listen, my son, and be wise; keep your mind on the right course.

Matthew 22:37-38

He said to him, "Love the Lord your God with all your heart, with all your soul, and with *all your mind*. This is the greatest and most important commandment. (from Holman Christian Standard Bible® Copyright © 1999, 2000, 2002, 2003, 2005 by Holman Bible Publishers.)

I used these scripture passages and more to preach a message last Sunday (July 17) on getting one's mind right with God. The Bible tells us to have the mind of Christ and in order for that to happen; we must rely on the conviction of the Holy Spirit. He must conduct our thoughts and supply the strength and power to establish the priority for our life. We must consign our control and trust to Him and the Apostle Paul reminded us in Romans 11:33 thru 12:1-2 not to be trapped by the world's thinking. Who can know God's thoughts unless He reveals them to us through the Holy Spirit?

I recognize there is a constant battle for our minds. Ephesians 6:12 identifies our true enemy. Paul challenges us to be strong and stand firm. The only way we will accomplish our standing is through God's strength to each of us as believers. It is redundant to say these last six months and especially these last three weeks have been challenging. But I am resolved to stand.

Three weeks ago this afternoon a large number of family and friends gathered at Tom's Creek Baptist Church to memorialize Nancy's life. I sensed the presence of the Holy Spirit from the time I got out of the mortuary's family car. When I walked into the sanctuary with *Great is Thy Faithfulness* played on the trumpet and piano, I praised the Lord for His faithfulness to my family. The bagpiper ended our gathering at the graveside with an *Amazing Grace* walk-off. Truly, God's grace sustains us from day-to-day, and when we let Him, God showers us with His love. So true are the words Karen sang, "*My God Will Always Be Enough.*"

Thirty-three years ago today, Barry Burrell, of Vintage Mobile Homes in Cornelia, Georgia delivered our first home. It was fully furnished and we thought we were living in heaven. Nancy and I lived in that home for four and a half years before purchasing the land and house in which I continue to live. Brian and Fonda (Gibbs) Hume bought our mobile home when we were through needing it. My, how those days have flown past. I am excited to see what the next thirty-three years have yet in store. Ha! Ha! Some of you think ole' Bill is being presumptuous to live that long. Well, either I will or I won't, but I'll be in heaven if I don't.

Today, I reviewed the final proof for a full-page tribute of Nancy. The Stephens, Franklin, and Hart County newspapers are publishing it for this week's edition. In it is a genuine thank you to everyone that has loved on us these last six or seven months. There are several pictures of Nancy … just being Nancy. I have said it before and will continue to say, "This story is far from over!"

• Monday, August 1, 2011

Two questions get directed to me often lately. The first question is, "How are you doing?"

Last week went pretty well. I went to a funeral and was greeted by several friends each asking me how I was doing and sharing genuine concern for me and the family. It was very nice of them to share their warm greetings with me. However, for some unexplained reason, I became more and more uncomfortable as the service progressed. I do not know why I felt the way I did, but as soon as the benediction was pronounced, I excused myself and bolted for the door. I have never felt that way before or since. I had been to a funeral two weeks ago without any uncomfortable feelings with the exception of sadness or sympathy for the bereaved family.

The rest of the week went remarkably well. Wednesday evening I was invited to preach a revival service at the Middle River Baptist

Church in Carnesville. There was a great spirit within the church, and I felt the freedom to preach God's Word boldly. The visible result was observing several people make decisions of recommitment to their relationship with Jesus Christ. The pastor reported to me Thursday that a young married man came to him after the service and prayed to receive Jesus. Praise the Lord!

Thursday Jay, Ben, and Daniel invited me to play golf and even paid for my game. It was kind of them to share their time and resources with me. I returned the favor by not beating either of them on the scorecard. I teasingly told Jay that with a score like mine, I had a pretty good defense proving I was not spending "too" much time on the golf course.

Thursday afternoon I contacted a book publisher and sent them a wad of money in order to publish the CaringBridge journal. What that means is now I need to get to work and fine-tune some of the entries and get them sent off soon so the book will be available for Christmas presents. In fact, I don't mind saying you could even pray about that with me.

Thursday evening was even better. Sometime around 10:15 PM, my six-year old granddaughter, Ashtin called me on the telephone. She reported that during the family devotions and prayer time, she prayed to ask Jesus into her heart. Wow! I was so happy for her and so thankful for my godly children and sons-in-law. They continue to model what they observed in our home and the benefits are eternal. I had to laugh when Ashley called me Friday and told me while she was taking the children to day-care that Ashtin said, "Mom? Elliott (her four-year old brother) is not saved yet is he? We need to pray for him don't we?" Ha! If only all of us as adults could be as passionate for lost people as six-year-old converts.

Friday morning I met Danny and we rode to Murrells Inlet, South Carolina for a Booth Brothers concert. It was therapeutic to share a meal with them, meet new people, and hear some of the best talent Southern Gospel music has to offer. Thanks guys.

Saturday morning I got home around 5:30 AM from the above mentioned concert and slept a couple of hours. Jessica and I went to Nancy's parents' house for lunch. It's hard to beat any kind of meal with fresh fried okra, tomatoes, green beans, and cornbread. We enjoyed our visit and got caught up on some of the family news.

Sunday I was able to preach during the morning service. It was the first time since Nancy's illness that I made it to Sunday School. After the service, the church hosted a one-year anniversary meal for our associate pastor and his family. Nate, Heather, and their children have been such a blessing not only to our church but to our community.

Earlier in the week I resumed a health care program that I was already several weeks into when Nancy got sick. I don't have any stirring results to share but I am working on getting myself into a healthier state of being. You may want to add that to the pray list too. Ha!

Today, I awoke to a broken air conditioner unit. It was a quick fix, and after replacing a switch it started working correctly. I had a ministerial meeting with a local pastor, and I have been on the phone with several other people going through challenges of life.

I guess one could answer the above question number one by saying, "Ole' Bill seems to be doing pretty good with all things considered." I miss Nancy tremendously and have continued to adjust to her absence. It has been five weeks already and there are moments that it seems like five years.

The second question that is directed to me often is, "Has Jessica and Josh set a wedding date yet?" No, not yet. I don't know when it will happen, but I am confident that in time, you will know, and we will welcome you to the celebration of their marriage.

In the meantime, this story is far from over!

- **Friday, August 12, 2011**

Just a few thoughts from a seasoned soldier ...

Onward, Christian Soldiers is an old standard among hymns of the Christian faith. In fact, it was composed as a processional for children. While one does not normally think of children as being soldiers, as believers, we are in reality God's children, and according to the Apostle Paul, we are engaged in spiritual warfare. The second stanza reads:

"At the sign of triumph Satan's host doth flee; On, then, Christian soldiers, on to victory! Hell's foundations quiver at the shout of praise; Christians lift your voices, loud your anthems raise!"

Through my experience, I have noticed that as I praise the Lord, the emptiness of my situation subsides. It seems as though when I genuinely give God the glory for all the things He continues doing, my life becomes more bearable. I live with the reality that the love of my life in this world has gone to her heavenly reward, but the more I praise the Lord, the sting of that reality seems easier. The battle I face then, is will I praise the Lord or settle to live in despair? I am praising the Lord. He provides hope during days of lonesome futility. He provides the strength as I continue ministering in the hallways of a hospital or sharing grief with families in their bewilderment. Yes, it is a battle sometimes, but our victory is in Jesus. I am committed to live it as well as preach it.

2 Timothy 2:1-4

You, therefore, my child, be strong in the grace that is in Christ Jesus. And what you have heard from me in the presence of many witnesses, commit to faithful men who will be able to teach others also.

Share in suffering as a good soldier of Christ Jesus. To please the recruiter, no one serving as a soldier gets entangled in the concerns of everyday life.

(from Holman Christian Standard Bible® Copyright © 1999, 2000, 2002, 2003, 2005 by Holman Bible Publishers.)

The last ten or twelve days since the last journal posting have been interesting. The adjusting to Nancy's passing continues as the "small things" are examined and dealt with as though they were "big things." Yet, life as we knew it and know it goes on. Last Wednesday (August 3), I was asked to preach a funeral for a total stranger. My connection was through one of our church members, but I knew no one else. The fifty-six-year old lady went to bed Sunday evening, telling her husband she would call the doctor the next morning due to her feeling poorly. She never woke up. I was able to encourage the husband in a way, that previous to our recent situation, I was unable. Praise the Lord!

People continue asking how I'm doing. I have recognized the question as one of concern and desire to check on my inner peace. I responded to one such text with transparency. I'm doing well—I believe genuinely well. However, Nancy and I were constantly interacting throughout every day. I don't know how many times during the course of a day we told each other, "I love you." It was not a passing phrase, but it was a genuine statement of our love for the other. We also playfully interacted in physical ways. We constantly were poking, thumping, tickling, or teasing the other. While I sit here at my desk, I reflect on the numerous times Nancy would pass by while putting clothes away or doing other chores and she would thump my ear or poke my ribs playfully. I miss not being able to playfully sneak up on her while she was preparing a meal or doing another household task. I am well. I sleep well. I eat well. I'm interested in grooming and not embarrassing the family with poor fashion choices. Ha! Ha! But I still miss my Nancy-fixes.

Last Friday (8/5), I diligently sat down to do some rewrites and additions to the CaringBridge journal in preparation for publication. I got trapped into reading the story and re-living some of the moments of those days. After three hours, I got up from the desk without having written a word. The publisher needs it soon to stay on our projected schedule. Some of it is still a little too fresh or raw with which to deal. You may pray that I will stay on schedule and process the work in a therapeutic way. My desire is that I can produce it in a ministry or healing format for others going through family crisis. I would appreciate your prayers for its completion.

Wednesday (August 10), I stopped by Tom's Creek Baptist to pick up the edited audio version of Nancy's memorial service. It is a two-disk CD set, and I popped the first one in as I was driving to the Stephens County Hospital for a visit with one of our church members. I soon found myself driving down Broad Street with tears pouring from my eyes. They were not all tears of sorrow, but many were tears of affirmation. It has been six weeks since her funeral, but I found that listening to the comments from the speakers and relishing in the memory of the Holy Spirit's presence was rewarding. The singing was electrifying, and the words from those songs have found a resting place within my heart. I could never ask Nancy to come back knowing what she went through and what she is now experiencing. I am praising the Lord that His Word is truth and the promises are real.

God has placed upon some of you nudges to send a card of encouragement or phone calls of concern or invitations to meals. They have come in timely fashion and have ministered to my heart. Thank you for thinking of me and the rest of the family. I know you are a part of God's Kingdom and are simply being faithful to His leading. Some of you are also going through difficult times within your own life. The last stanza of "Onward, Christian Soldiers" reads:

"Onward, then, ye people, join our happy throng; Blend with ours your voices in the triumph song. Glory, laud, and honor unto Christ, the King; This through countless ages men and angels sing. Onward, Christian soldiers, marching as to war, with the Cross of Jesus going on before."

Yes, it continues being true. Because of Jesus, "this story is far from over!"

• **Monday, August 22, 2011**

Today begins another school year for the students of Stephens County School system. While it's true Nancy was counting the days for retirement, it is equally true she wanted to work a couple of more years. The faculty and staff at Big A Elementary embraced Nancy when she was having to make the difficult career adjustment of moving to the elementary school after having spent twenty-three years teaching and coaching the middle school ages. It was not her choice, and I vividly remember her phone call to inform me what the superintendent required of her. I remember our conversations after that first year adjustment, and how she had endured, but was determined to make the best of her situation. She fell in love with the school and gave it her best effort. Those last seven years have flown by.

Now, I sit here working on a journal entry in the reflection of the last seven weeks. Life provides a classroom in which to learn. Some of the subjects are easier in which to make a passing grade than others, but the experiences learned are seldom forgotten and they carry with them the knowledge required for the next level of understanding. I have discovered a new-found respect for my peers in the classroom who have taken the same course study on loss-of-spouse adjustments. As I choose to use Jesus for my instructor, I observe how He illuminates the situation and drives out the shadows of gloom and despair. I am most blest to read His Word as the curriculum and follow the guidelines He has placed before me.

On to lighter fare: I have almost completed the preliminary procrastination section of the book. There are more than a few reasons for that section. Mostly, I have been busy catching up on church-related tasks and have not prioritized my time allotment. That issue continues being a good prayer request if you have run out of things for which to pray. Ha! Ha! The girls and their families seem to be doing well. We got together for a meal and sleepover Friday night. Saturday, we tried to narrow down the details for ordering a headstone. Yesterday, (Sunday) we enjoyed two good services at church. I am looking forward to a radio interview, a guest preaching assignment, an upcoming mission trip to Haiti, followed by our church revival. Other than those items, I sit and twiddle my thumbs while watching the grass grow. Ha! Ha!

Finally, let me address the educators of the community. I hope you have an enjoyable teaching year, and that you will not forget the impact and influence your presence has upon our children and youth. Thanks for the great job you do and to quote Nancy, "After 3:00 PM today, we will only have one hundred and seventy-nine more days before summer."

Enjoy the year and remember, this story is far from over!

• **Saturday, September 10, 2011**

I spent the morning reading scripture about biblical characters living in marriage relationships. I would concede the story of Abraham and Sarah is a love story. While they had some rough patches within their relationship due to poor choices, it is evident they truly loved each other. The entire chapter of Genesis 23 is dedicated to the mourning and burial preparations Abraham secured for his lovely wife. The first sentence of chapter 24 makes me a little nervous. It says, "Abraham was now getting old ..." Ha! Ha! The rest of the verse is so important. It says, "The Lord had blessed him in everything."

As I reflected on these last thirty-five years today, it is so very obvious that the Lord has truly blessed me. I thought about how Nancy and I threw caution (and old wives tales) to the wind as we broke tradition. We were standing shoulder to shoulder on the morning of our wedding day while we were helping prepare food for the reception. I distinctly remember spooning out melon balls. I don't remember what she was doing, but we were following the direction of her Aunt Annie Jim, mother, and others. I never looked back. Nancy stood shoulder to shoulder with me through the next thirty-three years.

Like Abraham, there have been times of mourning. I have discovered the closer I move my relationship to Jesus, the easier I can endure the pain of her passing. The problem for me is in keeping the clouds of discouragement and loneliness at bay. If I let my guard down for (it seems) even a minute, I am smothered and stifled without her. I have been running on our elliptical machine. While I am probably not as competitive as Nancy, I race against the clock, the number of calories burned, and distance. The other day I decided I was actually running from loneliness. The running has kept me exercising and a healthier body is obviously a healthier me in every aspect. The girls have been helping with household chores, filing insurance claims, picking the right headstone, and managing their own personal responsibilities.

Yes, it has been nine weeks and in most school systems a report card would soon follow. If I were to evaluate these last nine weeks, I would like to think I was adjusting well within reason, having gone through the last seven months. I have purposefully kept a busy calendar but I have also had some down days that were difficult to even get going. The Lord has blessed the ministry in spite of the preacher, and we have had the enjoyment of salvations and baptisms. The church has done well in maintaining form and function without me, and instead of feeling insecure, I am elated that people picked up responsibilities during a serious time of the church calendar year. Nate has done well coordinating nominating meetings and so forth.

The above portion was written a week ago on September 2. Now, it's Saturday, September 10. It has been a stifling week in many ways. I remind our church family of Paul's writing to the Ephesians 6:10-ff. He says to Be Strong in the Lord. He also reminds us who the enemy of life and happiness is in reality. *It's not flesh and blood, but against the rulers, against the powers, against the world forces of this darkness, against the spiritual forces of wickedness in the heavenly places. Therefore take up the full armor of God, that you may be able to resist in the evil day, and having done everything, to stand firm.*

This week started with two baptisms, a moving of the Holy Spirit during the Sunday morning service, and another person receiving Christ at the close of the service. It was after a huge family gathering at Nancy's parents' house that I went to Ashley and Dustin's church for the privilege of baptizing Ashtin and then preaching freely and boldly there. Wednesday morning Marlene and I went to the Athens Regional Hospital Guest House Foundation meeting. The coordinators were hosting a reception of perspective financial donors and invited me to share a report of how the guest house benefited my family during the crisis and long-term stay of Nancy's illness. I was honored to report how their services were instrumental in allowing us to spend more time with Nancy. Wednesday evening during the prayer service and AWANA club, three more people prayed to receive Jesus. I truly believe the devil knows that I am involved and traveling with a group of men from the Georgia Baptist Disaster Relief today, and he has done all the discouraging things he could think of to keep me from going. With all the good things going on at church, and the mission trip to Haiti, along with our workers with the Hispanic ministry and Child Evangelism, I don't think he likes what is taking place.

Let me share a few examples... For over two weeks I have tried to get my health insurance reinstated due to an error in the state health office. Supposedly, I got clearance of continued coverage just before five o'clock yesterday (Friday). There has been a series of events that have happened here at the house. Thursday Marlene called me while I was visiting Nancy's aunt who is recovering from a broken hip, to inform me we had been infested with ants. They seemed to come in from everywhere all at once. The floor in the utility room was wet due to a malfunctioning water drain. Then, the main-line water filter needed changing due to limited water flow. Later, I went to use the lawn mower only to find it had a dead battery. I finally got it started and cut the grass so the neighbors didn't think we had moved away. When I got to the edge of the yard, I noticed the mailbox pole was broken and it was lying in the ditch. I guess I forgot to mention the air conditioning unit that was stolen from the church or the melanoma spot on my chest that had been removed two weeks ago of which I just learned the results. I can promise you, I haven't lost a wink of sleep due to that because the doctor said it was completely extracted.

In the midst of all those things, I heard some challenging messages at the Tugalo Baptist Evangelism conference, and they helped prepare my heart to preach in Haiti this Sunday. Pray the Lord uses me to share His Word with impact and for life change. I just led Indian Creek through a series of messages committing to be "All-In" for Jesus. There were some forty names turned in at the altar of people needing salvation in our community. Our revival will begin Sunday, September 18, with the preachers and choirs from New Hope, Middle River, Tate's Creek, and Eastanollee Baptist Churches sharing through the Word and song. Pray with me that those forty people will come to church and hear what God can do for them through salvation.

Admittedly, I haven't sat still long enough to dwell on Nancy's passing. I miss her so much. My trip to Gatlinburg last week to reflect on what would have been our anniversary was special. I spent many hours thinking, praying, and reading God's Word. He continues to comfort me, but I miss the humor, wisdom, love, and affirmation that Nancy shared with me on a daily basis. I have sat to write a CaringBridge journal for several days, but I can't seem to have the words to write in order to best express the feelings of my heart. I realized this week that while Nancy was living, the CaringBridge was largely about her. It obviously is not a news flash that she is gone, but now I notice the CaringBridge journals are more about me and my feelings. I am not comfortable writing about my feelings without Nancy. She has been my inspiration and my passion was sharing my love with her.

Well, I have finished packing for the trip, and now at 4:15 AM it is time to wind this journal post to a close. I want to personally thank those of you who have continued to reach out to me and the family. When you write those notes of care and thoughtfulness on CaringBridge, others receive benefit from your kindness as well. I have witnessed the effect your responses continue to have on others. I have also received some personal cards this week that came to me in a timely way. The words of encouragement accomplished the intention of you who sent them. God's Word says to stand firm. I am able to continue standing and fighting with Him and for Him because of the Holy Spirit's enabling, but also because of the shoulders I have leaned upon. I have bent several ears during these last weeks, and I continue to covet your prayers. Thank you for "listening" one more time.

You can be assured that I will continue writing because this story is far from over!

• **Friday, September 23, 2011**

I came into my room in order to read around 9:00 PM this evening. Well, actually, now that it is past 5:00 AM, I guess it was yesterday (Thursday) evening. Sometimes I like to listen to music or even preaching while I am studying. Tonight was no different. I selected Nancy's funeral service because I knew it had both music and preaching. I soon found tears streaming down my cheeks in reflection of such a beautiful life memorialized in such a special way. The remarks made by her peers continue being informative, humorous, and touching reminders of that "one-flesh" which was/ is a huge part of me. Now, twelve weeks later, I find myself in the midst of an all-nighter for no apparent reason. During college days the all-nighters were necessary for those procrastinated term papers and last minute attempts for bettering test scores. It is while neither the required assignments, nor test-cramming, that I must admit the intentioned reading surrendered with flashes of cherished memories charging through my mind as some of the stories of Nancy were revisited. When the recording of her service finished, I flipped on some praise and worship music and continued the reading. I was plowing through some pages of CaringBridge. No, this time they were not from our story, but rather from another guy going through difficult and random feelings. His name was David. His CaringBridge is recorded within the Psalms and I chose to read those journals starting with chapter fifty-one and continued through chapter seventy. In those journal entries are the emotions of David and the moving of God as he admits "impropriety" (society does not like to call it SIN) with Bathsheba and fear of Saul. Much of it is in recognition of his own weakness and total dependence upon God as he stays a step ahead of his adversaries.

I rediscovered the treasure of a well-worn Bible as I poured over David's journals and God's Word. I could not help noticing the highlighted and underlined areas I had previously visited in sermon preparation or simply seeking comfort of my own. At some point, in two of the three Bibles being studied, I previously highlighted Psalm 55:22 *"Cast your burden on the Lord, and He will support you; He will never allow the righteous to be shaken."* Psalm 62:2; 5-8 echoes the same promise. *"He alone is my rock and my salvation, my stronghold; I will never be shaken ... Rest in God alone, my soul, for my hope comes from Him. He alone is my rock and my salvation, my stronghold; I will not be shaken. My salvation and glory depend on God; my strong rock, my refuge, is in God. Trust in Him at all times, you people; pour out your hearts before him. God is our refuge."* I am confident that if David found comfort in his trust and hunger for God, I can find the same comfort. My adversaries have not been in people, but rather in the face of loneliness and discouragement. Let me explain.

I left the church on a tremendous high back on September 4. We were able to baptize two people, preach a bold message of how Jesus was "All-in" while fulfilling prophecy by coming to earth to provide us with salvation through his shed blood, and then we enjoyed a special communion service. It concluded with another individual realizing a need for a savior and then praying to invite Jesus into a life-fulfilling relationship. I received several texts sharing how people valued the worship service in such a meaningful way. That evening at Bethany Baptist Church, I had freedom to preach a message of discipleship along with the distinct privilege of baptizing my granddaughter, Ashtin. The following Saturday I boarded a plane with eleven strangers that God obviously put together in order to accomplish a mission assignment at the epicenter of the earthquake in Haiti. I fell in love with the team members as I preached God's Word, worked with nearly one hundred youth and children in Bible school, and helped do light construction in two church sanctuaries. The heat and humidity was nearly unbearable without any air conditioning, and there was only a thimble-full of water with which to shower. The result was in seeing over twenty people accept Jesus and making friends with other brothers and sisters in Christ as we continue building His kingdom. Third-world mission trips tend to sap the spiritual, physical, and emotional strength out of most people, and I was no different. When our plane touched down on Georgia soil Saturday evening, I knew I had a Gideon speaker scheduled for Sunday morning followed by four pastors and their choirs to lead our services in revival through Wednesday night. My discouragement surfaced with a lack of attendance from those people who had previously pledged being "All-in" with their renewed commitment to reach our community of unsaved family members and coworkers. My burden for the lost enlarged during the invitation Sunday evening. The devil seems to know when we are weak, and he tends to pile on other stuff to capture our attention and get our focus off of Jesus. In my case, on Monday, he used a newspaper article from the Georgia Baptist Convention's Christian Index informing me of the tragic death of my friend Max New. Max was killed when a hit and run driver struck his motor scooter. To further the sorrow, Max's forty-year old daughter died unexpectedly in December with a blood clot. I called his wife to share my sympathies and tell her of Nancy's passing. My burden continued growing during the invitation Monday evening of the revival. Tuesday I spent much of the day re-reading the CaringBridge posts that people sent to our family. I found a great source of strength in being reminded of the prayers, scriptures, and songs with which people encouraged us. My pastor friends were calling me to offer words of encouragement. During the singing Tuesday I remember getting a release from the personal part of my burden while the choir was passionately singing, "*How Great Is Our God.*" My eyes began physically watering with tears, but spiritually refocusing on Jesus. Thank you, Lord, for your tender touches when we need your refilling and refreshing of your Holy Spirit. Wednesday I attended a funeral of an elderly woman who had prayed for her son for years that he might receive Jesus. Her prayers were answered about five years ago when I was able to lead him to Christ and baptize him. I found both comfort and challenge in each of the messages during revival. The music each night was uplifting and worshipful.

I love what I do. The ministry is not for the faint of heart in dealing with the heartaches of individuals' poor choices, broken relationships, or financial ruin. But it is a joy to counsel the recently engaged as they prepare for marriage. It is a thrill leading people to Jesus regardless of their ages. And it is rewarding in being a shoulder in which to lean upon during grief. I do not always love what is required, but I love what God has called me to do. Nancy was a major part of the support network that helped keep me focused. I miss her playful teasing, her willing servant's heart, and the wisdom which balanced my thoughts. The handfuls of cards have understandably trickled to a few each week, but it seems God knows when I need one. A couple of weeks ago Nancy and Tommy sent a word of encouragement at the right time. Today I opened a letter from one who lost a spouse ten years ago. Again, it was at the right time and I appreciate people being sensitive and acting on their notions. Your responses to CaringBridge are treasures in and of themselves. I value each of them and pray God's blessing on you for sharing time with us.

It's true; this story is far from over!

• **Monday, October 3, 2011**

A year ago today, (Saturday) the Atlanta Braves lost to the Philadelphia Phillies by the score of 11 to 5. It was the last home series of the 2010 season, and the Bobby Cox era was drawing to a close. Nancy and I had decided about six weeks earlier to get tickets and take her mom and dad to the game as well. It was the first time her mother had ever been to a professional baseball game, and she is an avid Braves fan. Oddly enough, it would be the last time Nancy would see a pro game. It was an early birthday present for her mom and for good measure we made sure to pose for the "professional" picture with the ball field as the backdrop so Nancy and I could present it as an extra Christmas gift. I stopped to visit Nancy's parents this evening and saw the picture. I had to pause for a minute and regain some composure. It is a precious memory of a seemingly carefree time.

The previous paragraph was written Saturday night just before I received a text message from the Franklin County Sheriff informing me of the building that was on fire at one of the neighboring churches. The New Bethel education and fellowship building was heavily damaged when I arrived shortly before 11:00 PM. I offered the pastor an option to relocate their daily preschool to our facilities approximately five miles away. It seems the main worship center is useable once it has been properly inspected.

Wow! It has been another interesting week. There was a mixture of ministerial challenges sprinkled with a handful of emotional feelings. Pre-Nancy's illness, visits to the infirmed was almost second nature to me. Now, the emotions are tender and require a bit more strength to hold them in check. I was blessed with the spiritual gift of mercy, and God allowed me the presence of mind and heart to minister in confidence. I am adjusting in order to regain that strength of ministry. There were a couple of days that seemed comfortable being reclusive and not greeting the public. Personal motivation was nearly nonexistent. For those of you that know me personally, I usually thrive in the public setting. Now, not so much. I am adjusting and purposefully scheduling dates which require my attendance and interaction with peers, friends, and family. Towards the end of the week I was studying the book of Ecclesiastes and rediscovered a passage which I suppose addresses loneliness. Chapter 4:9-12 *Two are better than one because they have a good reward for their efforts. For if either falls, his companion can lift him up; but pity the one who falls without another to lift him up. Also, if two lie down together, they can keep warm; but how can one person alone keep warm? And if somebody overpowers one person, two can resist him. A cord of three strands is not easily broken.*

It was while I was studying those verses, that one commentary reminded me that loneliness is a choice. Moments of being alone may not be a choice, but lingering in the house of loneliness is. God has given us His Son, His Word, and His people—all of which are antidotes for loneliness. Throughout the Bible, scripture shares examples of individuals who felt alone at times. In the last journal entry I mentioned how David wrote concerning his loneliness. Elijah felt abandoned soon after the mountaintop experience of calling fire down from heaven. He wanted to die. Jonah felt alone too. Even Jesus Himself cried out, "My God, my God, why hast thou forsaken me?" He was carrying the weight of sin for the world and found it a lonely, lonely place. My point is not in misery loving company, but rather godly people are going to have challenges of loneliness in the midst of life. Understanding the issue helps me be hopeful that the current stage of grief will pass in time. I am looking forward to looking back one day and seeing how God delivered me from the quagmire I am currently plodding through. I am moving forward and adjusting.

The Lord blessed us with answered prayer yesterday, (Sunday) as we had prayed for the Holy Spirit's presence in our church services. One of the best ways to begin a service is with baptism. We had three. During the Praise and Prayer time, I introduced Cody. He is a soldier serving our country in Afghanistan, but has come home for a few days. Cody sporadically attended Indian Creek as a child without too much encouragement from his parents. On Friday he contacted me through FaceBook that he was waiting in Kuwait to board a plane for the fourteen-hour ride home. He came into our Sunday School class to quietly and humbly request prayers for his buddies and families. Earlier in the week some soldiers were on a routine patrol when an explosive device hit their transport vehicle. Three were killed instantly and two others were transferred to Germany in critical condition. Cody knew these men personally. One had just received word a week ago that he was a first-time father. While I am not a prophet, I am confident his wife will experience loneliness in the days ahead as she tries to wrap her mind around unexplainable grief.

Our Sunday evening service was equally touching as we heard testimony from two guests sharing what God has done through them in recent months. They were both totally unrelated and of different backgrounds, and yet, there was common ground that put them together for the evening. They both had temporarily died and then had been revived. One's death was due a serious heart condition, and the other was caused by an industrial accident. Their stories were gripping and they were shared with tearful humility as they praised the Lord for sparing them. Now they willingly tell others about the Lord and His goodness to them. It was quite a blessing.

Here I sit as the clock chimes in the background of my reflections. I have played various CDs during the early hours. It has been a cadre of Southern Gospel, Eighties Love Songs, Rascall Flatts, and the "Live In Paris" Diana Krall jazz. Yes, that is quite a diverse listening appetite. Nancy and I would hold hands while driving home from a date night, ministry visit, or just a quick trip to Wal-mart. We listened to a wide variety, but mostly just enjoyed our time together as we shared conversation of the day or the recent enlightenments from the wisdom of our grandchildren. Ha! Ha!

Your timely calls and notes on CaringBridge are far more rewarding than you might imagine. I have poured over each one while reading and re-reading of your interactions with Nancy or the struggles and joys of your life. I have unsuccessfully attempted on more than one occasion to finish the book, but for now, please know I am okay, and this story is far from over!

• **Saturday, October 15, 2011**

I have teased a friend with coining a phrase Nancy's mama has used over the years. It is used when one does not sleep, awakens for an extended period during the night, or simply stays up on purpose. When one does one of those, they are described as having the "big-eye." It was a phrase that we have used especially during the time Nancy's health required assistance with turning her body every two hours. Sometimes it was easier for me to stay up during my watch than it was to sleep with one eye open so as not to overlook her care. Nancy was always kind if one of us would miss a rotation, and on a few occasions she would request skipping a turn to let us all sleep. Well, tonight, or better defined as this early morning, I have had the big-eye. Sometimes I would rather stay up and read, listen to music, play a game on the computer, or a combination of all three. During the last twenty-four hours I have been doing a great deal of thinking through several reflections as well as formulating plans for future days.

It has been a good day in many ways for me, and yet, I am aware of several circumstances in which people have had to deal with a myriad of emotions today. I can think of one family that has waited with anxious anticipation for the clock to tick away from the required days and hours before the perspective child they have adopted finally becomes official. I can only imagine the emotions of the biological family that chose to share their child in adoption due to diminished resources and other circumstances. It is tremendously rewarding to realize they chose life for the child and elation for the welcoming family instead of abortion. In an unrelated situation, my heart is broken for the family of a seven-year old son who died suddenly after a very brief, three-day illness. The ripple effect from the stone being dropped into the proverbial pond reaches beyond the sorrow of that family. Their situation has reminded many of us of the brevity of life itself. A fellow pastor shared his remorse in attempting to offer comfort while trying to help answer the "why" questions posed to him. A busload of professional counselors will never be aptly equipped to provide those answers. The school teachers, fellow students, and general community will share the sorrow but may never know why it happened.

Yes, it has been a good day for me in many ways, and yet, this week has been chock-full of heartaches from broken relationships, joblessness, or forced terminations, to terminal illness, and accidents that have robbed individuals of a certain quality of life that was previously enjoyed to its fullest. Let me share what it is that I have observed during these last, most recent hours.

Our lives constantly change. Many times circumstances beyond our control are the culprits that cause a decision that will inevitably bring change and adjustment. People often cannot help the circumstance in which they find themselves, and yet they can control the response with which the change or adjustment used affects the end result. A perfect example was shared with me this week. A woman was diagnosed with a cancer by her family doctor. She was immediately and understandably thrust into shock and bewilderment as she listened to the results, and then set up an appointment for a specialist to thoroughly examine her and prescribe a suitable treatment. Since she is a believer, she admitted her fears and asked a few of her closer friends to pray with her concerning the upcoming appointment. One friend noted the seemingly helpless feeling the woman was experiencing and challenged her about her faith. She asked, "Where's your faith?" That one, single question caused her to make a decision to fully trust the Lord regardless of the outcome. When the examination and determination of what needed to be done was completed, the specialist commented that she was handling the news remarkably well for what she was about to endure. Her response was that she would trust the Lord regardless of the outcome and faithfully believed God would see her through the problem. The woman said it was obvious the doctor was surprised at her response, but did not probe for more explanation until the follow up visit after the procedure was done. Some time passed, and it was then, after a successful procedure and testing that she was told she was cancer-free. It was also then, that the doctor broke down privately, and admitted he, too, was believed to have cancer. He told her he wanted her to pray for him because he was scared of the outcome with which he was facing, and he *knew* she was a woman of faith.

I do not imagine the doctor would have asked for her prayers if she had caved into helplessness. Yesterday (Friday) I was re-reading some CaringBridge journal postings and came across the one for March 8. Our niece and RN, Kendra, spent the day with us and shared the "Word of the Day." She was reading from the Internet and the word was "*puckish.*" Naturally, we inquired its meaning and learned it is being *impish or whimsical.* I teasingly texted Kendra and asked her what the "Word of the Day" was for Friday. Her reply was "*cosmogony.*" Its meaning is: *the creation or origin of the world or universe.* Hmm … I thought about that definition for a minute. I began to contemplate all the huge burdens with which people in my circle of influence were made to carry. In Galatians 6:1-10, the apostle Paul through the inspiration of the Holy Spirit admonishes us to help carry the burdens of our fellow believers. Some of you readers have done some heavy-lifting for our family these last ten months. Paul reminds us to build each other up and encourage for restoration when others fall or fail. I believe that it can happen once our view of God is large enough to fit comfortably under the shelter of His wings. It is when we acknowledge He is a big God and fully capable to enable us to endure the trials along the paths of life we might face. It is then, the adjustment and change can take place in our given circumstances that the end result will be for His glory regardless of the outcome this side of heaven. When we attain that understanding, we can, like the psalmist David say, "*My lips will glorify You because Your faithful love is better than life. So I will praise You as long as I live; at Your name, I will lift up my hands. You satisfy me as with rich food; my mouth will praise You with joyful lips. When, on my bed, I think of You, I meditate on You during the night watches because You are my help; I will rejoice in the shadow of Your wings. I will follow close to You; Your right hand holds on to me*" Psalm 63:3-8. Praise the Lord for His ongoing goodness to each of us, even in the face of turmoil and trials.

God is the coordinator of our strength. Wednesday I went to get a haircut. I have walked into Debra's shop for over thirty years. We have an agreement that she can cut my hair as long as she does not cut me. Over the years there have been a few nicks, but not bad enough to draw blood. We laughed about it on several occasions. Wednesday was one of those days, that as a pastor, I have cautioned others in bereavement about. Grief will be the farthest from one's mind and then, a picture, a song, a fragrance, or some other item will cause the memory of the loved one to come rushing back to the forefront of thoughts. While sitting in Debra's beautician's chair

Wednesday, my mind did the same to me. I could not help it. I got sad. I thought about all the various times Nancy and I would meet at Debra's after work while Nancy was getting her hair styled and then go out to eat or run some errands together. Now, I did not tell Debra I was sad. In fact, I tried to act like everything was fine, but I doubt my acting would have won any awards Wednesday. But God is the coordinator of our strength.

While driving back to the church after getting my hair cut, a friend who had lost his wife a few years ago to a massive heart attack called to check on me. He reminded me that I had checked on him during his initial days of change and adjustment and that he felt impressed to do the same Wednesday. Folks, I do not believe that was coincidence. I got a card in the mail from another individual that wanted to encourage me. I am looking beyond the tangibles and watching or feeling God enable me to get through each day. I am encouraged with the way in which He reaches down and strategically places reminders of His presence and purpose all around me.

Like the psalmist, I can reverently and confidently say, "My lips will glorify You because Your faithful love is better than life. So I will praise You as long as I live." And with that, I can report to you the reader, this story is far from over!

• **Thursday, October 27, 2011**

Observations—Reflections—and Inspirations

Now that you know where heaven is; you wouldn't trade that world for this ... Those words are from the song "Now That You Know" as made popular by the sterling performance of Karen Peck Gooch. Last Saturday I was getting ready to host a family birthday party, and I was listening to it and several other songs which I had downloaded to my phone. The cleaning was nearly to satisfaction, so I decided to spend a few minutes by changing out the seasonal floral arrangement at Nancy's grave. The cemetery is just over a mile from the house. I had been reflecting all morning and decided it was time for a visit.

Let me flash back to Labor Day weekend. That was our wedding anniversary weekend. I had decided about a month previous that I did not want to be home during our anniversary so I made reservations for Gatlinburg, Tennessee and the big gospel singing that Ray Flynn and Abraham promotions hosts each year. I further decided to wait until our anniversary night and remove my wedding band. Except for a brief time working in a textile plant with safety regulations requiring no jewelry around the machinery, I had worn my ring continuously for thirty-three years. Nancy and I repeated our wedding vows and exchanged rings during a 7:00 PM ceremony on Saturday, September 2, 1978. After giving it a great deal of thought, I realized we would not be spending any more anniversaries together, so without telling anyone I decided to remove it. It is a rather odd feeling making adjustments in order to maintain one's sanity and move on through various life crises. There were several A-list talent groups performing at the singing. I did not have a specific plan or a particular group in mind, but I wanted to make the removing of the ring as memorable as the first night I wore it. Triumphant Quartet is one of the classiest groups in Southern Gospel music as well as one of the crowd favorites. They began singing "Saved By Grace" and as I listened to the words, I decided it would be the perfect song in which to remove the ring. It was in realizing Nancy's presence is no longer available to comfort me, but rather it is in knowing God's grace will continue to offer comfort and assurance of better days ahead. The first verse says, "*I was alone in the darkness; I could not find my way. Jesus shined His light on me and turned my night to day.*" The focus is redirected from my loneliness and discouragement and re-centered on Christ and what He has done and will continue to do for me and others that have trusted Him. I suppose I should mention I am not the only one that likes the song as it has climbed to number one in the recent *Singing News* survey. When I got home from Gatlinburg I had to explain to the girls that my love for their mother was not diminished in any way, form, or fashion. It was simply what I felt like I needed to do. They have been great in understanding and supporting me through it all. We have each had our moments, as have other family members, friends, and Nancy's coworkers. But we all seem to be moving forward each day.

Now, the story returns to Saturday. I was playing the songs from iTunes, and a feature it has is called "shuffle." There are many songs but when it is in the shuffle mode, they are played randomly. After Karen's song was played two piano instrumentals followed. I was nearing the cemetery and a thought flashed through my head that it would be interesting if "Saved By Grace" played. When I opened the door to the backseat and reached in to get the flowers, a sudden surge of sadness swept over me. I pondered, "What am I doing bringing flowers to the grave of my Nancy?" How does that make any sense? She was healthy and we were enjoying life only months ago, and now she is gone. How is that fair? Interestingly enough, the piano medley finished playing and you guessed it, "Saved By Grace" started blasting through the earpiece. I leaned against another headstone to let those words and God's Spirit penetrate my heart. Soon the despair was gone, and I was refocused. The next song could not have been more appropriate. It was Susan Whisnant singing, "Even In The Valley God Is Good." *Even in the valley He is faithful and true. He carries His children through like He said He would.* I will admit that I was weeping at Nancy's grave while the song played on, but they were not tears of sorrow as much as they were tears of appreciation for the way the Holy Spirit had ordered my day and coordinated my steps. I found such huge affirmation of God's love to me and reassurance that things were going to be okay. It is difficult to relay all the emotions and feelings, but I want people to understand God's Word is true and His promises are proven often to me. His mercies are new every morning.

Well, I need to get on with another day today. The birthday party went well and the kids were excited spending time together while opening their gifts. I would encourage you readers to Google the songs I have shared with you and listen to them if they are unfamiliar to you. I believe you will find comfort in the words. In the meantime, this story is far from over!

- **Tuesday, November 8, 2011**

(200,187 Visits—3,028 Posts) That's unbelieveable!!! Thanks for your continued interest.

Random Thoughts—Fond Memories—and Purposeful Prayer

It has been twelve days since the last journal posting, but then, who is counting? It has been one hundred twenty-eight days since Nancy passed from this world to her heavenly reward, but then, who is counting? The girls and I have been processing the loss in various ways. One suggested it seemed as though she was on trip and would soon be home. I have not been looking out the window with expectancy. No, instead I have been trying to wrap my mind around the scripture the apostle Paul wrote when he said, "to be absent from the body is to be present with the Lord." It stretches my mind especially as I look into the clear, starry skies of the fall season evenings. I suppose my mind has wandered and wondered just where the geographic location of heaven could be found on the map of God's vast creation. I will let the world know once I have discovered the answer. I am comfortable waiting, but my prayers are increasingly intentional in seeking His return. I do not know when He will return, but I am subconsciously counting those days as well.

The last twelve days have been action-packed by design to move me farther past the beginning of the last one hundred twenty-eight days. I was privileged to spend a few hours with ministers in an appreciation luncheon with Dr. Henry Blackaby as the featured speaker. I was especially moved with emotion as I joined in the worship singing of "How He Loves" as made popular by the David Crowder Band. It was yet another reminder of affirmation that God is in control and, "how great *His* affections are for me." It was gripping as five hundred other ministers sang from their hearts the acknowledgement that the Father loves us. I would challenge the readers of the journal to find a genuine love that supersedes the love of the Lord. I can rest assured in knowing there is not a love that exceeds His love. Scripture states that we love because He first loved us. I miss my Nancy-fixes and the tender embraces, but I am smothered in God's love and I do not take it for granted.

I was invited to address the body of deacons for the New Holland Baptist Church of Gainesville during their annual retreat at the Georgia Baptist Conference Center in Toccoa. It was enjoyable to share scripture and thought in developing God's ordained leadership. Their attentiveness and dialog was refreshing. Indian Creek hosted the annual Fall Festival complete with the traditional Oyster Stew. One person who shall remain nameless suggested his "chowder" was a favored addition to the menu. I think he continues living that idea down. The stew was prepared well, but it tasted better once the score of the UGA–Florida game was posted with Georgia on top. I must admit the same guy with the chowder idea delivered on another or better idea. He has been leading a Bible study each week for the last three weeks. The menu was prepared by Francis Chan's *Crazy Love* and the spiritual nutrition is better than any chowder. Thanks Nate.

I managed to squeeze a couple of sessions with a grief counselor in the schedule to keep me centered. After four meetings he suggested I was as balanced as one could be, considering the process of laying a spouse to rest. He further suggested in his years of observing surviving spouses that they tend to have rough patches during three-month, six-month, and twelve-month anniversaries of the deceaseds' passing. I remember struggling during the three month period. Looking back, it was almost exactly during those days in which the wind came out of my sails. The difficulty of the six-month passage will come with the added feature of the Christmas holidays. At least I will have a better understanding of why the days seem so hard. I am not looking forward to "those" days, but I am looking forward to getting through them. The love and support through cards, texts, emails, calls, and visits are so encouraging. Sharing meals with folks like the Woodrings and others have been tasty and uplifting. It was fun visiting with them and their special guest Celia as we reflected on our days in the Atlanta church.

This past weekend was equally packed with activity and spiritual development. I joined six others as we drove to Birmingham for a visit at David Platt's Church at Brook Hills for a *Secret Church* session. We were joined by those present and some fifty-thousand others through simulcast. There were people from fourteen other countries listening and watching as we spent seven hours in an intense Bible study. The topic was *Marriage, Family, Sex, and the Gospel*. In those hours we filled in blanks for one hundred-fifty pages. It was like trying to take a drink of water from a fire hydrant, but David did an excellent job of covering the biblical perspective from God's intention for healthy families, to abortion, homosexuality, polygamy, and so forth. It included discussions for widowed as well as single and divorced people. I found it to be a helpful perspective chocked-full of scripture to show what God's Word had to say in addressing the various subjects. We got out of the sessions at one o'clock in the morning. Nate and the others made provision for spending the night while Steve Raffa and I decided to make the four-hour trek back home. I rested for two hours and then met Jeff for a ride to Athens to watch the Bulldogs run wild through the weaker team of New Mexico State University. As we made our way into the stadium, I could not help reflecting on the first trip I made to Sanford Stadium. It was on September 17, 1977 for huge rival game between Clemson and UGA. (Okay, I'll admit that I had to look that date up on the Internet for those of you concerned about my memory. Ha!) Nancy's cousin James Earl and his date ushered us into our seats that day. Back then, the stadium was open at both ends with the famed bridge at one end and the railroad-track crowd at the other. It was a rainy day in which the running of UGA's Willie McClendon was matched by the quarterback play of Clemson's Steve Fuller. Clemson scored early and then held on until the last minute when Georgia finally found the end zone. In those days if the score was tied at the end of the contest, it would remain tied in perpetuity. Vince Dooley had a decision to make. Should he take a fairly sure extra point to tie the score or should he send his grid-iron troops back out to attempt the two-point conversion? He opted for the two-point conversion attempt. It was a failed attempt and Clemson defeated Georgia in the rain by the score of 7-6. When we slogged our way back to the car a decision was made to eat at Charlie Williams Restaurant. The food was far better than the score and has left a fond memory of our first division one game. That was thirty-four years ago.

Sunday was the thirty-fourth anniversary of another memorable day. The dam above Toccoa Falls burst in the early hours and flooded through and unsuspecting campus. Thirty-nine souls perished in the muck and mire of the devastating tragedy. I had not yet gone to sleep and had only minutes earlier crossed the very bridge that some of my friends were monitoring moments before they drowned. It was a sobering, mind-boggling, gut-wretching time for our family. Nancy's family invited me to move in with them until our family could get relocated and re-established. It was three months before I would return to what was home in a different location. The Lord spared my life then and on other occasions since that day. I believe my life continues to move forward due to the prayers of many. One such prayer is taken directly from scripture as Paul wrote to the people of Ephesus.

Ephesians 3:14-21

For this reason I bow my knees before the Father from whom every family in heaven and on earth is named. *I pray* that He may grant you, according to the riches of His glory, to be strengthened with power through His Spirit in the inner man, and that the Messiah may dwell in your hearts through faith. *I pray that* you, being rooted and firmly established in love, may be able to comprehend with all the saints what is the length and width, height and depth *of God's love*, and to know the Messiah's love that surpasses knowledge, so you may be filled with all the fullness of God.

Now to Him who is able to do above and beyond all that we ask or think—according to the power that works in you—to Him be glory in the church and in Christ Jesus to all generations, forever and ever. <u>Amen</u>. (from Holman Christian Standard Bible® Copyright © 1999, 2000, 2002, 2003, 2005 by Holman Bible Publishers.)

Prayers such as that are what keep me focused and centered. Prayers like that offer the love of God through the work of Jesus Christ and enables me to move forward as I sort through the plans God has yet to reveal to me. Prayers like that help me encourage the readers of the journal or others through the experiences in which I have already been molded.

Prayers like that allow me to declare, this story is far from over!

P.S. Don't forget to vote today and then be sure to THANK the Veterans for their unselfish sacrifices so we may continue to vote.

• **Sunday, November 27, 2011**

It's A Wonderful Life...

Depending on how one tabulates or counts, Nancy has been deceased for a while now. If one was counting weeks, it would be twenty-one. If it were months, it would be five, and if it were days, it would be either one hundred forty-eight or forty-nine depending on where the sun rose in relation to your position on our big, yet small, small world.

Whichever way one counts, Thanksgiving 2011 is now a memory and for me a reflection of the many Thanksgivings Nancy and I shared together. A typical day would begin with a few minor chores while simultaneously reading the paper and watching the Macy's parade on television, while Nancy finished preparing food to take to my parent's home for the evening meal. One such year has the added (now humorous) story of Ashley picking on Andrea.

Andrea was just over four or five years old and was playing in the living room floor while I was reclining in my chair reading the *Anderson Independent* newspaper with the parade on TV. Ashley entered the room and began interacting with Andrea, but soon started antagonizing as little sisters do sometimes. I don't remember specifically what issue was starting or even what she was attempting to get from Andrea, but as a father half-way paying attention to them and doing my thing, I observed things getting a little heated. I told them to settle down. I said, "You better stop or somebody is going to get hurt and somebody is going to be crying." I was not closely monitoring the pesky playful interactions, but previous childhood experiences led me to believe someone was going to get upset and someone else might even get angry. Sure enough, Andrea had taken all she was going to take from Ashley, and she balled up her fist and struck her nine or ten-year old sister soundly on the end of her nose. I still chuckle when I recall the amazed astonishment Ashley's face revealed. She inhaled a huge breath of surprise, shock, and confusion. Knowing she had gotten more than she anticipated, she jumped up in a huff, and stomped off to her room while slamming her door. Andrea's eyes were big as saucers as she was impressed with Ashley's response and fearful of how I would react. I too was bewildered by what I had just witnessed and wanted to use it as a good teaching moment.

I had to stifle a laugh at my previous prophetic cautions and warning. I didn't want to encourage physical outbursts or condone violence, but at the same time, I wanted to let Andrea know it was fine to defend herself in a similar given situation. I further wanted to teach Ashley the impact of ignoring parental warnings and cautions without using the "I told-you-so" phrase. One would need to ask Ashley for sure, but I think we have ALL looked back and chuckled at that story over the years.

Another reflection of past Thanksgiving days with Nancy is the viewing of the American film classic entitled, *It's A Wonderful Life*. It usually followed one of the network station's parade coverage. Sometimes it was interchanged with *The Miracle on 34th Street*. I did not watch either of those movies this past weekend. I have reflected on the wonderful life of my time with Nancy. The *Wonderful Life* movie portrays George Bailey (played by Jimmy Stewart), as a guy who never got to follow his dreams entirely. However, upon review with the help of his guardian angel, Clarence Odbody (played by Henry Travers), George soon realized he had had a wonderful life. It would be presumptuous for me to speak on behalf of Nancy, but in our special moments and later reflections together, I got the affirmation from her that she lived life without any true regrets. Her mental strength was astounding as she fought the cancer without showing any fear or defeat. She was rightfully proud of her accomplishments as a mother and grandmother. She took her job as a teacher seriously, beyond the requirements of meeting a standard, and excelling to make a difference within the lives she was privileged to influence. Naturally, she and I had unrealized plans for the future that were interrupted with the life-changing experience that a terminal disease causes. There were trips we wanted to make, people we wanted to help, and more lives we still wanted to influence together. The affirmation of Nancy's life being in the classification of "wonderful" is when I hear from readers of CaringBridge, or from students she influenced years ago who share a story or memory of their interaction with Nancy.

Earlier today I was listening to a discussion and hearing testimony of individuals whose lives had been impacted with the direct interaction of angels. In two of those eyewitness testimonies, the issue was of personal protection in the midst of persecution. In both cases, the individuals themselves were not immediately aware of the physical presence of the angels, but years after the fact, their perpetrators admitted to supernatural beings that hindered their mischievous and detrimental tactics and freed the individuals. Hollywood's film industry can recreate the imaginations of various screen writers in order to allow people like George Bailey cross paths with his guardian angel, Clarence Odbody. However, in real life, while being a pastor, I would not claim to be an authority with absolute insistence of how our heavenly bodies interact with the physical. I honestly don't believe people "become" angels when they die because scripture indicates they are created beings in and of themselves. However, I did chuckle back a few laughs when I reflected and tried to imagine what Nancy was doing in her current spiritual form.

This weekend was the first Thanksgiving in thirty-five years that I was unable to share with Nancy. I have had the pleasure of traveling thirteen time zones from where I laid Nancy to rest, and was able to remain in contact through modern technology with my families and friends. Within the last forty-eight hours I traveled by plane, auto, taxi, scooter, and bullet-train. With technology I have been able to visit by phone, Skype, texting, and email. I was able to watch my favored UGA Bulldogs tame those pesky Yellow Jackets yet once again. Steve and Penny opened their home and shared their friends to help me make some new memories at Thanksgiving. As I sit on their high-rise balcony overlooking a hazed-filled Taichung sky, I realize that George Bailey is not the only one with a wonderful Life.

For me that wonderful life begins with Jesus and because of Him this story is far from over!

• **Saturday, December 10, 2011**

Interesting Thoughts Due To A Cold Night

It is cold outside. That is not a newsflash to most of you living around this part of the world. The wind has kept the air fresh, crisp, and cold. I have been working on some sermon preparation in my bedroom office and decided I would go warm up next to the gas logs in the living room. The grandfather clock has been chiming those shorter, single digits, chimes of early morning, and the room was lit only by a small lamp we leave on for a night light.

I was peering around the dimly lit room and caught myself in an unexpected moment of reflection. My back was to the fire, so I was looking across the room at a large box used to store our artificial Christmas tree. I brought the box in Thursday night along with several other storage containers of various decorations, lights, and tree trimmings. What caught my attention was the irony of its location. Nearly six months ago, that area of floor space was filled with a hospital bed which held my precious, yet ever weakening, sweet Nancy. I stood still as I let the warmth of the fire heat my hands and feet, but I was distracted with the memories of her last few hours. In my mind I saw the Margaret's attending help as she skillfully and carefully monitored the diminishing life of Nancy and made us aware of what to expect in those waning moments. The fire was getting too warm on the backs of my legs so I turned and looked up at the ceiling as my memory raced ahead in thought. I tenderly remembered the preciousness of her caring family as they individually, one-by-one, brothers, sisters, in-laws, parents, and children, came to her bedside to softly and gently declare their love to her. It was a very moving memory. It is one I cherish. It is not a memory that I have thought of in several weeks or maybe even months, but it was all there while those gas logs brought warmth into the room.

I have the task of putting that tree up. Nancy usually took care of the inside decorations while I handled the outside chores of lighting the eaves and nearby trees. I'm sure if I talk nicely enough those girls of mine will make sure the tree is well balanced with a mixture of lights and ornaments. While I was warming next to the fire the

thought struck me how peculiar a box could bring all those memories back as fresh as the day they were lived. I found it interesting
how that at the foot of Nancy's bed is the location of where the tree
is annually placed. Now, I want the readers to understand we do
not consider that area a shrine or special floor space. We have not
cordoned it off and left it as an exhibit. No, it is all part of our home
where in fifteen days we will be celebrating Christmas with food,
family, and fellowship.

I am not sure why those memories were triggered. I wonder if
it was experiencing another "first" of many firsts a surviving family
of a loved one goes through during the grief process. Friday night
Jessica and I went to church for the purpose of having our picture
taken to be included in a pictorial directory. Yes, it was a bit odd.
The lady taking the pictures did not ask, and we did not tell her
that there was supposed to be another person in our family photo.
We both just oddly smiled and posed upon direction and moved on.
Humorously, I suppose a life-sized cardboard cutout of Nancy like
the ones I have seen featuring NASCAR drivers at the auto parts
store could have filled up a space, but it seems it would be difficult
carrying her around without bending her.

All-in-all, we are doing well and continue being thankful for the
friends who take time to call or write. I can promise that it makes
a difference and the family genuinely appreciates all the kindness
that is shown. I am going to go ahead and sign off for now. I need
to get to sleep and get ready for all that Christmas decorating stuff.
If I remember correctly, I was a little grumpy about having to do it
last year simply due to laziness. Without enough sleep I can only
imagine how pleasant I will handle the task. Ha! Ha!

Stay tuned because this story is far from over!

• Saturday, January 7, 2012

Servants, Singings, & Sentiments

I am not sure how to explain the absence of journal postings.
I 'spose I could blame it on the rush of the Christmas season's
schedule, but really the reason is more of a personal challenge. I

told some of you my reason for not writing is not in having a subject but rather, it is in getting the feelings of my heart to process through my mind, and coordinate with my fingers, which in turn, enables the typing of the emotions onto the printed page. Humorously, I suppose I need to admit I have turned another year older since the last posting, and well, you know the rest of the story. Ha! Ha!

On December 13, Ashley, Jessica, and I made a presentation of $25,000 to the Stephens County School Board members to establish the Nancy Adams Stacey Scholarship. An annual scholarship will be awarded to a deserving Stephens County "Top Five" graduate during the awards night hosted in the spring by the high school. A selection committee of school administration and our family members will determine the deserving student. During the week of Nancy's funeral several people asked us about doing some type of memorial fund, and the scholarship seemed to be the best way to accomplish it. Contributions in Nancy's memory or appreciation are accepted when written to the Stephens County High School and directed to the scholarship fund. The scholarship was our way of keeping Nancy's memory fresh in the student population as well as helping us show the community our gratitude for the support they gave us during the last twelve months.

The Christmas season came and went without too big of a hitch. The decorations and tree trimmings were managed with the girls' diligence to "do it like Mama" would have done it. They did a great job. I finally accomplished getting the outside decorations up in time for the family gathering on Christmas Eve. For the last eleven years we hosted everyone, and this year was no different. Well, with the exception that it's hard to host a party without the "Hostess." One head-count reported around seventy people in attendance and I think everyone had a fun time.

Emotionally I have done okay. I got through the week of Christmas fairly well. I had the privilege of baptizing my niece and nephew last Sunday on New Year's Day. I was excited to start the calendar year with baptisms. I usually schedule baptism at the beginning of our service so I can greet any guests and visitors after service. Last week I did the same, so after the baptism I changed out of my robe and re-entered the sanctuary in time to hear Ashley, Jessica, and Andrea sing "Amazing Grace (My Chains are Gone)." A flood of emotions swept over me that I thought would require me leaving in order to pull myself together. It plunged me into a whirlwind of thanking God for His amazing and loving forgiveness, while simultaneously making me miss Nancy so very much that words are inadequate to express from my heart. I guess those moments of being blind-sided is the part of the grief experience that leaves me without an explanation. Fortunately, those extreme moments do not expose themselves too often, and I generally am doing well.

This past week has been busy with church-related schedules. For Southern Gospel enthusiasts, many attend various events during the last week in December and the first week in January. Recently for example, I have traveled to Gainesville, Vidalia, Marietta, and tonight I am headed to Spartanburg. As I inventory my thought process I believe the reason for doing as well emotionally as I feel that I am doing is because I try to keep a busy schedule while selectively steering away from events in which Nancy and I shared. A year ago tonight Nancy traveled to Spartanburg with me. She loved gospel music but she often went with me so I would not have to go alone. Nancy had a quiet servant's heart that she sometimes masked with her teasing or bold exterior. She and I would greet people with an Indian Creek flier and a smile as they exited the Memorial Auditorium. I am going to Spartanburg tonight with fond memories and a tug on the heartstrings. A year ago tomorrow night, Indian Creek joined services with New Hope Baptist of Toccoa, for the annual Watkins Family and Karen Peck and New River concert. We went together last year and had a great time. While visiting with Karen earlier this week, I told her I just did not think I wanted to put myself in that emotional position this year.

2012 has already made its mark on several of you. Some are rejoicing with a new job promotion, a new child, or other celebratory events. I hope you have the best year yet. Unfortunately, some have already had to embrace the year with grief and the loss of one of your loved ones. I can think of three families in grief while I am writing. At the close of 2011, the Ginn funeral home in Carnesville sponsored a memorial service at the city hall. They asked me to share a few words with the ones in attendance. I reminded them of the apostle Paul's words through the inspiration of the Holy Spirit when he wrote Philippians 4:8 "Finally brothers, whatever is true, whatever is honorable, whatever is just, whatever is pure, whatever is lovely, whatever is commendable—if there is any moral excellence and if there is any praise—dwell on these things." I am going to keep good thoughts and focus on the blessings rather than the absences and losses.

Happy New Year!!! Remember this year is just beginning, but this story is far from over!

P.S. FYI ... we do have a wedding date for Jessica and Josh. It is Saturday, March 24 at Toms Creek Baptist Church. Time is yet to "officially" be determined. Stay tuned.

- **Friday, January 13, 2012**

I Can Only Imagine...

Surrounded by Your glory, what will my heart feel
Will I dance for you Jesus or in awe of you be still
Will I stand in your presence or to my knees will I fall
Will I sing hallelujah, will I be able to speak at all
I can only imagine

Life is full of events, opportunities, promises, or sorrows that are hard to imagine. I am sitting in the early hours of another day. For some it is "just" another day. It is a day of work or a day of school or maybe it is a day of appointment. I can only imagine what the day may bring for you. I remember all too well what this date brought for me and the rest of the family one year ago. Snow remained on the ground from the blast that covered our area three days earlier. The alarm clock sounded, and as was customary, I simultaneously reached to silence it, while gently nudging my Nancy awake to begin our morning routine.

However, on this morning a year ago, the morning routine ran amuck due to Nancy's abnormal behavior. Oh, it was not so bizarre that I noticed it right away. In fact, nearly three hours would pass before I actually understood something was wrong. Our family doctor agreed to see Nancy, and by late afternoon it was apparent she was going to need some special attention. A test was scheduled for the next day but as we were driving home, through phone conversations, our daughters strongly urged us to go to a larger facility and have the test done immediately. I called our family doctor for additional direction and she was kind enough to reopen her office and forward Nancy's medical records to the Athens Regional Hospital in order to have the test done expeditiously. It was around the midnight hour of January 13, 2011 that we would hear the disconcerting news that a mass had formed in the frontal lobe of Nancy's brain. The emergency room doctor carefully and gently told us that while it was not his area of expertise, he had observed enough similar cases to know we were headed for more, extensive tests and that Nancy would be admitted into the hospital immediately.

Another hour passed and we were introduced to Carol. She was the charge nurse on the fifth-floor Neuroscience wing. We fondly chuckle at the first impression we got with Carol. She had spent several years as a military nurse, and it did not take long to learn she was a no-nonsense person who would tell us what to expect from her staff. It obviously was not her first day on the job, and in the days following we grew to love her as we observed her "extra-mile" way of caring for those in her charge. I cannot say enough about the staff of caregivers on the fifth floor and how they helped us adapt to a serious and heartbreaking situation.

Now, I am sitting in reflection while listening to selections from Greg Buchanan's harp. Yesterday (Thursday) I was doing sermon preparation for Sunday. I reached for a song CD in the night stand beside my bed. I got distracted with an old dilapidated jewelry box Nancy had long ago placed on the lower self. I had not looked at its contents in years. As I lifted the lid and peered inside I found a treasure trove of memories. Oh, the monetary value would doubtfully reach much above fifty dollars. There were not any precious jewels or gems, but there was a fistful of love notes and cards. Nancy had organized some of my high school memorabilia that included Georgia State Quartet medals, track medals, and ribbons. I even found the receipt for our marriage license and marriage certificate.

One of the love letters I had written to Nancy was dated January 11, 1978. It was fun remembering what I had written and the circumstances which prompted it.

It was a distraction. It was a good distraction. This week has had its challenges of letting life go on while reminiscing about the past. Life really is hard on people. There are tough decisions and life-changing choices that alter one's path forever. I spent a couple of hours reading and reflecting on the choices Nancy and I have made. Several families close to me or related to the church have been in grief this week. In each case, they left a void in their families that only the love of God can fill. I spoke at Brooke Wiese Eby's funeral Wednesday. It was thirty-four years after I had written the above mentioned love note to Nancy, that I would stand before Brooke's family and reminded them of God's sustaining love and mercy. Jon Penland Jr. sang as did Matt Farrow's daughters. Jon sang "I Can Only Imagine" made popular by the Christian group MercyMe. The song gripped my heart as I tried to imagine what Nancy and Brooke were doing at that moment. Were they dancing for Jesus or being in total reverence and awe? I can only imagine ... These last three hundred sixty-five days have been a literal blur. Yet, I rest in the peace of God while knowing and believing the words of Isaiah 55:8-9, "For My thoughts are not your thoughts, and your ways are not My ways. For as heaven is higher than earth, so My ways are higher than your ways, and My thoughts than your thoughts."

In these early hours, I have replayed Buchanan's harp CD three times and it has run its cycle again. This coming year may run by faster than last, but I continue trusting God's thoughts and God's ways. He knows the outcome of the story, but for now, this story is far from over!

• **Monday, February 6, 2012**

Getting Beyond Reliving the Reflections

The last journal posting was a reflection of Nancy's day of diagnosis. When I wrote it, I was already determining how best I would "get through" the day a year removed from the shocking news. It just so happened that my good friend, and Southern Gospel darling, Karen Peck Gooch, debuted in a movie called the *Joyful Noise*, and it was opening in theaters around America on Friday, January 13, 2012. Her part was admittedly a small one, but she met the challenge and made her peers proud with her fashionable outgoing charisma and powerful voice. I told my girls of my plans and how I decided to see it alone, but after Andrea implored she really wanted to see it with me, I gave in and agreed to let her.

Interestingly enough, I sat watching the movie and if it is possible to reflect upon reflections, my mind raced back to the mid 1980's when our church choir from Tom's Creek Baptist performed in competition similar to the one in the *Joyful Noise* story line. Our competition took place on the same stage as where Karen belted out *Mighty High* with her polished professionalism. We did not win on that Sunday afternoon in Atlanta, but it provided over sixty choir members a moment in time which has not been forgotten. The movie provided excellent singing and one of its co-stars, Dolly Parton, wrote and sang a song that kind-of blindsided me. Her character sang to the memory of her deceased husband (Kris Kristofferson) in a song "From Here to the Moon and Back". Wow! I did not see that emotion coming, and I was glad Andrea was in the theater with me. Yes, in some ways it was a reflection which in truth was one with which was hard to deal. Yet, that scene in the movie reminded me of the special love Nancy and I shared for thirty-five years. Reliving our happy moments even in reflection is an exercise in which I have learned to cherish and enjoy.

This coming week is no different in reflections. Last year in February was an extremely challenging time for our family. Nancy's initial brain surgery recovery did not go as planned and on the eighth, the proverbial dam burst with what would in fact be the beginning of the end. I do not know when enough is enough with the CaringBridge posts, nor do I intend to write about re-living each of those emotional, fatiguing, or deplorable days. I have re-read some of those journal postings and have rerun those memories while sitting here in the solitude of my bedroom/office. In my mind it would be very easy to dwell on the eventual outcome in bitterness and despair, but that is not where my heart takes me. While broken and understandably slow in healing, my heart takes me back to those moments of personal friends surrounding the family physically with love and nurturing. My heart overrules my mind by reflecting on the unimaginable number of CaringBridgeguest postings that affirmed our family with love and promised prayer. It is with my mind I realize the emptiness and hollowness the direction of my life could be taking. However, it is with my heart that I continue following the Lord while patiently waiting to answer the "whys" or the "how-comes."

With all of that said or written I am progressing down life's road with the understanding that unless God chooses otherwise, I still have a lot to accomplish and more to do. It is with Valentine's Day approaching that I fondly remember those thirty-four special days with Nancy in which we exchanged cards and kisses while expanding our love for each other. It is also a reminder of those hard times when last year I yearned for a hug from her but due to her critical health condition; it was reduced to a handshake. I want to use CaringBridge to once again encourage you, the reader. To those of you that are happily married, remind your spouse why you love him or her, and relish in the moment of your love that can be expanded. To those of you struggling in your relationship, take an inventory of where things seemed to get off track and be willing to take the first step in restoration. Often an unobvious selfishness or unrecognizable prideful attitude overwhelms the relationship and it soon is reduced to tears and irreparable feelings. Put those petty things aside and practice forgiveness. Take time to reflect what put the two of you together and build on the spark of love that once was an unquenchable flame. The best way to meet the challenge is to first make sure your relationship with God is pure and healthy. Once the vertical relationship with Him is restored and secure, the horizontal relationship with your partner can begin healing and be strengthened. Admittedly, I am not a professional counselor, but I have witnessed through experience a loving wife and healthy relationship in which Christ was the center.

For those left single due to death or unwanted divorce, I am learning to adjust to the uncontrollable circumstances that rob me of the joy once experienced. I have a long way to go in feeling "whole" after sharing nearly two-thirds of my life with the one who joined me in becoming one flesh. Someday maybe through more life experience and careful study of God's Word I will have an answer to lift you from the pain in which you suffer. I have leaned heavily upon some of you that have endured the pain of loneliness and grief. I have listened carefully to your stories and found encouragement in realizing some of you have rediscovered the heart that you once gave to your spouse. I recognize I am still gathering the pieces of my heart. I have found I can weave those heartfelt feelings together with God's Word, inspiring music, and the hope of loving again. It, in no way diminishes the love or high esteem in which I hold Nancy's memory. She was my treasure and I thank God for my time spent with her. Understandably, for some who have endured their pain longer, they may never desire finding a soulmate with whom to share their refurbished heart. I recognize it may be a long time in gathering those pieces and it may be even longer in finding one in whom I could entrust that heart once again.

In the meantime, I am staying busy with church schedules, mission trips, Jessica's wedding details, and various family gatherings. I would welcome hearing your stories of the past year and what you have learned about yourself or your relationships with others while walking down the road of life. I believe writing has provided a certain element of therapeutic healing for me, but I have listened, read, and really enjoyed your experiences as well.

HAPPY VALENTINE'S DAY!!!

And remember, this story is far from over!

P.S. Yes, I realize Valentine's Day is February 14th. I was hoping to jostle the memory of your significant other so they would treat you special. Ha!

• **Thursday, February 23, 2012**

Faith versus Futility

Some habits are hard to break. I do not exactly immerse every day with the reflection of last year's shared date. However, on occasion, I will take a quick look back to a time that caused an undeniable reshaping of who I am or will become. It is true that life's road has a way of winding around difficult and sometimes unforeseen obstacles which in turn vary our planned goals and teach us to adjust to the situations at hand. Earlier in the week I had planned to write about the adjustment of last year's third week of February. Nancy lay totally dependent upon the support of her family and the I.C.U. staff at the hospital while she was fed through a tube inserted from her nose to her stomach. Her days were simultaneously interrupted with the disconnection of all the various apparatus apparel so she could be shuttled by a team of transport personnel to the daily radiation treatments in another building. Due to her condition, the doctor ramped up her dosages to three-times a regular treatment and she would endure ten days of those.

This past Tuesday I peeked back to last year and recalled with satisfaction the journal posting entered on that date. I am in "a place" emotionally that I could reflect the songs I sang to her in our moments of quiet solitude. At the time, she was almost too weak to say much, but she would look at me and wink her approval. While I will be the first to humorously admit that in general few men ever know what women are thinking, I would at the same time argue Nancy was thinking she was loved and cared for with few limits. I rest well at night in knowing her family, closest friends, and medical staff provided the best care available. To sum up, we did all we could do to assist in her recovery. No, I did not get the result I was hoping or passionately praying to receive, but in its place I got a supernatural peace that enables me to move forward without bitterness, anger, or second-guessing the "woulda, coulda, shoulda's" of life's journey. Naturally, I still sometimes find myself nearly paralyzed with blind-sided emotion. I continue to adjust to life without my Nancy as well as my Nancy-fixes.

I have volumes to learn about life. I realize I look at life through different lenses than some. Some only see the hapless, hardened, or hollow results of a challenged life. Their life is grizzled by disillusionment and despair. I find in my quiet reflections the peace of God that I not only read or preach about, but it is also the peace that has sustained me through many of life's challenges. The lenses I look through reveal strength found only in the promise of God's Word and the comfort of having it seen lived out through my peers before me. I humbly recognize I have evolved into one of those role models for the peers that will follow me. I guess by looking at life through those lenses, I will observe both the encouragers of those around me as well as the ones in which I may yet encourage.

I chose not as a pastor to keep a close count of weddings, funerals, or the dunking of those claiming salvation with which I assisted. Since Nancy's passing there seems to be a keener awareness of the funerals that I have either attended or performed. I honestly do not know the number of them, but already this week I have been to two funeral homes and will assist in performing a third funeral on Friday. During the last eight months I have observed the sorrows of families going through the grieving process with slightly different perspectives than before June 26. I cannot say that I am more caring, but perhaps simply more aware of the sensitivity death brings to a family. For some it is a celebration of a life well-lived, while for others it is a concern of the unknown choice their loved one made during their life.

I have been challenged by some who have not understood the peace with which I move forward. Oh, they have heard or read about the kind of peace I am experiencing, but they have not captured it for themselves. I recently read a familiar passage in 1 Corinthians 2:6-16. It seems verse nine is sometimes misrepresented as a scripture defining the promise of heaven. I would rather believe the passage reminds believers what God has done for us through the Holy Spirit. Read the following carefully:

However, among the mature we do speak a wisdom, but not a wisdom of this age, or of the rulers of this age, who are coming to nothing. On the contrary, we speak God's hidden wisdom in a *mystery*, which God predestined before the ages for our glory. None of the rulers of this age knew it, for if they had known it, they would not have crucified the Lord of glory. But as it is written:

What no eye has seen and no ear has heard,
and what has never come into a man's heart,
is what God has prepared for those who love Him.

Now God has revealed them to us by the Spirit, for the Spirit searches everything, even the deep things of God. For who among men knows the concerns of a man except the spirit of the man that is in him? In the same way, no one knows the concerns of God except the Spirit of God. Now we have not received the spirit of the world, but the Spirit who is from God, in order to know what has been freely given to us by God. We also speak these things, not in words taught by human wisdom, but in those taught by the Spirit, explaining spiritual things to spiritual people. But the natural man does not welcome what comes from God's Spirit, because it is foolishness to him; he is not able to know it since it is evaluated spiritually. The spiritual person, however, can evaluate everything, yet he himself cannot be evaluated by anyone. For:

who has known the Lord's mind,
that he may instruct Him?

But we have the mind of Christ. (from Holman Christian Standard Bible® Copyright © 1999, 2000, 2002, 2003, 2005 by Holman Bible Publishers.)

I hope this scripture will shed light on some of the questions you as a reader may have had concerning the working of the Holy Spirit and the wisdom of God. The gospel is a mystery to those who have no desire to understand it in faith. Many celebrities cannot understand it. They often try to say "spiritual" words thinking they will make them appear holy or biblically intellectual. Yet, when a crisis or conflict rises in their lives, confusion overrules the situation, and they have nothing with which to hang upon for comfort.

Other people live life in the strength on their own wisdom or physical stature. What they end up realizing is that problems and crisis can hugely overshadow any of their limited human power. They will struggle in trying to make logical sense out of the scriptures instead of accepting them in faith and observing them lived in life before them. My desire is for people to grasp hold of a faith that will not fail them. The light of God's truth will dispel darkness and chase away doubt. My challenge to those searching for answers is to surrender living in their strength and allow the Holy Spirit to lead them into a life of peace.

Like the apostle Paul stated in Philippians chapter three, I have not yet attained all the answers of spiritual maturity, but I have learned the necessity of surrendering my way and embracing God's instruction. Humorously, I should interject that common sense is often available but sometimes rejected. For example, Jessica and I visited a funeral home earlier in the evening. On our return home we decided to stop in for a cup of coffee at the Café Kava. I got one of those fancy brews with a few extra shots of espresso. The waiter handed it to me while grinning and said, "I hope you are not planning to sleep any time soon." Here I sit winding up a journal posting and expecting the sun to pop up soon. Interestingly enough, Sweet Beulah Land just started playing over the iTunes selections. Many of you know that was a song Nancy played while I sang in comfort to many bereaved. It tells of a day when my faith will end in the sight of glory. It is a great story and like this one, it is far from over!

- **Monday, February 27, 2012**

Patience May Be More Than a Virtue

Patience is a word that describes a character trait. Oddly enough, it is esteemed in the four major world religions. Christianity, Judaism, Islam, and Buddhism place a large acclamation on its value. Currently I am preaching through a series of the Fruit of the Holy Spirit. Those familiar with scripture will remember the letter the apostle Paul wrote to the church in Galatia in which he expounded upon the benefits of surrender and the allowing the Holy Spirit to direct one's life. In it, he describes the qualities that are visible in one living a life who seeks the Holy Spirit's direction and leadership. The evidences of such a life are revealed through the attributes or qualities of the Holy Spirit. Patience is one of the nine Paul mentions in Galatians 5:22.

I wrote all of that to tell you I appreciate your use of patience in waiting for details of Jessica's and Josh's upcoming wedding.

Some of you have traveled through some of the rough adjustments life can present. Compounded with reflections of what our family went through this time last year, the building of a new house, and life in general, Jessica and Josh have chosen to postpone their wedding date until July 28, 2012. The plans include having the wedding ceremony at Tom's Creek Baptist Church in Martin, GA with the reception to follow at the Currahee Campus of North Georgia Technical College near the church. Unapologetically, I admit this past year and especially these last eight months since Nancy left us, have been difficult.

Thank you for practicing patience with our family as we continue making adjustments. All the current wedding showers, and so forth. are still scheduled without hesitance or interruption. Jessica genuinely appreciates the encouragement and love shown to her during these days of wedding planning, house building, and so on. Thanks for loving on us with the virtue of patience and understanding.

For now, that is the story, and as you well have heard, this story is far from over!

P.S. Thanks for practicing patience with the author. One of these days it will get published. Hmm ... patience is good, but in his case prayer might even be better. Ha! Ha!

- **Monday, March 26, 2012**

Random Ponderings from 35,000 Feet

The environment of home, occupation, or even pleasure is filled with a cadre of items that are overlooked and undervalued. It seems some of the items in which I am thinking are taken for granted or used only when an assignment requires its input or usefulness. When is it that a task evolves into a different priority in one's life? What transpires to cause one's value of life and its odd little facets change from one of earlier age? For example, my writing has become more therapeutic for me personally, and a collection of journal reflections have had benefits for others since the beginning of Nancy's illness and departure than in previous times. Writing assignments for school was simply that. It was a way of meeting the requirement for a passing grade and a stepping stone for the next level of education or personal development.

I suppose one should prepare himself with an understanding the discoveries of peering into the mirror of life's experiences may reveal more than he is ready to uncover. For me it seems the wells of emotions and previously un-penetrated personal barriers kept me from examining the deeper thoughts that are prevalent in superficial relationships. I am addressing the emotional as well as the spiritual core of my personhood. As life happens, adjustments change us and alter our priority. Nancy and I were remarking a few years ago how differently the addition of children and grandchildren changed us. When the added ingredient of aging was factored into the equation, we were quick to agree "softball" was not as important as it was when we were in our teens and early twenties. Admittedly I am still a youngster when viewed through the eyes of octogenarians.

I am sitting scrunched up and twisted slightly to the right to avoid the reclined airline seat ahead of me. The information monitor reveals the plane is flying just over 35,000 feet from the earth at a speed of 519 miles per hour. The temperature outside the cabin is 72 degrees below zero and the plane is overcoming an 89 mile-per-hour headwind. The earphones are turned down to a soft jazz tune, and my mind is racing ahead with figuring how best to write some recent ponderings. Japan is the destination, and the purpose is to offer hope to the devastated people who were blindsided by a major earthquake followed by a tsunami reaching record proportions of disaster and destruction. In a unique way, I can relate to those individuals who were merely in the ratchet-jaws of life completely oblivious of how quickly their lives would change in just a matter of hours. Video clips have shared personal testimony of the suddenness and help-lessness their lives changed on March 11, 2011. Those surviving lives will never ever be the same as they were previous that date. Reality shows us that each day our life will force adjustments on us, and the direction we choose can and will have eternal consequence to our decisions.

My point may be better expressed by observing the outside con-ditions of this airplane. Without the proper equipment life would be next to impossible to sustain itself. Inside, I am comfortably wearing a tee shirt and sipping cranberry juice in a climate-controlled environment. An emergency door is only a few feet away, and I was pondering that if it were opened before readied, tragedy would result in the sudden decompression of the cabin. Yet, that same door would be the perfect way of escape in the event of an emergency landing. During the early part of last week I was working in my home office while listening to my iTunes library. I started subscribing last year while passing time in the hospital with Nancy and I was needing the encouragement music often offers. I think the very first song I downloaded was an oldie from the Greater Vision Trio entitled, "God Wants To Hear Me Sing." A couple hundred songs have been added, along with voice recordings and miscellaneous other recordings. One specific addition was the two-part CD of Nancy's funeral service. Last week during the iTunes shuffle, her service started playing. I had the ability to fast-forward to another song, but as the service started playing "He Is Here," sung by me and my daughters, I asked myself, "Do you want to listen to this today?" I was busy working on some gospel singing preparations for our church's Memorial Day weekend singing and decided I could bear to listen once again.

Soon the tears were trickling down my cheeks but they were not exactly tears of sadness. In retrospect, I think they were tears of appreciation as one-by-one Nate, Melinda, Michael, Lucy, and George went to the microphone and expounded upon the Nancy's qualities that were so endearing to each of us listening that day. Those funny moments Nancy shared with us with her priceless sense of humor and timing mixed with the testimonies of her grit and determination with which she modeled and made us better people by having observed her life. Once the first half of the service finished, iTunes shuffle went directly to a Country Music song Aaron Tippin wrote and sang called "Always Was." Since I am traveling nearly six miles above the earth, I am unable to download the lyrics right now but I will leave a space for them here and add them before I post this entry.

Always Was:

I look at you and I remember
The way I felt on the day we met
That same old feeling washes over me
It's hard to forget

Nothing has ever changed for me babe,
Nothing changes for you,
I still want you just as much as I did
When I said, "I do."

I'm still wrapped up in that ring around your finger,
Without you, baby, I would be lost,
I'm telling you the truth I'm still
As much in love with you as I always was.

I'm a slave to your every desire,
I worship the ground where you walk,
I'm telling you the truth I'm still
As much in love with you as I always was.

You still stir up that old desire,
I can feel it now as we speak,
Nothin' I ever felt before prepared me
For a love this deep.

Yeah, I'm still crazy about you, baby,
In my heart and in my soul,
Yeah, I'm still mesmerized
By two brown eyes and a band of gold.

I'm still wrapped up in that ring around your finger,
Without you, baby, I would be lost,
I'm telling you the truth I'm still
As much in love with you as I always was.

I'm a slave to your every desire,
I worship the ground where you walk,
I'm telling you the truth I'm still
As much in love with you as I always was.

Oh, I'm telling you the truth I'm still
As much in love with you as I always was,
Always was, always was,
As I always will.

(Recorded on the *People Like Us* album in 2000)

Needless to say, the tears started pouring again with the reflection of not only the song itself, but why it was special to us. I heard the song on the radio when Aaron was making it famous. I decided to buy the CD, and I secretly placed it inside Nancy's CD player of her car and queued it to play when she started the car. By having an extra set of keys, I was able to set it up while she was at school. I left her a note to "listen carefully," and I once again pledged my love to her. To get the full effect of the moment one would need to listen to the song. Mr. Tippin has an interesting and distinguished country-twang in his presentation but it worked for me and Nancy, and it was just one of those "special moments" I wanted to share in reflection. (By-the-way, guys, it is never too late to do something special for your wife to let her know how much you appreciate her. Write her a note, do something that has been on that "honey-do list", or let her know in some other way, that you are proud to call her your wife. It's just a thought.... Ha!)

I have also been pondering about my girls. They are scheduled to sing at Pleasant Hill Baptist Church tonight. It is an exciting day for the church as they have built a new worship center and are celebrating with a dedication service this morning and revival service into the rest of the week. Our ministry allowed us to serve ten years and ten months with that group of people. I do not think anyone is any more excited about their new building than I am. It has been a long time in coming to fruition, and I am glad I can rejoice with them.

One other "pondering" is my trip to Japan. By most standards taking three international trips within a nine-month period is probably exceeding the comfort zone of what is considered appropriate for a church/pastor relationship. When the Georgia Baptist Disaster Relief leadership called me to see if I could serve, I went to our leadership and sought their guidance. They not only agreed I should go, they insisted the trip should be financed through the church's mission fund. Robert Crump has joined me, and together we are traveling with four other Disaster Relief teammates. Our primary focus as I mentioned before is to aid healing and offering hope to them through the gospel of Jesus Christ. Our work will partner with the Samaritan's Purse group. Before the tsunami, the particular area with which we are traveling was not receptive to outsiders. Now, there has been a softening of hearts and a willingness to at least listen to the gospel as it is being presented. They are a lovely group of people who simply need to see other believers who have lived through the struggles of life while embracing the love of Christ and receive the hope and peace that passes understanding. In a matter of hours is the nine-month anniversary of Nancy's passing. I miss her greatly and yet I have lived in that above-mentioned peace. I have not liked having to make the adjustments these recent months have evolved me into making, but I have done it with God's grace. If I can share some of those promises with the people of Japan and it impacts them with eternal value, then the sting of Nancy's passing will not be quite as great. It is with the vision of the people like those of Indian Creek, and the other friends who have stood close by with strong shoulders, that I am able to move forward and remind you that this story is far from over!

P.S. The above was written while traveling to Japan. Now, I've landed, recovered my suitcase with its broken zipper, and eaten our dinner meal. Robert is getting ready for bed. I have contacted the folks from home to report safe passage, and now I will post this journal entry and call it a day.

- **Thursday, April 26, 2012**

It's the 26th of the month today...

Phone texting allows quick notes for information, brief updates, greetings, and so forth. This morning Jessica sent me a reminder that today was the ten-month anniversary of Nancy's passing. She also suggested a better way to think about today was the eighteenth anniversary of Andrea's spiritual birthday. Jessica's same year anniversary was yesterday. While reflecting on her reminder and those consecutive nights at Pleasant Hill Baptist Church with Dr. James Lee preaching at the invitation of Dr. Billy Owensby, I thought about another significant April 26.

April 26, 1975 was on a Saturday and the high school quartet of which I was the lead-singer, was scheduled to sing at the youth event of a local Baptist church. We were unfamiliar with the name of the church or any of its members. It was because we were from a neighboring high school that their youth were unfamiliar to us. Toccoa Falls College produced a good number of youth workers, pastors, and missionaries. One young lady was Kathy Britt (Penick), and she invited us to sing. After a few hot dogs, hamburgers, and chips were consumed at the home of James and Sue Stowe, we went a few blocks away to the home of W.T. and Henrietta Segars. They had a son, James Earl, a daughter, Angela, that were in the Tom's Creek youth group, and a piano. James Earl had an escort that evening whose name I don't remember, but he also had a cousin with which I became acquainted. She had long dark brown hair, beautiful blue eyes, and a quick wit that captured my attention. She was wearing a red/white striped shirt with the half-inch stripes going east and west around her body. Blue jeans and tennis shoes completed her outfit, but I cannot remember if her Converse shoes were red or white. My hair was over my ears but off my collar so as not to go against our school's dress code. I was wearing a Mr. Goodbar tee-shirt recently purchased from Hershey Pennsylvania's chocolate factory while we were on spring choir tour. I added my blue-suede elevator shoes and elephant-leg blue bell-bottoms. Um-hum, we decided to wear our own clothes instead of the school-provided polyester leisure suits that night. I am grinning as I write today because of the fond memories I have of those guys with whom I sang. Jon Penland sang bass, Tim Lilly was our baritone, Dean Bogert sang tenor, and Wes Steiner was our pianist. We spent a little over five weeks together that summer singing in Georgia, Florida, and Alabama churches with Eldon and Cheryl Arndt as our chaperones. Those were fun times and provided great memories.

Unlike today, we did not have cell phones, text messaging, emails, or other modes of today's instant communication. If it was necessary to talk more than five or ten minutes on the phone, our parents encouraged us to visit the person rather than stay on the phone too long. During our summer tour, I received either four or five letters snail-mailed to me at the different churches with which we performed. Nancy had our itinerary and allowed enough time for the letters to reach their different destinations. Our last concert was at the Bethlehem Baptist Church in Clarksville, Georgia. Nancy got special permission to drive Angela, Wanda Stowe, and Angela Anderson to our concert rather than attend church at Tom's Creek that night. I was in a pickle of a decision as to what to do.

My family was leaving the next morning to travel to Ohio and visit some of our relatives. While we were gone, I had time to think about my relationship with Nancy. We had not officially dated but there was some obvious chemistry between us. I weighed out my options and made my decision. Granted, over the years Nancy reminded me it was a stupid decision, but it was the one I chose. Ha! Ha! Let me explain. I did not have a car. In fact, though I was old enough, I did not have a license to drive or money to pay for insurance. Nancy was going off to play college basketball at Gainesville and I had no idea she was coming home every weekend. So, I decided when I got back from Ohio I would not contact her. Yeah, I know, I probably deserve the hate mail some of you are thinking of sending, but really, I think the year apart taught me a greater lesson. My birthday falls later in the year than Nancy's did, so I started school a year later. She was in college and I had my senior year to fulfill. It just seemed like the right decision. Again, admittedly, I should have explained some of that thinking to her, and maybe things would have been different. Either way, I am glad things turned out the way they did. They certainly have produced great thoughts and memories to me even this morning as I write.

It was while I was reflecting on the previous story and thinking about Jessica's and Andrea's salvation dates that I read my devotional for the day. I use one provided through the *Singing News Magazine* that links to my cell phone. Today's scripture is from Romans 11:33-36.

A Hymn of Praise

Oh, the depth of the riches
both of the wisdom and the knowledge of God!
How unsearchable His judgments
and untraceable His ways!
For who has known the mind of the Lord?
Or who has been His counselor?
Or who has ever first given to Him,
and has to be repaid?
For from Him and through Him and to Him are all things.
To Him be the glory forever. Amen.

(from Holman Christian Standard Bible® Copyright © 1999, 2000, 2002, 2003, 2005 by Holman Bible Publishers.)

God's Word brings comfort to me regularly. His timing is never coincidental. I have not yet seen His purpose in taking Nancy; yet, I have experienced His comforting peace throughout the last fifteen-plus months since her diagnosis. Life is not easy for those of healthy bodies and for those care givers to the infirmed I encourage you to trust Him in every aspect and detail. Since Nancy's passing I have visited with several people going through similar life changes and adjustments. Some were not health related but simply difficult times of seeking God through the crisis of job changes, relationship challenges, and so forth. It is when one is able to totally trust the leadership of the Almighty that they are able to rest in the comfort of His peace which passes understanding.

In reflection to God's timing, I recognize I was not yet ready to ask Nancy out for a date after our initial meeting. Our first official date was mentioned in an earlier journal entry, but that is another story and this story is far from over!

• **Monday, June 25, 2012**

(210,184 Visits - 3,073 Posts)

Moving in the Right Direction

There is a line from an old Steve Martin and John Candy movie that bears repeating. It is from the movie entitled *Planes, Trains and Automobiles* and is delivered from Candy's character after they just ran their car between two tractor-trailer rigs in oncoming traffic in which the car was sideswiped on both sides. When they pulled over to examine the damages and regain their composure from such a frightening situation. Candy looks the car over and says, "Oh that will buff right out." The laugh line hits the mark as the camera pans over the car, and reality meets common sense, the movie watcher knowing that the car will never be the same. Ever the optimist, sometimes reality is in simply realizing that life is never quite the same.

Our family is coming up on the one-year anniversary of Nancy's passing away. We've ridden in planes, trains, and automobiles, and yet life has sideswiped us with irreparable damage. Just like the movie character's autobody mechanic will work hard to make the crumpled pile of metal resemble a car once again, the reality is in knowing there are scars and wrinkles which will never get buffed completely out. The positive outlook is when one can use the same optimistic approach to that of the apostle Paul when he wrote a letter from his prison cell. Philippians 1:21 For to me, to live is Christ, to die is gain. Paul's life endured many hardships. Some of which are probably not recorded in the laundry list of life-threatening experiences he reflected upon in 2 Corinthians. And yet, in Philippians 4:4 Paul, through the inspiration of the Holy Spirit wrote, "Rejoice in the Lord always. And again, I say rejoice." It's almost as if Paul is saying life is hard, it has its difficult days, but with the Lord's help and guidance, I'm going to buff it out and move on. He does not deny the scars. He does not claim his life will totally avoid rough times in future days. He simply lived one day at a time and thanked the Lord for His constant companionship and unconditional love.

As a family we have chosen to move on. The scars will remain but we have chosen to buff out the wrinkles and smooth over the rough edges of life. God has placed within me a peace of both heart and mind. While I do not enjoy the shadows of loneliness or the lack of wisdom my life partner offered me for thirty-five years, I am learning to adjust. To be sure there remains plenty of opportunity for more reshaping and smoothing. An intentionally planned schedule with full agendas have enabled me to keep getting up each day and moving forward with purpose.

In the days since the last journal posting the activities have included several promotional engagements for Indian Creek Baptist Church's Memorial Day Weekend Gospel Singing. The family has endured both special occasions of Mother's Day as well as Father's Day without too many emotional meltdowns. The three girls and I went to Stephens County High School's Senior Awards Night to award a deserving Top Five honor student with the first $1,000 scholarship in Nancy's memory. We decided to give the additional gift of a new leather-bound student study Bible with the student's name engraved on its cover. It will be around as a reminder of achievement and accomplishment long after the scholarship money has been submitted to the institution of higher learning. Final drawings were endorsed for the completion of the Stacey memorial monument, and it is scheduled for delivery June 28 which is the day before the one-year anniversary of Nancy's funeral.

In addition there have been numerous birthday parties, a grandson's pre-school graduation attended, and various other opportunities to stay busy with purpose and invest in other people's lives. Ministerially, there have been hospital rooms visited, funeral parlors offering shoulders upon which to lean, marriage counseling to help encourage staying together, and pre-marital counseling to help form a basis of sustaining a healthy marriage. We were able to negotiate through a week of Vacation Bible School, overcome a church financial crisis, and participate in a tent ministry. There have been blown tires to change, bills to pay, and an air conditioner requiring replacement. In other words, life goes on. It is the choice of the individual as to how they choose to allow life to go on. One can choose to embrace life knowing it will have challenges that seem insurmountable and buff out the rough edges while claiming the victory of accomplishment. Or one can lie crumpled, broken, and ruined in the wake of a head-on crash from an unforeseen truck wreck and dwell defeated in its result.

More thoughts... Same post—6-24-2012

The previous paragraphs and thoughts were written from the deck of a cruise ship headed to Cozumel, Mexico two days ago. The trip has been a family outing with sixteen members from my side of the family getting together to celebrate the March 20, eightieth birthday of my mother. It has been twenty-one years since my last cruise and the general particulars are the same. We have experienced great and pampered service, scrumptious meals and snacks, and for the most part decent family entertainment. There are some stark differences from the previous trip besides the obvious geographical destinations. For one difference, I am the grandfather of four of the passengers, and I have two sons-in-law on board. My girls have chosen good life mates and they are seeing firsthand what over sixty-two years of wedded bliss can look like through the role model of my parents. While it is refreshing to examine the longevity of such a marriage, it is also important to realize that eighty year olds continue working on their relationship of give-and-take in order to sustain their marriage.

Out at sea we have encountered the fallout from a huge tropical storm. The ocean is anything but calm and the white capped waves are like snowflakes in that there are no two the same as they relentlessly beat against the ship and cause it to pitch and roll with the ticking regularity of a grandfather clock. Another stark difference to the cruise of 1991 is that my life partner is not with me to enjoy the shared time together. Oh, there are plenty of activities to keep one's mind occupied and hands busy; however it is noticeably different in the adjusting of cruising without her. I escaped the upper, pool deck when the sky opened up a torrential rain that gave the title "pool deck" new meaning. I waded to a drier deck and stopped by the ice cream counter for a small cone before I moved on and found refuge in a lounge with secluded seating and privacy. It is adjacent to the afternoon art auction that is selling several Thomas Kincade prints as well as those of some of his contemporaries. When I found my spot in the lounge it was quiet and quaint which allowed me to reflect over the last thirty-six years: Thirty-five years with Nancy being the center of my earthly focus and this past year with her huge absence. The rain has driven other pool deck patrons into my newfound lounge and a televised soccer match from two European teams has captured the attention of some of my shipmates. All of those activities are reminders that life does indeed go on. The ship is moving forward while carrying a couple of thousand vacationers to and from their destination in the midst of the uncontrollable circumstances of a weather storm. It carries me back in thought to what I wrote at the beginning of the trip. Life goes on and we must choose how to make the most of the life we have been given.

The trip has been an emotionally educational experience for a couple of reasons. I have fully embraced the time spent with my family and enjoyed their company during the hours spent revolving around mealtimes and kids' activities. I was like any other grandfather when my heart swelled with pride as Ashtin brought the house down with her accapella rendition of "Jesus Loves Me" during karaoke night. I chuckled with approval as Jessica and Andrea raised enough noise to get the game-show host's attention and onto the main stage for a friendly competition. The difference has been in traveling with a group of loving people and yet finding myself pitching and rolling with loneliness. I am not oblivious to the tender touches I observe other couples very naturally sharing as they walk along the deck in front of me. In fact a wave of sadness swept over me at the Greenville/Spartanburg airport soon after mom, dad, and I seated ourselves and got buckled up to fly south. The woman sitting across the aisle from me innocently and unknowingly reminded me of my Nancy. She was in similar age, similar body frame and shape, and seemed well educated and confident in whom she was as an individual. Before anyone gets the wrong or warped idea, let me explain that my behavior was gentlemanly. I did not gawk or stare. I did not even try to strike up a conversation with her. In fact, I kind of wish I had not seen her at all because the overwhelming wave of loneliness that swept over me. I did not have an emotional meltdown or shed a tear. I did not tell anyone in the family or ask if they thought she reminded them of Nancy. Instead I sat in my seat and thought of all the special trips Nancy and I were privileged to enjoy and how this particular trip would have its moments of emptiness and loneliness because of her absence.

I am writing these thoughts in an effort of testimony that one can get through difficult times. I have wondered, even while on the cruise, at the number of other individuals having recently lost their mates. I have wondered when, if ever, the feeling will transform into pleasant, satisfying memories rather than hollow, empty, lonesome feelings during the special times of remembering. In all honesty, the emotions I am experiencing are not paralyzing. I am able to continue functioning and hopefully performing my ministerial duties without any hiccups or significant judgment lapses. The experiences of the past year have enabled me a clearer understanding of emotions with which I previously thought I had understood. It has been with a personal need I have felt the scripture take root for a purpose of significant need rather than for academic information. Even in the bouts of loneliness I have sensed the encouraging warmth of God's presence and the affirming comfort of His love. The soccer match is drawing to a close and the dinner bell will soon sound. The excellent service will resume where it left off at lunch and an entertainment night of Broadway-style proportions will showcase the talents of rising performers hoping for a big break to help them follow their dreams. Meanwhile the publisher has urged me to submit my writings and put closure on the book project. The book may be coming to an end, but this story is far from over!

Epilogue

*W*hen I was a young boy, I remember watching more than a few of those black-and-white television westerns. They usually concluded with the good guys, in the white hats, riding off into the distance on the Wild West plains seeking their next adventure. In living the Christian life and reading from God's Word, I am reminded that His mercies are new every morning.

Lamentations 3:21-24

Yet I call this to mind,

and therefore I have hope:

Because of the Lord's faithful love

we do not perish,

for His mercies never end.

They are new every morning;

great is Your faithfulness!

I say: The Lord is my portion,

therefore I will put my hope in Him.

(from Holman Christian Standard Bible® Copyright © 1999, 2000, 2002, 2003, 2005 by Holman Bible Publishers.)

It is only because of my relationship with Jesus Christ and the realization that I need forgiveness from my sin through His cleansing blood that I am able to don a "white" hat and ride off into the distance seeking my next life adventure. I recognize the promise from scripture that comforts me in knowing whether I marry or remain a widower, He is with me and I am not alone. The path I choose daily is to follow His leading and join Him in the various adventures of life itself. To me, the Christian life is not one of boredom but rather it is adventuresome in watching and observing what God is doing in and around me. He continues blessing me with a caring family and Christian friends to help me stay centered and balanced while I investigate the possibilities of the next chosen path. Regardless of the path, it is because of Jesus Christ that **This Story Is Far From Over!!!**

About the author...

*B*ill Stacey was born in north-west Ohio but his family moved to northeast Georgia in 1965. He graduated with an Associate of Arts degree in music from Truett-McConnell College in Cleveland, Georgia and later earned a Bachelor of Arts degree in Pastoral Ministries from Toccoa Falls College, Toccoa Falls, Georgia. He interrupted his Master of Divinity studies from New Orleans Theological Baptist Seminary during his pastoral administration. Rev. Stacey currently is Senior Pastor of Indian Creek Baptist Church of Carnesville, Georgia and has served three other Georgia Baptist churches during his 34-year ministry. He has sat on the Boards of Toccoa Falls College Alumni, Believe Ministries, Northeast Georgia Special Mission's Outreach, and the North Georgia Pastor's Counseling Center. He has led international mission teams and participated in gospel pre-sentations through singing, preaching, teaching, or disaster relief to more than ten countries and four continents.

His secular employments have ranged from owner/operator of a logging and sawmill business to supervisory positions in textile manufacturing. In his personal life he met the late Nancy Adams Stacey, and their marriage produced three daughters, Ashley, Jessica, and Andrea. Ashley married Dustin Strickland and their children are Ashtin and Elliott. Jessica recently married Joshua Moore. Andrea married Christopher Segers and their children are Clayton and Jackson.

Stacey enjoys giving himself away through encouragement to others through interpersonal relationship building. He also enjoys reading, family gatherings, various sporting events, and listening to a wide variety of music.

CPSIA information can be obtained at www.ICGtesting.com
Printed in the USA
LVOW100458201112

308031LV00001B/3/P

9 781624 194719